MANAGING CHURCH CONFLICT

MANAGING
CHURCH CONFLICT

HUGH F. HALVERSTADT

WESTMINSTER/JOHN KNOX PRESS
Louisville, Kentucky

Book design by Publishers' WorkGroup

First edition

Published by Westminster/John Knox Press
Louisville, Kentucky

PRINTED IN THE UNITED STATES OF AMERICA

9 8 7 6 5 4 3 2 1

Library of Congress Cataloging-in-Publication Data

Halverstadt, Hugh F. (Hugh Fleece), 1939–
   Managing church conflict / Hugh F. Halverstadt. — 1st ed.
      p.   cm.
   Includes bibliographical references.
   ISBN 0-664-25185-4
   1. Church controversies. I. Title.
BV652.9.H42 1991
254—dc20   91-15211

Contents

84751

Preface

In his author's note for his book *I Love You, Let's Work It Out*, David Viscott writes, "There are some books that can be written only at a certain time in life. This is one of them. . . . I knew the principles for living together, but I'd had an unhappy marriage."[1]

This is also a book that could be written only at a certain time in my life. I worked to write it earlier, but could not. I knew the principles of managing conflict, but I often still behaved reactively in conflicts. The core of this book comes from what I have learned in twenty-three years of coaching church leaders' hands-on efforts to manage church conflicts. I am deeply in their debt for my own growth and learnings of ministry in conflictive situations.

The concepts and prescriptions of this book's model are still evolving in this school of church experience. I expect readers to use this book's model as a starting place for their ministries in conflicts, building on it as part of an ongoing inquiry into a Christian management of conflicts in church and society.

Although this book's model focuses on conflict in church systems, it is also applicable to managing conflicts in other nonprofit, voluntary systems. Based on students' experiences with this model in philanthropic and community organizations, the model's values and ethical understandings of conflict have been found to apply even when parties do not necessarily subscribe to the Christian beliefs underlying these values.

CHAPTER 1

Can Church Conflict
Be Christian?

The minister was leaning on the door frame of her church office, pain and anger written large across her face. "It just kills me when people are this ugly in any community, especially the church. What happened in the nominating committee last night was bald-faced character assassination. Nobody stopped it until I finally stepped in. Even then, they just sat there. Today Joan is still at it, spreading her poisonous lies about Sheila all over the congregation. What hurts so is how the people of this congregation play dead and let her keep on. I can't believe it. At times like this, it makes me sick to be the pastor of this church."

Christians fight. Conflicts erupt between a minister and an enclave of church officers, between "the first family" of the congregation and a pastor, between the associate pastor and the head of staff. Rival congregational factions feud over church officer nominations or lock horns over giving communal funds to an in-house nursing service for people with AIDS. A church board polarizes over providing a meeting room for a twelve-step group on sex addiction. A church educator and a pastor clash over each other's ministries until the educator abruptly submits a resignation. A group of church officers organizes a campaign against national church staff because of a denominational position on abortion or on homosexuality.

Christians not only fight, they also often fight dirty. Issues are personalized. Gossip and hearsay fog up reason and common sense. Enemy-making wounds parties' spirits and shreds long-standing friendships. Moralistic judgments vaporize trust. Labeling parties suppresses openness and candor. Roberts' Rules are misused to polarize members of governing bodies, making political alliances more influential than reason or spirituality in determining leaders' votes.

It is no wonder that so many thoughtful Christians avoid church conflicts like the plagues of Egypt. The question is not whether Christians fight
or even whether Christians fight dirty. The question is whether church
conflicts can ever be Christian.

Christian Sources of Church Conflict

Why are church fights so often so devastating? To be sure, early in his
public ministry Jesus observed, "I have come to call not the righteous
but sinners" (Mark 2:17b). Are Christians, however, more sinful or crazier
than non-Christians? Are church staff more destructive than secular employees? Indeed, why do church folk who may fight fair at work often fight
dirty at church? Apparently, certain forces shape the feelings and behaviors
of parties in church conflicts.

For one thing, parties' core identities are at risk in church conflicts.
Spiritual commitments and faith understandings are highly inflammable
because they are central to one's psychological identity. When Christians
differ over beliefs or commitments, they may question or even condemn
one another's spirituality or character. Their self-esteem is on the line.
That is why parties slip so easily into taking differences personally, even
launching personal attacks. When church folk feel that their worldview or
personal integrity is being questioned or condemned, they often become
emotionally violent and violating. Any means are used to justify their goal
of emotional self-protection.

For another thing, parties to church fights profess a gospel that is vola-
tile. "I came to bring fire to the earth," said Jesus. "Do you think I have
come to bring peace to the earth? No, I tell you, but rather division!" (Luke
12:49a, 51). Jesus Christ is in the business of social and personal change.
He calls us to turn away from sin to salvation; from meaningless religious
rituals to meaning-filled action; from indifference to the earth's ecology
to stewardship of all creation; from social violence to social justice; from
human isolation to human community; from personal despair and compul-
sion to personal hope and responsibility; from serving the idols of national
culture to serving the transcending Rule of God. Church conflicts are often
generated by acting on such faith agendas for cultural or social change.
While Christian religiosity often operates to preserve the status quo, Christian faithfulness operates to challenge and change the status quo. In itself,
such inner conflict between religious security and spiritual risk taking generates emotional conflict between believers.

Finally, church conflicts occur in voluntary institutions whose structures
and processes permit and even entice unaccountable uses of power. In the
name of individual conscience or vision, church members may embark on
ministries without going through institutional channels. Neither authoriza-

tion nor coordination is secured. When the word gets out or when the ministry involves controversy, others may feel used, misrepresented, or betrayed. Indeed, vague job descriptions for staff and unstated role expectations for members leave all church parties vulnerable to conflicting assumptions about one another's callings. Moreover, an imbalance of economic dependence between church employees and church volunteers further confounds church conflicts. Those whose incomes depend on church offerings have more to win or lose than those who make their livelihoods elsewhere. This imbalance of financial dependence sets up manipulative exercises of power between them. Church systems are particularly vulnerable to abusive uses of power in conflicts between staff and volunteers.

In summary, threats to self-esteem, pressures for and against personal and social change, and vulnerability to power plays in voluntary systems all combine to exacerbate the sinful humanness of parties to church conflicts. Indeed, one marvels that any church conflicts are ever Christian or constructive.

And yet, there are church fights that are. For example, church officers with strongly differing convictions control their emotions and begin listening respectfully to one another. As they do, they come to understand and appreciate their differing interests. They acquire new perspectives from which they create genuinely workable win/win solutions. And again, church staff, without blaming or patronizing one another, level with one another over their competing professional commitments. The focus of their exchanges shifts from defending differing professional commitments to exploring ways of pursuing their differing professional commitments collaboratively. Rather than abandoning their differences, they learn to benefit from their differences. Yet again, a church governing body adopts a process of fact-finding that puts a stop to distorting gossip and character defamation. Creative problem solving replaces self-serving rhetoric. Over a three-month period of dialogue and reflection, a consensus emerges about the wise thing to do.

What can make church fights Christian? To begin with, a constructive process is vital. What can start differing Christians on a path of Christian conflict is *a way* of interacting that elicits and utilizes more godly traits and gifts in them and in the larger faith community around them. The purpose of this book is to prescribe such a process, a process for ethical responses to church conflicts.

Making Church Conflicts Begin to Be Christian

The Chinese characters for "crisis" mean both "danger" and "opportunity." One character is "wei" (danger), a face-to-face encounter with a powerful animal. The other character is "chi" (opportunity), the blueprint of an open universe. In the same way, church conflicts present us simultaneously with a danger of divisiveness/disintegration and an opportunity for wholeness/reconciliation.

Conflicts are power struggles over differences: differing information or differing beliefs; differing interests, desires, or values; differing abilities to secure needed resources.[1] As Jay Hall puts it, "Thus, conflict is defined here as essentially the circumstances—both emotional and substantive—which can be brought about by the presence of differences between parties who are, for whatever reason, in forced contact with one another."[2]

Power is to the social process of conflicts what oxygen is to the biological process of our physical bodies. However different parties' issues or feelings may be, they all use power. They will exercise their power either to overcome one another (dirty fighting) or to collaborate with one another (fair fighting). In virtually every case, parties will use power both ways in church fights. But the critical ethical question is which way of using power predominates.

The fundamental axiom of this book is that the key to making church conflicts Christian may be found in fashioning a faith-based process for differing parties to use. *How* Christians behave in conflicts is of critical moral and spiritual consequence for *what* they seek. As John observed, "Whoever says, 'I am in the light,' while hating a brother or sister, is still in the darkness" (1 John 2:9). A process that Christians use to deal with their conflicting differences will need to be an ethical process that is consistent with standards of Christian morality. Ethically constructive behavior does not make a conflict Christian. But without such behavior, the substance of a conflict's resolution will surely be sub-Christian, if not actually un-Christian. This book prescribes an ethical process—a model—by which a Christian works with conflicting parties for constructive constraint or creative resolution of their differences.

In this regard, one faith understanding underlying this book's model is that the constructive management of a conflict cannot rely only on the individual righteousness or virtue of the parties in conflict. This model sways parties' personal moral ambivalences with a covenant-making process that establishes agreements between them that elicit their human goodness while restraining their human sinfulness. These process agreements between parties open the door for constructive treatment of their differences. How parties agree to fight becomes as much a matter of their faith's expression as the conflicting convictions over which they are struggling. In fact, parties' destructive behaviors in conflicts often speak so loudly that they will not hear whatever is constructive in the positions being advocated.

The viewpoint that ethical process is a critical means for making church fights Christian begs the question. What is a Christian definition of constructiveness in conflicts? What is a Christian vision for managing conflicts? What ultimate Christian definition informs a penultimate ethical process of managing conflicts? Is this ultimate Christian vision a matter of reconciliation? redemption? justice? forgiveness? liberation? compassion? kindness? or what?

The view taken in this book is that a Christian vision of *shalom* is the most fitting goal for an ethical process of conflict management. This is because *shalom* incorporates all of the values named above for a Christian standard of good and evil in a church conflict. The vision of God's peace portrays a wholeness that incorporates God's reconciling love, justice, redemption, liberation, truthfulness, and compassion. As Jack Stotts explains,

> A persistent and pervasive symbol in the Old Testament materials for indicating the relationship that God establishes and intends of humans . . . and nature is *shalom*. We ordinarily translate that word as *peace*. It represents in the biblical texts, however, a broad range of meanings. The core meaning is that of wholeness, health, and security. Wholeness, health, and security do not mean individual tranquillity in the midst of external turbulence. *Shalom* is not peace of mind, escape from the frustrations and care of the surrounding environment. Rather, *shalom* is a particular state of social existence. It is a state of existence where the claims and needs of all that is are satisfied; where there is a relationship of communion between God and humans and nature, where there is fulfillment for all creation.[3]

God's peace provides the ultimate Christian vision for what makes a church fight Christian. The approximation of *shalom* is what an ethical process of management aims to realize.

God's peace is an ultimate but not a humanly achievable property of church conflicts. God's peace is a divine gift, not a human capability. Although Christians often unthinkingly assume that being Christian means being godly, that is not the case on this side of the grave. Human beings are not godly. Human beings only approximate God's life-style. *Shalom* is a "north star" for making conflicts Christian—a transcending orientation toward which to steer an ethical process of conflict management.

Christian ethicists have consistently urged that Christians not separate their ultimate values and beliefs from their penultimate ones. Just because we are not capable of *shalom* does not mean that we do not aim for *shalom*. In the case of church conflicts, we can make connections between the ultimate vision and the penultimate responsibilities of dealing with conflict situations. We make connections between

- the vision of God's love of the parties and a process that requires respectfulness between parties;
- the requirements of God's justice for parties and a process that requires assertiveness between parties;

- the realization of God's truth among parties and a process that requires accountability between parties; and
- the healing of God's reconciliation for parties and a process that incorporates their differences within the framework of a larger good affecting all.[4]

These connections generate for us a Christian ethic of conflict management that constitutes the core of this book's prescribed process.

Christian understandings of God's love mean much more than interpersonal respectfulness, but parties' respectful behavior in a conflict is a necessary way of approximating God's love. Christian understandings of God's justice are much greater than the meanings of human fairness, but parties' assertiveness in a conflict begins to reflect God's unconditional love for all parties. Christian understandings of God's truth recognize that Ultimate Truth far exceeds human comprehension, but precisely for that reason, human accountability that checks for parties' distortions and self-deceptions in conflicts is required in approximating God's truthfulness. These "middle axioms" for behavioral respectfulness, fairness, and accountability do not incorporate all there is to making a conflict Christian. However, without such middle axioms for parties' behavior, there is little chance of making a conflict Christian. Middle axioms for moral behavior bridge the space between ultimate and penultimate values, connecting behavioral prescriptions with the directives of ultimate values and putting the meanings of ultimate values to work in approximate human activities.

In summary, no conflicts are purely or perfectly Christian. But a conflict can be judged to be more or less Christian by how parties exercise power in dealing with their differences. Behaviors of respectfulness, assertiveness, and accountability and the inclusion of a larger common good serve as standards of behavior in a Christian's calling in conflictive situations. Together these behavioral standards define what this book's model means by fair and dirty fighting.

A Fair Church Fight

Consider a case in point. An angry church member was circularizing a petition in the fellowship hall of Good Shepherd Church during the coffee break before morning worship. Two days earlier the woman who was the church secretary had been frightened by encountering a male stranger in the church kitchen. The petition demanded that the governing body immediately install locks on all outside doors of the church facility so as to prevent any further surprise encounters with street people.

By the end of that Sunday morning's worship service, the emotional climate among members was bristling with distrust, confusion, anxiety, and hostility. Enclaves of partisan groups were clustering in the halls and in the parking lot. The "traditionalist party" and the "modernist party" in the congregation were rapidly coalescing into their accustomed formations for war. That afternoon the phones of the pastor and church officers buzzed with escalating rumors and accusations. By the time the governing body convened the next evening for its regular monthly meeting, church officers were in highly emotional and polarized states. A battle line had been drawn between faith issues of ministry to the homeless and faith issues of ministry to the congregation's own staff and members.

As soon as the petition had been read to the board, an effort was made to "jump start" the board by using the parliamentary procedure of "calling for the question" without debate. At this point, the pastor advocated that the governing body vote to reject the motion and move out of the polarizing dynamics of parliamentary rules of debate into an exploratory discussion as a committee of the whole. A power struggle ensued between those on both sides of the issue who wanted a quick win/lose resolution of the conflict and those who wanted an open exploration of the issues for possible win/win resolution.

At that point, what would make the conflict Christian depended on which process for resolution was chosen, rather than the resolution of the issues. By a narrow vote, the board adopted the process of becoming a committee of the whole, thus beginning a two-month dialogue, the outcome of which will be described later in chapter 11. The point here is that a change in the process of the conflict transformed it from being a win/lose power play to a win/win process of power sharing. A polarizing congregation was changed into a unifying congregation with a new sense of hope and trust among all parties.

Managing as Intervening to Cut the Costs
or Reap the Benefits
of Church Conflict

An ethical process of dealing with church conflict is concerned both to constrain human sinfulness and to realize human goodness. This book's model offers ways of intervening to constrain a malevolent cycle of conflict and ways of intervening to empower a benevolent cycle of conflict. A malevolent cycle of conflict is entropic, a mindless, escalating pattern of power struggling for a win/lose outcome (see fig. 1.1).

Without reasoned intervention, a malevolent cycle of conflict moves toward an all-or-nothing outcome. All natural conflicts evidence this process. Many social conflicts do too. Some behavioral scientists like Lorenz have considered this "natural" pattern of violence both necessary and desirable in social conflicts because it provides the mechanism for the survival of

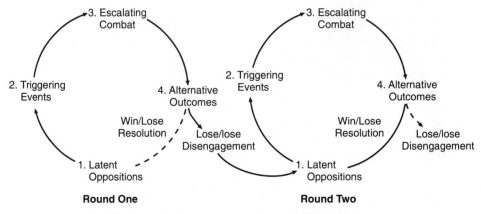

Fig. 1.1: The Malevolent Cycle (Dirty Fighting)

the fittest.[5] Others, including those holding the perspective of a Christian ethic, hold that one can intervene with a rational, creative, problem-solving process that is both feasible and preferable to letting things simply run their instinctive course.[6] Indeed, interrupting the malevolent cycles of a conflict has become essential for human and ecological survival in a nuclear, technological age.

Such intervening is also needed as part of the church's survival in our age. In the case of the church conflict over locking the doors, just such a malevolent cycle had begun to play out, devastating a congregation that was already cratered from previous malevolent rounds. Years of accumulation of unresolved emotional and substantive differences between factions in the congregation lay behind the eruption over the kitchen incident. That incident triggered these issues and feelings out into the open. Fighting habits from previous malevolent rounds began scripting the behaviors of all parties. The kitchen incident did not create this malevolent round of conflict; it only triggered it.

Once in the open, the conflict escalated with the polarizing effects of the circularizing of a petition—a petition advocating a solution rather than the exploration of concerns. A parliamentary motion to prevent debate threatened to reduce the situation to nothing more than a political contest between competing factions for control of the congregation. The outcome would have been one faction's winning at the expense of the other. A damaging residue of distrust, cynicism, and disaffection would have been left for members on the losing side. Malevolent cycles are destructive not only to the principals but also to the larger communities that host them.

Fortunately, a constructive process for this church conflict was initiated. A reactive, mindless pattern of increasing irrationality was interrupted by the proposal and adoption of a benevolent process (see fig. 1.2).

The pastor/manager changed the power struggle from one over solutions to one over the process for dealing with differences. The pastor/manager moved to abort the win/lose outcome of a malevolent cycle by mobilizing the common sense and good faith of the governing body for a benevolent cycle. By removing the threat of having to vote the petition up or down, parties could begin to explore the information, views, and values underlying their differences. What had been a power contest over locking doors became an exploration of a congregation's changing identity in a changing neighborhood.

In this case, management of the conflict resulted in a resolution of differences. This is not always the case in church conflicts. There are times when differences between parties constitute genuine dilemmas, as when there are not enough resources to maintain equally valued programs of service.

There are also cases when one or more of the parties to a church conflict refuse to follow a benevolent process, as when a governing body refuses constructive debate as a basis on which to find a creative solution.[7] When win/win solutions are neither possible nor sought, a Christian ethic of conflict management prescribes ways of blocking or minimizing the costs of win/lose outcomes. A Christian vision of *shalom* for conflict management pursues the resolution of differences. A Christian realism for conflict management also prescribes alternatives when resolution is not apparent.[8]

In this regard, the very term "management" may suggest manipulation of or control over parties in a conflict. Managing may sound like moving parties or their circumstances around as if one were moving pawns on a chess board. In this book the term "managing" signifies coping with rather than controlling conflictive situations. Dealing with conflicts is called

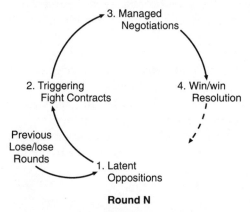

Round N

Fig. 1.2: The Benevolent Cycle
(Fair Fighting)

managing rather than resolving conflicts precisely because managers cannot force unwilling parties to make peace. If an Almighty God stands at
the doors of human hearts knocking (Rev. 3:20), how should Christians
presume to do otherwise? In this book, managing conflicts means coping
constructively with parties by constraining those who fight dirty and/or
assisting those who fight fair.

Managing conflicts signifies both constraining win/lose resolutions and
obtaining win/win resolutions. A Christian ethic for managing conflicts
requires trust of God because one recognizes one cannot control the parties. A Christian ethic, however, undertakes the risks of managing conflicts
because one recognizes that unmanaged conflicts do not go away. They just
increasingly yield evil.

In summary, managing conflicts is a process of intentionally intervening
by proposing constructive processes by which to deal with differences.
Rather than reacting emotionally to the issues and mobilizing politically to
overcome others as "enemies," a Christian ethic prescribes how parties
may adopt a process of shared control for respective self-control. Parties
are helped to move from enemy making to problem solving. This model
for managing church conflicts offers those indirectly affected by church
conflicts ways to constrain or support those directly involved in church
conflicts.

Distinguishing Concepts of This Book

Readers may wonder why they should read yet another book on managing church conflicts constructively. The insight that process is key to making conflicts constructive is not unique to this book. Virtually all models of
conflict management focus on process as the primary tool for making conflicts constructive. Other concepts in this book's model that are not unique
include

- the concept of identifying what parties have in common as the founda-
  tion for working out their differences
- the concept of setting behavioral ground rules for respectfulness and
  productive communication between principals
- the concept of using the steps of the problem-solving process as steps
  for identifying and negotiating resolutions to conflicts

The more unique features of this book's model for managing church
conflicts are these:

First, this model prescribes a way of dealing with conflicts as a moral,
ethical endeavor: a self-conscious applied Christian ethic in light of a

Christian worldview.[9] The concept of enlightened self-interest found in secular theories of conflict management is not here rejected.[10] But it is enhanced by moral understandings and commitments of ethical and theological import: an ethic of fair fighting. Parties to conflicts are seen as Christian "responders" to conflictive situations, responsible selves before God.[11] This model for managing conflicts is advocated as a practical way of exercising a ministry of reconciliation rather than only as an expedient way of securing personal or ecclesial survival. This model incorporates a doctrine of the church as a communal power and spirit that is critical for managing church conflict. What is proposed here is more than a formula or set of general rules to follow. What is offered is a method of thinking theologically and responding ethically to conflictive situations.

Second, this model uses a systemic way of thinking about and intervening in conflictive situations which understands and mobilizes communal spirit for managing church conflict. Attention is given to more than just those who differ. The first step prescribed in this process is to deal with oneself as a Christian manager before trying to "fix" anyone or anything else in the situation. Attention is also given to the faith community that has a constructive or destructive influence on all parties to a conflict hosted within its context. Parties' behaviors are understood as part of larger communal processes rather than as just their personal or group traits. This book's model for managing conflicts recognizes that often changing the family rules of a congregation or other church body can yield more Christian reconciliation than just dealing with the behaviors of the immediate parties to the conflict. Prescriptions for changing contextual factors are seen as one strategic intervention that changes the "rules" and structures of communal process so as to change the behaviors of conflicting parties.[12] Furthermore, the interests of both parties and of their hosting communities are taken into account in this book's ethical prescription for fair fighting:

- the values of both individual rights and the larger communal good in which they participate
- the requirement of truthfulness through both personal honesty and communal accountability
- the realities of both individual choices and familial processes in becoming a responsible self in a conflict
- the insights of both psychological and sociological perspectives on parties' motivations in conflicts

The third distinctive trait of this model is its recognition and use of communal power for managing conflicts. Church systems do not have the controls of business (utilitarian) or civil (coercive) organizations.[13] Often parties to church conflicts cannot be made to fight fair by threats of being fired or by threats of being taken to court or imprisoned. This model for managing church fights mobilizes power for managing a church conflict from the faith community hosting it. Members of the larger community who are affected by the impact of the course of a conflict are mobilized to bring their interests to bear on the parties to the conflict. This communal aspect of the model is both realistic in a voluntary organization and faithful to the theological nature of the church. This model for managing church fights incorporates and utilizes the power of covenanting for realizing the Christian life. Covenanting ground rules and procedures mobilize communal power for responsible constraint or resolution of conflicts as a people of God.[14]

Fourth, the model vests in an ethical process the commonality needed among parties to negotiate their differences.[15] Parties' commonality of interests and faith commitments are formulated around fair ways of fighting per se. The rationale is that until parties fight fairly for fair fighting, they will not fight fairly over their substantive or emotional issues. Fair fighting commitments create the initial commonality required to realize additional commonalities over differences.

Fifth, this model draws from a variety of scholarly disciplines relating to church conflict: disciplines of biblical interpretation, theological reflection, and sociological, organizational, psychological, and political sciences. In actual church conflicts, all of these perspectives bear on conflictive situations. The problem is that each of them involves a mastery of scholarly knowledge not claimed here. In this model the author takes the risk of being less scholarly for the sake of integrating a broad range of academic perspectives for concrete implementation. As indicated above, the book prescribes an interdisciplinary method for understanding and coping with church conflicts that draws on sources specific to church systems and to Christian beliefs.

Finally, with the exception of dealing with chronic interpersonal conflicts, this model prescribes how in many cases parties to a church conflict can manage their conflicts themselves rather than having to use a paid consultant, at least initially.[16] The invitation is made to parties to exercise third-party functions themselves, rather than requiring them to secure an outsider to provide these functions. Many parishes do not have the time or money to bring in an outside expert or consultant to manage their conflicts. In this model, the originating parties are equipped to manage their own conflicts, seeking the services or arbitration of outsiders only when their efforts fail. In most cases, outsiders cannot resolve conflicts for the original parties. The arbitration of a conflict simply resolves matters so that members of the larger community housing it are no longer held hostage by it. As necessary as arbitration may often be in church systems, a constructive management of differences by insiders is much to be preferred. It should at least be attempted before outsiders are brought in. This book is written primarily for insiders' use in dealing with church conflicts.

Although no one of these characteristics may be unique to this book's model for managing church conflicts, together they provide a distinctive approach to managing church conflicts with more attention to their ethical and systemic dynamics.

How to Use This Book

This is a book of high density. In an effort to respect the reader's time and to take into account the complexity of actual conflictive situations, the book's material is concentrated. Readers will probably need to read repeatedly the sections of the book that address their conflictive situations if they are to get the usable help they seek.

Readers who have glanced ahead may be less concerned about the density of the book's material than about whether the model is actually practical and workable. At first glance the model seems terribly complicated and time consuming. How can a reader do all this thinking and planning when all one has is a ten-minute coffee break to determine how to deal with an erupting situation? How can a reader follow *three* tasks of Step One introspection when being angrily confronted in the church fellowship hall? How can a reader use a model to manage a conflict when no one around will admit that there is one?

Learning to use this book's model for managing conflicts is like learning to walk. At first the steps seem complex and laborious. But with just a little practice, the steps become almost second nature. That is because the model is fundamentally one of common sense informed by Christian values. Presumably, readers of this book are imbued with both qualities. One can sit in a meeting and intuitively grasp the presenting power and ethical factors at work as the parties heat up. One may not be able to read others' minds or know their hearts, but one can quickly recognize their increasingly destructive behaviors and know that it is time to call on the group to interrupt exchanges that are generating more heat than light. Indeed, learning this book's model is not so much a matter of acquiring new knowledge as of recognizing and mobilizing what one has already learned in the school of life about both constructive and destructive conflicts.

The book is organized around the three steps of a method. Chapters 2 through 4 present Step One tasks for managing oneself as a conflict manager, whether as a combatant or as a concerned member of the community in which the conflict is taking place. Chapters 5 and 6 describe Step Two tasks of assessing a conflictive situation, both its communal context and its principal parties. Chapters 7 through 12 describe the five Step Three ways of intervening to manage a conflictive situation: three strategies to cut costs by constraining parties' win/lose behaviors and two strategies to reap the benefits of empowering parties' win/win behaviors for reconciliation. A final chapter explores how an ethical process of Christian conflict management can be used to precipitate fair fights for personal and social change in serving the vision of *shalom.*

All three steps of the model flow together. One moves from step to step, often in an informed trial-and-error way, as one manages the social and spiritual complexity of church conflicts (see fig. 1.3).

One may begin with Step One self-reflection and proceed into Step Two appraisal, only to flow back into further Step One self-reflection before proceeding with a Step Three strategy of intervention. The point is that each step in the model prepares a manager for the step following, and the consequences of undertaking each step of the model may lead one to undertake another portion of the model. Conflictive situations are dynamic. So is the process of their management. Therefore, the model is presented as a flowchart that works for the manager like a wiring diagram works for electricity. In this flowchart boxes contain tasks and diamonds contain questions for the reader's decisions. Although this flowchart may seem overwhelming at first, it will become less so as one reads and works with the explanations of each step through the book. As one gets to know the model, it "wires" one for the kind of quick thinking and acting often required in conflictive situations. Taking time to understand and use the model now saves time and confusion later.

For the sake of communication, a glossary of terms provides working definitions of some key terms used in this book. No claim is made that these definitions exhaust the meanings of these terms. They only specify the meanings of terms as they are used in this book.

When all is said and done, however, the value of this book remains a matter of how faithful it is to Christian values and how practical it is for Christians to use in Christ's ministry of reconciliation. Mindful of God's grace and human limitations, one is invited to seek to understand and to use this model for the good of the church, toward the wholeness of the world and to the glory of God.

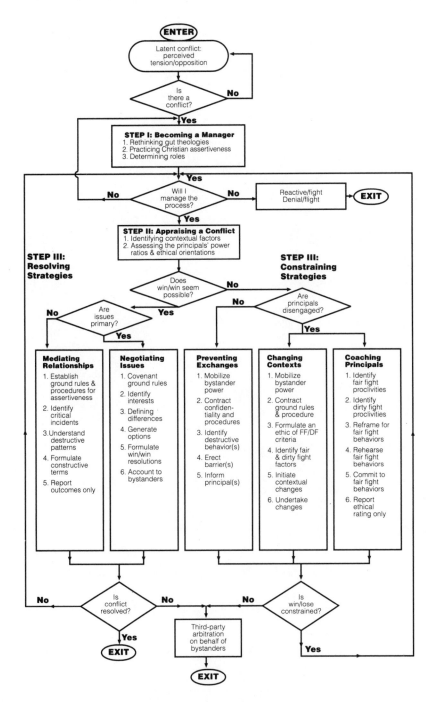

Fig. 1.3: Flowchart for Managing Church Conflict

PART ONE

STEP ONE:
BECOMING A
CONFLICT MANAGER

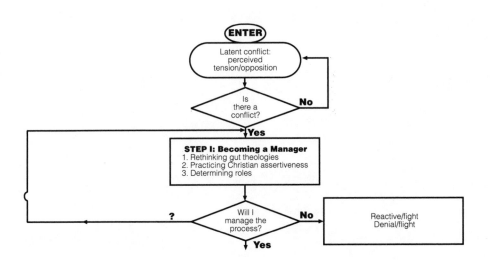

CHAPTER 2

Step One, Task One: Rethinking Gut Theologies of Conflict

When a conflict arises, most of us automatically begin to concentrate on who is at fault or what the issues are. We study the situation until we decide what our Christian position or solution is. We focus on what is going on outside of us rather than within us. Step One of this book's model for managing conflicts changes this habitual response to conflictive situations. It directs our attention first to ourselves as managers (see fig. 2.1).

Registering Feelings to Detect Their Underlying Messages

Conflictive situations arouse negative feelings in most people. People sense the presence of conflict even when things seem calm on the surface; parties deny that anything is going on, but their behaviors tell otherwise. A latent conflict feels like the eerie quiet before a storm. A minor difference of opinion comes up, and suddenly people are silent. People literally clam up. Someone may make a loaded comment, but no one picks up on it. Or someone's temper may flare out into the open, but it is quickly extinguished with a tepid apology. These kinds of behaviors around a latent conflict make people feel uneasy, tense, wary.

Many Christians feel uneasy for an additional reason: They have qualms of conscience. Before they were six years old, many Christians learned that it was unkind, even selfish, to stand up for themselves. In short, many may have learned that good Christian girls and boys don't fight. As they grew older, these Christians often found that such beliefs did not work on the playing fields of life. Here they learned to fight "by hook or crook" for what they wanted, while feeling guilty about it. They hoped Jesus would forgive

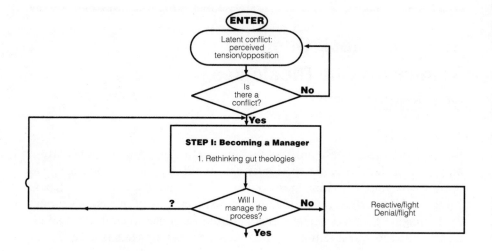

Fig. 2.1

them but often also felt hypocritical about asking for such forgiveness. Other Christians may take the opposite tactic. They decide not to fight even for what they legitimately deserve. They chose to be Christian wimps rather than ungodly fighters. To this day, when such Christians run into conflicts, they feel anxious over the dilemma between being Christian or being combative. Either way, they want to ignore their anxious feelings.

For various reasons many of us may resist this model's directing us to begin by paying attention to our own feelings in a conflictive situation. We rationalize that conflicts are matters too dangerous or too urgent to permit us to spend any of our time "navel gazing." We figure our feelings are childish and therefore out of date. Thinking like a five-year-old is fine when one is five but dangerous when one is thirty-five.

That is precisely the point. One's feelings are undeniable evidence that one's childhood experiences are still at play. Feelings provide us with clues for detecting what we learned to believe and think when we were too young to choose or test what to believe or think about anything. It pays to pay adult attention to our childish feelings so that we can update our childish beliefs and thoughts underlying our feelings.

The first task of becoming a Christian conflict manager, therefore, is to follow this directive from David Viscott: "When you look at any situation and have feelings about it, note . . . your reactions and understand what they mean."[1]

Respecting our feelings does not mean obeying them. The meanings of our feelings are not self-evident. I may feel angry with someone else because he or she has violated me. But I may also feel angry with someone else because of what I am laying on him or her from inside me. When we pay attention to feelings, we are put in the position of discovering to what degree they arise from our own habitual messages of the past or from our current circumstances. Exploring and understanding the inner beliefs and thoughts underlying our feelings arms us to distinguish between current reality and our projections onto reality.

Although we may think that feelings underlie our thoughts, the opposite is true.[2] Thoughts underlie our feelings. David Burns puts it this way: "You feel what you think."[3] When we think in exaggerated ways, we distort reality. When we think in all-or-nothing terms, we will see all conflicts as challenges to either win or lose. When we find ourselves labeling others in a conflict, we will see them as all good or all bad. When we catastrophize our own or others' circumstances in a conflict, our fears pollute our reason. When we find ourselves jumping to conclusions about others' intentions or positions in a conflict, we will fail to hear or respond to them accurately. When we overgeneralize or personalize others' interests in a conflict, we reduce all the substantive differences to issues of face or self-esteem.[4] Our exaggerated feelings in a conflict, especially negative ones, signify our exaggerated thinking about conflictive situations. Until we detect the thoughts underlying such feelings, we cannot know what we are really dealing with in conflictive situations. As we discover such habitual, unconscious thoughts within us, we can then know what is coming from us and what actually exists in the circumstances outside us.

For example, one may have just hung up the phone after talking with a furious parent of a child in the church school class one teaches. One feels a dizzy-like chagrin inside. That parent is angry over one's upsetting his daughter's beliefs. One has refused to back down, yet one feels *so guilty.*

Why? What automatic, unconscious thoughts have come to mind? A possible answer is that one is thinking what one may have learned as a child: that when others are angry, it is one's own fault. Or that when one is not a perfect teacher, one is no good. Or that standing up for oneself with an angry parent is un-Christlike. Or that one is sinning by not apologizing to this parent. Any such habitual message about another's anger automatically makes one feel anxious or ashamed, regardless of what actually exists in the situation. Having uncovered one's automatic inner thought, one can now decide whether one's feelings are justified or not in this particular situation.

Or again, during a church governing board's debate, an officer finds himself increasingly furious with the pastor. He finds this young pastor not only idealistic but also arrogant. Her ideas about inclusive language in worship services feel like an insult to his intelligence. Saying "mankind" does not mean only men to him. He is offended. Why? What habitual inner thoughts are making him so upset about all this? Perhaps he is thinking about what he learned from his grandmother about "good ole-time religion." He is thinking that this young woman pastor is discounting the faith of his beloved grandmother. He is thinking that anyone who wants to change things is condemning the way things have been. In loyalty to his grandmother and her faith, he must defend the faith language of our fathers, and he means *fathers*![5] He resents this young woman with her feminist theology. He now discovers a basic inner message that he habitually thinks to himself: that anyone who disagrees with his upbringing belittles his upbringing. He can now decide whether to hold on to this message or to pay attention to what his pastor is actually giving as her reasons for wanting to use inclusive language in worship services.

One may wish at this point to take the "Inventory of One's Gut Theology of Conflict," found in appendix 2.

Understanding Family Systems as Theological Teachers

Early family life is everyone's first school of theology. In family fights we acquire our basic attitudes and beliefs about conflict.[6] What happened to us, how authority figures behaved and dealt with us, and what we were told or not told about it all generated our gut theologies of conflict. As we uncover these childhood beliefs buttressing our inner thoughts, we acquire the opportunity to choose what we believe now as adults. We can put away childish thoughts without losing the wonderful openness and trustfulness of a child.

Much of what we learned to believe as children arose from our position in the family—being physically and emotionally dependent on "big people." In terms of power, we were underdogs in the power politics of family conflicts. Until we were at least six, our parents and older siblings towered over us with more knowledge, emotional maturity, physical and verbal skills, worldly information, and familial authority than we had. We were vulnerable to being overridden or shamed in conflicts with those on whom we depended for security, validation, affection, knowledge, and economic support.[7]

Should we feel dread around conflict, we probably had dreadful experiences of conflict when we were so vulnerable. Maybe there was physical, emotional, or sexual violence involved. If so, the thought behind the feeling of dread might be "Conflicts mean violence" or "Conflicts mean kill or be killed." Should one feel rage in a conflict, one may have experienced rejection or humiliation in family fights. Should one have been blamed for family fights, one might have learned "Conflicts are my fault, I'm wrong," or "Conflicts show I'm no good." The point is not that one's feelings are always simply the product of one's past. Indeed, one may feel rage in a current conflict not because of one's childhood but because one is currently being humiliated or violated. But until one identifies one's early learnings about conflict, one cannot accurately assess a current situation in which one is having feelings.

The gut theologies we acquire are rarely all wrong. We all have good reasons for our gut theologies, including the good reasons of painful or dreadful family experiences. However, whether relevant or irrelevant to current circumstances, all gut theologies are inadequate. They are too immature to serve as the sole basis of an adult response to conflict. We are no longer the relatively powerless children we were when we first learned to think and believe this way. As adults we have greater capabilities of thinking, assessing, and understanding information. As adults we can grasp and apply theological concepts in a much wider context than just that of our early family life.

We begin to acquire more adequate theologies of conflict when we understand our life situations with perspectives larger than our own childhoods. What we learned from our families of origin can be augmented now by what others have learned through the centuries in a family of faith. When we were young, we interpreted the meaning of a Bible verse or church belief only in the context of our childhood's limited circumstances. That was all we were capable of as small children. But now we can interpret the meanings of biblical ideas in a variety of contexts: church, occupational, and family of choice. In other words, we can see from the vantage point of the insights of millions of life experiences across thousands of years. In this way, we may acquire much more adequate perspectives with which to make "faith sense" of a conflict we face. We update our gut theologies by informing them with the perspectives of both Christian tradition and contemporary behavioral science.[8] Such rethinking broadens and deepens our understandings so that gradually the thoughts behind our feelings change and we mature spiritually as well as physically. As the author of Ephesians would see it, "We must no longer be children, tossed to and fro and blown about by every wind of doctrine, . . . But speaking the truth in love, we must grow up in every way into him who is the head, into Christ"(Eph. 4:14a, 15).

Christian Perspectives for Rethinking Gut Theologies

Because of a rich diversity of faith traditions and cultural contexts among Christians in a global church, Christians hold to differing beliefs about many things. However different the range of beliefs among Christians, Christians share a context of faith perspective on which to claim that a belief is Christian. This basic context consists of Christian perspectives on human creation, sin, atonement, community, and fulfillment.

What follows is an understanding of the cumulative meanings of conflict from these five Christian perspectives.

Human Creation and Experiences of Conflict

A context of Christian communal perspectives on human creation suggests at least three faith meanings for one's understandings of parties in church conflicts. First, Christians believe that this earth and its inhabitants were created good, not evil. Second, Christians believe that human beings were created in God's image to be responsible stewards of God's good creation. Third, Christians believe that human beings were designed as a species to be interdependent, social beings.

Because humanness is created good, no one's humanity is defective or second rate. Whatever inner messages we may have learned in family conflicts, the communal belief of Christians is that everyone is of inherent worth. God's copyright on our humanity constitutes a universal birthright for personal dignity and self-respect among and between parties to a conflict.

Because human beings are created in God's image, we possess the transforming capacities of spiritual beings. Integral to our humanness is what Niebuhr has called "the reflected image of God."[9] People are not robots. People are finite, but they are not programmed like mindless computers. People can make changes around them by their capacities to think, imagine, construct, invent, communicate, learn, pray, and negotiate. From a Christian perspective, parties to a conflict are innately capable of resolving differences by creative negotiation rather than by irrational power plays or the use of brute force. This human capability also means that parties are morally responsible for their behaviors in resolving conflicts.

Because we are created as an interdependent, social species, we have conflicts. Our differences matter to us, both because we can bond emotionally and because we share dependence for survival on common economic, cultural, and ecological systems. Parties to a conflict may not be directly connected, but they are always indirectly connected. When parties' differences arise, they impinge on one another. They conflict. From a communal Christian perspective on human creation, social conflicts are inherent and inevitable in human experiences.

Human Sin and Experiences of Conflict

A context of Christian communal perspectives on human sin suggests at least two faith meanings for one's understanding of conflicts. First, Christians believe that all human beings sin at times by seeking to "lord it over" others to control them. Second, Christians believe that these sinful behaviors of parties in conflict create evil forces that both predispose parties to sin and hold parties hostage to communal structures of deceitfulness, greed, tyranny, violence, exploitation, or injustice.

It is no wonder that so many gut theologies harbor the belief that conflict is sinful and evil. Conflictive situations tempt parties to defend themselves and their interests at others' expense. The Christian viewpoint is that conflicts both confront us with moral choices and confound us with evil circumstances. Parties to a conflict can and often will try to settle differences by seeking to overpower one another. Like Adam and Eve, they will choose to exceed their finite limits by trying to control everyone else in their lives. And like Cain and Abel, they may end up with murder.

While conflicts, as such, are not sinful, conflicts provide opportunities for sinful behavior. A Christian ethic of conflict management takes seriously the destructive potential of conflicts and the oppressive, cumulatively evil influences bearing on parties who inherit the wind of previous win/lose resolutions of conflicts. Win/lose resolutions of conflicts generate oppressive forces of tyranny, greed, exploitation, injustice, violence, deceit, and death. A Christian perspective alerts a manager to parties' predispositions toward sinful behavior in conflicts.

A Christian ethic of conflict management includes constraining interventions with which to respond to the sinfulness and evil that may obtain in conflictive situations.

Human Redemption and Experiences of Conflict

A context of Christian communal perspectives on human redemption suggests at least three faith meanings for one's understanding of conflicts. First, God's self-giving intervention in Jesus demonstrates what perfect human assertiveness is. Second, God's self-giving intervention in Jesus demonstrates the godly uses of power for nurturing rather than controlling others. Third, God's persistent self-giving intervention in Jesus creates a new situation in which parties can repent of sin and challenge its evil results. God's intervention generates a saving option.

God's will for Jesus demonstrated ethical assertiveness. Jesus chose to die on his terms rather than live on the civil terms of Pilate, the authoritarian terms of the Sanhedrin, or the political terms of a mob. Jesus was assertive about, rather than a victim of, his earthly circumstances. He made choices within the limitations of these circumstances. His choices demonstrated that true humility is not helplessness but assertiveness. We learn from him that our power consists in knowing we cannot control our circumstances but we can make choices in response to them. This is a paradox. When one uses power to control reality, one loses touch with the finiteness of one's reality. When one accepts one's inability to control reality, one discovers the choices one can make in responding to one's circumstances. Parties to conflicts who know their limits can exercise power assertively.

God's power in Jesus outlived evil forces. God's way of dealing with human sinfulness is to outlast its deathly results rather than passively ignore evil or aggressively strive to eliminate evil. God's power is nurturing of God's creation, not overriding it. Rather than forcing people to repent or change, God chooses to invite them to hear and believe. Rather than overpowering them with spectacular miracles, God chooses to join and endure with them their limitations. Christian parties to conflicts are called to accept the same kind of vulnerability.

God's tenacious reconciliation in Jesus establishes a redemptive, win/win option for parties in conflict. As H. Richard Niebuhr put it,

> this Christian understanding of ultimate salvation or wholeness is less the establishment of innocence from transgression than the granting to the self of ability to move again toward perfection, toward the actualization of the power by which it is enabled to see God and live in His likeness.[10]

Because of God's reconciliation in Jesus, one's risking for reconciliation in conflicts is not unrealistic. What is unrealistic is to continue to fight dirty. Conflicts can have redemptive and constructive results, as well as evil and destructive ones. Evil circumstances deriving from human destructiveness have not been eliminated, but they have been decisively breached. What is unrealistic in conflicts is to assume that there is no way but power plays. What is unrealistic in conflicts is to wait for a no-risk way of seeking reconciliation. God's atoning intervention in human history has rehabilitated for human beings the reconciling option in conflictive situations. Christian parties to a conflict can be both realistic and daring as responsible selves.

Human Community and Experiences of Conflict

A context of Christian communal perspectives on human community suggests at least three faith meanings of conflict: the value of conflict as the necessary means of building genuine human community, the nature of human community as the incorporation of differences, and the redemptive power of communal "rules" to restore parties' personal wholeness.

Through constructive conflicts Christian catholicity and community are realized. It was through constructive church fights that primitive Christians were able to bridge their differing ethnic, class, linguistic, and religious backgrounds in realizing a oneness in Christ. Acts, the book of church history, tells of many conflicts among primitive Christians as they struggled with political factions within and imperial politics without. The New Testament epistles are replete with case studies of these church fights—first in Jerusalem, then between the Judaizers and Hellenists in the countryside, and finally within indigenous Gentile house churches that sprang up in cities around the Mediterranean.

For example, Paul writes with typical candor to confront the Christian community in Corinth:

> Now in the following instructions I do not commend you, because when you come together it is not for the better but for the worse. For, to begin with, when you come together as a church, I hear that there are divisions among you; and to some extent I believe it. Indeed, there have to be factions among you, for only so will it become clear who among you are genuine. (1 Cor. 11:17–19)[11]

In this and other Pauline epistles, Paul prescribes a commitment to a larger commonality in Christ that incorporates rather than negates parties' differences. Although these parties lived in different worlds, they fought through their ethnic, geographic, religious, and class differences toward a faith community that incorporated both males and females, Jews and Greeks, slaves and free citizens (see Gal. 3:28).

A Christian communal perspective on conflicts defines community as an incorporation of differences rather than as a homogenization of differences. The behavioral ethic for conflict in primitive church conflicts was to "speak the truth in love." In this regard, Joseph Haroutunian writes,

> If one engages in "sacrificial love" toward another whose love for one is indifference, one's sacrifice even if one gives one's body to be burned, is an affront to the creature and a damning act. Such sacrifice is neither human nor divine; it is the doing of a diseased mind at best and at worst a murder of humanity. Sacrifice presupposes the love of the creature, and such love seeks to be loved. I do not say that one loves in order to be loved; but I do say that one loves as one who depends upon the love of others for one's joy as a creature. One sacrifices oneself, if one does, for those one loves, for people whose love for one is not a matter of indifference but a matter of a most wonderful hope. Any sacrifice, any self-denial and self-sacrifice, is authenticated by a love that gives because it has already received. Sacrifice on the part of a person is an act of justice; a response meant to be according to the due of the loved one; of a person and a community, which are recognized as worthy of a sacrifice of one's time, goods, or any other good, and even of life itself.[12]

The moral aim for Christian parties to a conflict is self-investment in the good with others rather than self-sacrifice for the good of others. In a Christian communal perspective the desired outcome of human conflict is not harmony but community, not calm but synergy, not appeasement but justice. Church conflicts provide useful occasions for parties' learning to incorporate their differences into a larger social wholeness. In church conflicts one can learn anew how to give to another rather than give up or give in to another.

Finally, these stories of New Testament church fights illumine a fundamental principle of human change: Communal processes are prevenient in changing individuals' consciousness and behaviors. The Christian life in the New Testament is primarily a communal affair. When individual members are in pain, in need, or in error, the community is mobilized to reflect and work with them to resolve their problems. The pattern is more one of revitalized communities reforming their members than of reformed individuals vitalizing their communities. As we shall elaborate in later chapters of this book, the "rules" of communal processes are of great power in constraining parties' destructive behaviors and eliciting parties' constructive behaviors in conflictive situations.

Human Fulfillment and Experiences of Conflict

A context of Christian communal perspectives on human fulfillment suggests a major meaning for one's understanding of social conflicts. In this perspective, social conflicts are viewed as cosmic contests between the in-breaking Rule of God and the domination of self-seeking powers. This view applies to how parties use power as well as to what purpose it is put. Christians hope in and seek to cooperate with God's noncontrolling governance of this world and its history. In allegiance to God's rule, Christians pick fair fights for social change that approximate God's *shalom*.[13]

It has already been stated that Christians understand God-in-Christ to be in the business of personal and social change: from religion to faith, from chaos to coherence, from old humanity to new humanity, from self-righteousness (the law) to forgiveness (grace), from brokenness to wholeness, from violence to justice, from isolation to community, from despair to hope, from the governments of this world to the governance of God. God's vision for human fulfillment is a world in which people seek justice, enact kindness, and walk humbly with God.[14]

In a communal Christian view, all conflicts with which parties deal occur in a meantime world. Our era is a "meantime" in two senses: an in-between time and a difficult time. On one hand, one deals with conflicts in a time between God's intervention in Jesus and a time of that intervention's fulfillment at the end of time. On the other hand, one manages conflicts in a time of intense struggle between the healing power of God's self-giving assertiveness for humanity and the deathly power of compulsive social drives for winning at others' expense.

In this meantime era of human history, Christians see national and communal conflicts as casting eternal shadows. How people deal with their differences enlists one in a cosmic power struggle between forces of good and evil, life and death. How we deal with what appear to be quite modest conflicts actually contributes in a mysterious way to the contest between cosmic spiritual forces. Christian parties are called to echo and reflect God's wholeness in conflicts on a continuum from family violence to international violence. A Christian ethic of conflict management seeks to equip us for coping with daily conflicts in light of God's passionate commitment to heal the whole creation.

Rethinking Our Gut Theologies of Conflict

Communal Christian perspectives both confirm and correct parts of one's gut theology of conflict. One's own life experience is connected to those of a "cloud of witnesses." Rethinking gut theologies involves updating one's habitual, unexamined inner beliefs and ideas with Christian messages that incorporate these larger Christian perspectives. Sanders and Malony call such activity self-talk.[15] One takes the inner thoughts one has discovered from one's own life story and considers how they are affirmed and expanded by these larger Christian perspectives.

For Christians, then, the purpose of registering one's feelings is twofold: first, to recognize the underlying thoughts and, second, to discover the immature Christian beliefs supporting such underlying thoughts. In Step One work we first detect a feeling. Then we discover the inner message giving rise to that feeling. Finally, we recall our experiences with conflict as children in our families of origin and of faith to discern what Christian beliefs we acquired without critical assessment.

For example, Sanders and Malony compiled a list of inner messages underlying feelings that people frequently give themselves in conflictive situations.[16] One might intuit or remember learning Christian beliefs that reinforce these inner messages. Recognizing the inner messages can lead one to discover one's gut theology in conflictive situations.

Habitual Messages	*Possible Gut Theologies*
"I can't win."	God saves those who admit they are helpless.
"If you give them an inch, they'll take a mile."	Sinners can't be trusted.
"I must not be angry."	Anger is the root of all evil.
"They really don't mean those nice things about me."	God rebukes the proud of heart.
"S/he's just a [bleeding heart, fundie, communist, or the label of your choice]."	God despises the ungodly.
"If I'm not right, I'm no good."	Be ye perfect as your Father in heaven is perfect.
"In conflicts, it's kill or be killed."	Honor thy father and thy mother, no matter what they do.
"In conflicts, a true Christian always gives in."	Do unto others as you would have them do unto you.
"There's nothing I can do."	Wait, I say, on the Lord.
"True Christians don't fight for themselves."	Jesus says, "Turn the other cheek. Be good to those who persecute you."
"I have no right to criticize others."	Let whoever is without sin cast the first stone.
"Being loving means not hurting others."	I will repay, says the Lord.
"I give up."	Take up your cross and follow me.

"If I ignore conflict, things will work out."	Do not be anxious about tomorrow; tomorrow will take care of itself.
"Good Christians don't fight."	Blessed are the peace makers, for they shall be called children of God.
"I don't agree, but I'll cooperate."	Be reconciled one with another.

The connections we have drawn above between messages and gut theological beliefs illustrate rather than exhaust childish Christian understandings of conflict. The point is that the habitual inner messages we learned to give ourselves about conflict will have unconscious and usually unexamined religious beliefs supporting them. When our inner messages are distorted or exaggerated, they will be sanctioned by unexamined, uncritically acquired childish beliefs. Once we recognize the messages about conflict that we habitually give ourselves, we can discover and consciously examine habitual beliefs from our childhoods. We can then choose to update our beliefs by expanding or revising them in light of adult capacities to think and reason. Such Step One work of registering our feelings, recognizing their underlying messages, and discerning the childhood beliefs supporting them opens the way for more accurately perceiving both a conflictive situation and our Christian convictions about it. In other words, in Step One reflection we "put away childish things" in order to think, act, and love as spiritual adults (1 Cor. 13:11). One may want at this point to examine the "Primer for Updating Gut Theologies," found in appendix 3. We will work further with this part of Step One self-reflection in chapter 3 as well.

There are Christians, of course, who were not raised in Christian homes and who now go to Sunday school as adults. In such a case, one may think that one has no gut theology because one did not learn beliefs until one was old enough to think responsibly about the Christian faith. No one, however, can be raised without some kind of operational faith, some kind of belief system about what or whom to trust, how to behave, and what to seek in life. All people have a gut theology of conflict, be it humanistic or atheistic, cutthroat or genteel, religious or secular. Virtually all of us unconsciously filter Christian concepts and biblical texts through our childish belief systems unless and until we begin to consciously take them into account. We all need to do Step One work repeatedly as we work on Christian management of conflictive situations.

What follows are some Christian beliefs one may consider and choose to adopt from one's Step One introspection as a manager. One replaces childish Christian beliefs and the inner messages they support with consciously considered Christian beliefs and the inner messages they support:

1. Everyone, including me, is a worthwhile, nondefective party to this

conflict. I may have done wrong, but I am not wrong as a person. I may be guilty, but I'm not worthless.

2. Conflict itself is not sinful. Conflict is part of being a social being. Conflict is also an opportunity for ministry. The question is not whether to fight, but how to fight fairly for myself and with others.

3. In this conflict, part of me wants to win at all costs; part of me wants to run away; and part of me wants to stand up for my rights as part of a solution with others. God's way is to forgive the first and second parts and go with the third part.

4. In this conflict, I can trust God to help me as long as I want to do justice for both myself and others. I can't make others work differences out with me. Neither will I make myself be anyone else's victim. The middle way is to seek to work out differences with others for the well-being of all.

5. In this conflict, I can change myself. Other parties can change themselves. No party can force anyone else to change anything other than his or her surface behaviors. But God can change me and everyone else in ways I cannot demand or fully understand.

6. No one in this situation can ensure that this conflict will be resolved constructively. I can work with others to prevent a win/lose resolution, keeping open the potential for a win/win resolution.

7. Managing this conflict is a communal process. I cannot manage it alone. I can appeal to the larger community, not to settle the issues for the principal parties but to get the principal parties to deal with one another constructively. Then I can trust the communal process.

8. Ignoring, denying, or otherwise not managing this conflict will be destructive. It will not go away. It will get more destructive. It is my interest and calling to begin constructive management *now* before the conflict manages me and others destructively. God does not rescue me or others from conflicts. But God sustains those who seek, however imperfectly, to be responsible, assertive selves in conflictive situations.

Rethinking one's gut theology takes time. Even though one's mind changes, the new thoughts feel strange, seeming even heretical to one's customary feelings and thoughts. One may feel confused, unsure. "Maybe I'm betraying my upbringing." "I wonder if I'm wrong to even think about these things." "What if this book is wrong?" When we learn new things, we usually feel unsure of ourselves for a while.

But time will tell us whether we are on the right track or not. No book is perfectly right. No upbringing is perfectly right. No one's thinking is perfectly right. But we are all partly right. That is our spiritual birthright. If we ask for spiritual guidance in communication with others, we will be able to sift new thoughts and consciously considered perspectives until we recognize what is good and right for us as Christian conflict managers.

Rethinking gut theologies *informs* our minds as Christian conflict managers. It prepares us to think clearly and act faithfully. Now we are ready for another aspect of Step One reflection—to practice acting faithfully. Whereas our childish behaviors are often unconsciously reactive, our adult behaviors can be consciously formulated and rehearsed. In this second part of Step One, we seek to update our actions to match our updated beliefs.

CHAPTER 3

Step One, Task Two: Practicing Christian Assertiveness

The president of the women's fellowship was on the verge of tears. "I don't know what to do about Ruth. Every time we have a council meeting, she attacks me personally. It is embarrassing to me and everyone else. Outside of meetings she won't speak to me. I can't keep on being eaten alive this way. But I don't want to be ugly. What am I to do?"

The answer to the president's question is two words: Be assertive. She is feeling the need to practice Christian assertiveness: to respect and stand up for herself without putting anyone else down. The president of the women's fellowship is discovering that dealing with conflict requires personal assertiveness. The second task of becoming a Christian conflict manager is practicing being assertive (see fig. 3.1).

Conflicts are power struggles. Their management involves the exercise of power. One exercises power to secure a *process* by which to deal with parties' substantive issues. The question is not whether one exercises power as a conflict manager. The question is how one exercises power: aggressively, manipulatively, or assertively. Assertiveness about process opens the way for assertiveness over substantive issues. Similarly, aggression or manipulation over process tends to elicit aggression or manipulation over substantive issues. Witness the hours of frustration and anger when a church governing body is ensnared in parliamentary maneuvering. One has to fight fair for fair fighting before dealing with substantive issues.

A Christian Ethic of Assertiveness

A Christian ethic of assertiveness is like a triangle. Three behavioral standards are required, which define and limit one another: (1) personal

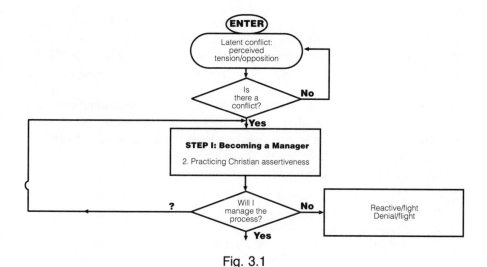

Fig. 3.1

assertiveness of one's rights; (2) respectfulness of others' rights; and (3) shared assertiveness for a common good.

Personal Assertiveness

Lange and Jakubowski define assertiveness in the following way:

> Assertion involves standing up for personal rights and expressing thoughts, feelings, and beliefs in direct, honest, and appropriate ways which do not violate another person's rights. . . . The basic message in assertion is: This is what I think. This is what I feel. This is how I see the situation. This message expresses "who the party is" and is said without dominating, humiliating, or degrading the other person. . . . Assertion involves respect—not deference. . . . respect for oneself . . . as well as respect of the other(s).[1]

"I'm not sure," we may say, "that being assertive is really proper for a Christian. I mean, aren't we supposed to 'turn the other cheek' and 'go the second mile'? Didn't Jesus command us to lay down our lives for others? How can assertiveness be Christian?"

Sanders and Malony have explored this question:

> Many of us have grown up with some strong stereotypes about what Jesus was like. Unfortunately, many of these are based more on motion pictures and other popular media than they are on the Jesus revealed in the Bible. . . . Much scriptural evidence indicates that Jesus was not only mild and giving but was also confrontative, openly angry, and positively assertive toward others.[2]

Indeed, reading the Gospels with a conscious awareness of assertiveness offers us a surprising portrait of Jesus' assertive style with friend and foe alike. Almost daily he squared off against the scribes, Pharisees, and Sadducees, bluntly confronting them with their spiritual self-deceit and their manipulative ways of being religious. Assertively, Jesus pushed aside powerful social prohibitions regarding race and sex: As a Jewish man he talked with a Samaritan woman, dined with traitorous tax collaborators who served the Roman occupation, and stood up for a prostitute who was about to be stoned. Jesus often fought with his disciples, confronting them with their spiritual blindness and resisting their impatient desires to unveil him as God's political heir for the throne of David.

A Christian perspective on assertiveness not only "permits" it but also supports it:

> To please others at the expense of oneself is misunderstanding meekness. The Old Testament definition of meekness is the "poor and needy." The prophets viewed the meek as people who were oppressed, not by their own decision but by the rich and powerful. The meek were dependent upon God for their liberation; meekness was not a condition to be chosen or cherished. The meek were praised, not because they groveled in the dust of oppression, but because they tenaciously kept their eyes toward God. . . .
> The New Testament gives the same meaning to meekness.[3]

Paradoxically, self-assertiveness is actually an act of ego-denial: denying one's ability to control others. Assertiveness recognizes one's limits as a finite creature. It consists in standing up for oneself within one's boundaries and limitations. As James Gustafson puts it,

> Self-denial . . . is not self-detachment or self-hatred; it is rather quiet acceptance, repentance, and cross-bearing in relation to the governing action of God through the beings that limit us. It is the acceptance of God's acceptance of human limitations. . . . It is the acceptance of our responsibility to limit others, even in the knowledge of the fact that our action is never fully right.[4]

Christian humility is not the command to be a human doormat. Christian assertiveness is a humility that accepts one's limits and one's worth as a child of God. One stands for boundaries created by God that prohibit one's controlling others and, by the same token, being controlled by others.

Once one understands humility as self-acceptance rather than self-sacrifice, it becomes clear that the Magna Charta of Christian assertiveness is the Golden Rule:

> One of the scribes came near and . . . asked him, "Which commandment is the first of all?" Jesus answered, "The first is, 'Hear, O Israel: the Lord our God, the Lord is one; you shall love the Lord your God with all your heart, and with all your soul, and with all your mind, and with all your strength.' The second is this, 'You shall love your neighbor as yourself.' There is no other commandment greater than these." (Mark 12:28–31)

To love oneself in place of others is aggression or manipulation. Aggression/manipulation sacrifices others for one's ends. To love others in place of oneself is passivity. Passivity sacrifices oneself for others' ends. To love others as oneself is assertiveness. Assertiveness recognizes a common intrinsic worth to all parties and calls for self-investment rather than self-sacrifice. Christian assertiveness leads us into struggles of giving to and giving with others rather than giving up or giving in to others.

Interpersonal Respectfulness

In their book *Responsible Assertive Behavior,* Lange and Jakubowski state, "In our view, personal rights should be presented in a way which promotes responsible assertive behavior, where one respects other people's rights, as well as one's own."[5]

In common with a humanist ethic, a Christian ethic of assertiveness balances self-respect with respect of others. Such responsible assertiveness approximates the second commandment of the Golden Rule: that we love our neighbor as ourselves. Christian assertiveness extends to others the same high esteem God has for all. Christian assertiveness makes clean distinctions between parties' behaviors and their motives, opinions and their worth, convictions and their spiritual inviability.

Shared Assertiveness for a Common Good

There is a third aspect to a Christian ethic of assertiveness that goes beyond a humanist ethic: the assertive pursuit of human solidarity, a communal common good that serves God in oneself and others.

What is decisive about Jesus' command was its aim: to serve a universal good to the glory of a universal God. In a meantime era, our assertiveness will not be perfect.[6] We will mistake the common good of the neighbor nearby for the common good of all human beings. We will make a little too cozy the coincidence between private and public interests. We will limit the meaning of goodness only to the experience of those most like us.

Nevertheless, a Christian ethic of assertiveness balances the claims of respectfulness between parties with the claims of a larger humanity with whom parties are interdependent. There is more to a Christian ethic of assertiveness than mutuality. A Christian ethic involves solidarity as well. As Douglas Sturm contends, "To act in the public good is not to deny the individuality of persons or associations, but it is to reject the indifference to others of individualism. It is to accept the obligation of being a gift to the entire community of being."[7]

A Christian ethic seeks the rights of persons within the benefits and limitations of the larger human community. To continue with Douglas Sturm,

The individual's political duty is not merely to respect the rights of other individuals. It is to contribute to the common good, the good of the polity. Rights are not ends in themselves. They are requisites to creative symbiosis. As requisites, they are abused when suppressed, for their suppression is a denial of human agency. But they are also abused if not employed for the common good.[8]

A Christian ethic of assertiveness is respectful not only of parties' rights but also of God's justice for all.

To sum up, a Christian ethic of assertiveness prescribes the exercise of power in ways that balance one's own rights with respectfulness of others' rights in pursuit of universal human solidarity. In conflicts we are tempted to take one of these behavioral standards to the exclusion of the others: to sacrifice our rights out of respect for others; to violate others' rights in pursuing our own; or to seek partisan solutions at the expense of a larger public good or human solidarity.

The Barrier of Shame to Practicing Responsible Assertiveness

Many Christians may agree with all these theological and ethical arguments but still find themselves blocked from behaving assertively. It takes more than cognitive understanding for them to behave assertively. The key to anyone's being assertive lies in one's fundamental sense of oneself: of shame or of self-worth.

Christians behave aggressively or manipulatively in conflicts when they are informed by habitual, unexamined beliefs they gained in childhood. Christians behave assertively in conflicts when they are informed and re-formed by Christian beliefs that they are fully loved by God. That is why learning to practice Christian assertiveness involves a continuing reflection about one's gut Christian beliefs.

What can block any Christian from being assertive is shame. Shame is a different form of sin than wrongdoing. Merle Fossum and Marilyn Mason explain:

Guilt is the developmentally more mature, though painful, feeling of regret one has about behavior that has violated a personal value. Guilt does not reflect directly upon one's identity nor diminish one's sense of personal worth. . . . A person of guilt might say, "I feel awful seeing that I did something which violated my values." . . . In so doing the person's values are reaffirmed. The possibility of repair exists and learning and growth are promoted. While guilt is a painful feeling of regret and responsibility for one's actions, shame is a painful feeling about oneself as a person. The possibility for repair seems foreclosed to the shameful person because shame is a matter of identity, not a behavioral infraction. There is nothing to be learned from it and no growth is opened by the experience because it only confirms one's negative feelings about oneself.[9]

Shame-based people cannot assert themselves because they secretly think of themselves as inferior to other parties in a conflict. They perceive of conflicts as occasions when their secret defectiveness will be found out. Therefore, shame-based parties experience conflicts as occasions when they must prove to be right at whatever cost. They are literally driven to be right.

Their goal in conflicts is to be a winner, so as to seem superior. Their terror is to be a loser, which they perceive as being defective.

Obviously, a shame-based mentality in conflicts sets up compulsive behavior. In some win/lose conflicts parties fight aggressively or manipulatively to get what they want at others' expense. They act sinfully. But in other win/lose conflicts one or more parties fight compulsively to be what they fear they are not: worthwhile beings. When parties act sinfully, they can repent and choose to fight constructively. But when parties perceive that they are not of worth, they must be healed before they can choose to fight constructively. Such parties fulfill the profile of a church antagonist drawn by Haugk:

> Antagonists are parties who, on the basis of nonsubstantive evidence, go out of their way to make insatiable demands, usually attacking the person or performance of others. These attacks are selfish in nature, tearing down rather than building up, and are frequently directed against those in a leadership capacity.[10]

Tragically, many antagonists cannot even consider repenting without experiencing self-hate. They don't know how to be different without being better or worse than others. When they shame themselves or others for being wrong rather than doing wrong in conflicts, they may regret their behavior, but they see no way to change the reality they perceive and defend at all costs. Reinhold Niebuhr's distinction between repentance and remorse is applicable here: "Repentance is the expression of freedom and faith while remorse is the expression of freedom without faith. The one is the 'Godly sorrow' of which St. Paul speaks, and the other is 'the sorrow of this world which worketh death.' "[11] Shame-based people hear God calling, and they hide. Shame-based parties do not hear God call their names because of the bedlam of name-calling going on inside themselves. The only way shame-based antagonists know to resolve conflicts is to determine who is right or wrong, good or bad. They cannot resolve issues without judging persons. Nor can they accept or offer compromises without feeling that they are acknowledging imperfections that might expose their defectiveness. Such tormented parties are often major players in chronically destructive church conflicts.

Fortunately, a majority of parties to church conflicts are sinners, not shame sufferers. Sinners can choose to be responsible selves. "Well, my problem isn't understanding but practicing assertiveness," they say. "I just can't get the hang of it. Sometimes I boil over and act crazy. But most of the time I just try to keep others from getting angry or hurt. And the next thing you know I've either lied to them or sold out to them."

Practicing Christian Assertiveness

Assertiveness is basically a mentality, a deep inner conviction that one is a creature of inherent worth and a loved one of God. That mentality can then become a skill through practice. As we learn to behave assertively, we learn to believe as God's loved ones. As we claim we are God's loved ones, we are freed to behave more assertively. Both thinking and acting faithfully are strengthened by practice.

In Step One work, we recover a sense of self-worth by remembering and receiving Christian perspectives on ourselves and others in a conflictive situation. As we uncover the negative messages underlying our feelings, we replace them with positive Christian messages based on our convictions:

1. I'm imperfect, but I'm as good as anyone else.
2. I'm a survivor, and I'm learning and changing.
3. Since God loves me, I will value and respect me.
4. Everyone has both goodness and craziness about them.
5. It's okay to make mistakes if I make amends.
6. I can be responsible.
7. I can't change others, but I can change myself.
8. I do evil, but I'm not evil. No one is.
9. Trust God, and trust the process.

Since we learned negative messages as children, we can learn positive Christian messages like these as adults. Our new inner messages do not immediately replace our old messages, but when we act on them, they gradually come to dominate the old ones.

The process of learning to practice assertiveness is like learning to play an instrument. One may believe that one is capable of playing an instrument, but learning to play it takes practice—repetition—rehearsals. Risking making mistakes. Accepting not being perfect. Similarly, any Christian in a conflictive situation may come to believe that he or she is worth being assertive for. Learning how to stand up for ourselves with others then takes practice—repetition—rehearsals—risking making mistakes—accepting not being perfect.

There is also another kind of risk taking involved in managing conflicts: risking not only to assert oneself but also to fight assertively for a constructive process of managing the conflictive situation one faces. One's own assertiveness does not make others assertive. Assertive parties can make the naive mistake of assuming that all other parties can and will behave with emotional reciprocity. They assume that if they are assertive, others will be assertive. If they fight fair, others will fight fair. They fail to appreciate the depth of wounded drivenness that shame can inflict on some parties. Precisely because an assertive party does not seek to control others, shame-driven parties can exploit and violate assertive parties in conflicts. This is the second risk of being assertive. Indeed, sometimes it almost seems as if those who fight fair are doomed to lose to those who fight dirty.

This would be the case without the countervailing forces of redemptive communal rules. While such rules do not eliminate risk, they minimize risk. As we shall see, a Christian conflict manager practices assertiveness not simply on behalf of self but also on behalf of interpersonal processes that protect the assertiveness of all parties, including the manager.

An Illustration of
Step One Work for Assertiveness

As he put the phone down, Hank felt tight and queasy inside. The other party had angrily hung up on him. He was feeling guilty. Hank was in a habit of feeling guilt when others were angry with him. For some reason he believed that others' anger was his fault. Hank was also scared. For some reason he believed that when he was in conflict with others, he would be badly hurt. These feelings were not new to Hank. They were all too familiar whenever he encountered or even sensed a conflict. But Hank's way of handling his feelings was to scold himself for having them. He'd tell himself that while real men cry, they aren't afraid of conflict. He'd then order himself to stop having such feelings and be rational. Even though his feelings often hung on, he would make himself think about how to handle the situation. Only in the middle of the night would his feelings take over again, causing him to lose a considerable amount of sleep.

This time Hank decided to explore his feelings rather than ignore or stuff them. He got out paper and began following the "Work Sheet for Step One Self-Talk for Assertiveness" (see appendix 4).

Hank listed negative feelings of guilt and fear. He was puzzled about whether his feeling guilty was actually his being mad or sad. At first he couldn't tell. But then he found himself realizing that for some reason he felt embarrassed over the caller's anger. Why? Why was he embarrassed and afraid over the caller's anger? Then it hit him. He was experiencing shame! His queasy feeling was shame, even though in reality he was not to blame for his caller's angry diatribe. He added shame to his list. Anger then welled up in him. He had been verbally attacked and had sat there taking it. He added anger to his list of feelings. Then he felt relief and joy over what he was doing. He added both feelings to his list. He began to feel a strange joy over recognizing that his habitually queasy feelings around conflicts were shame.

Hank then began to write down the thoughts he'd had with his feelings: "When someone's angry at me, it's my fault." "Let people blow off, and it'll be over." "Something's wrong with me." "Hurting others is dangerous." "I'm chicken, but I'm tough."

As these thoughts tumbled onto the paper, Hank recognized his past. His father had left home as a G.I., and no one had taught Hank how to fend for himself. No wonder he was scared. By the time his father came back, he was scared of him too. He remembered how his father, when angry, would walk out of the room. Then in a little while his family acted like nothing had happened. No one had shown him how to work things out. The family seemed to have a no-talk rule about conflict. Finally, Hank began to relive his childhood agony over the birthmark on his face. Sometimes kids had pointed at him. Sometimes a stranger would come up and ask him what was wrong with his face. At such times, Hank wanted to find a hole in the ground. His face flushed just thinking about it. But all his folks did was to tell him that he was fine just the way he was. No one in his family talked about his birthmark. It was almost as if they were too embarrassed to do so. At any rate, he knew that was where the shame had come from. He remembered the joy of finding a way to do his hair that covered the mark. He also realized now that he'd secretly felt he was somehow defective all his life. Hank wrote all of this down.

He then began to deduce the messages he'd learned about himself and others in conflicts: "Don't be sensitive." "You can take it." "Be strong enough not to hurt others." "There's something wrong about you that we won't talk about." "You lose in fights."

Hank's current inner thoughts and childhood messages began to make sense of each other. He'd felt guilt and shame on the phone because he was supposed to be strong enough not to hurt others and because he had been trained not to be sensitive.

He had learned to endure rather than challenge another's aggression. As he made these connections, it felt like a weight of negativity was sliding off his back.

Hank chose to give himself some positive messages. He wrote, "My birthmark does not make me defective. I'm okay." "My birthmark does not make me special. I'm just normal." "I can learn to fight assertively for myself." "I can fight with process to be safe in conflicts." "It's Christian to hurt others when setting limits on their hurting you."

He smiled to himself. "It all sounds strange," he thought. "I'm not really sure that this stuff is right." And yet his new messages for himself were very much like things he would have said to anyone else he was helping. Hank decided to try acting on his new realizations. He would begin practicing how to be respectfully assertive with himself and with others. He was a bit nervous, but the fear had dissolved. Above all, he was no longer feeling that it was somehow his fault that his caller was angry. He would now find a way to deal with this situation rather than ignore himself and his birthright as a child of God, birthmark and all.

In Conclusion

What is required for assertiveness is self-worth: knowing that one is loved and valued as an imperfect child of God. As we come to know that we are worthwhile, we learn to stand up for our ideas, feelings, and gifts without standing on anyone else. The skills come with practice, but the basic self-respect comes from experiencing God's valuing of us as mirrored by ourselves and others.

One is never through with Step One self-talk while managing a conflictive situation. Virtually all of us have wounds and destructive messages learned in an imperfect, sinful world. As one moves through the remaining steps in this model, one may frequently return to registering one's feelings, recognizing their underlying messages, and choosing new messages based upon one's Christian faith. The results of repeatedly doing Step One are not self-preoccupation or egotism but self-liberation for the assertive service of God, self, and all other parties in conflictive situations. The goal is an intentional Christian assertiveness about and for a responsible process by which all principals will resolve their differences constructively.

Having begun the ongoing process of updating gut theologies and practicing assertiveness, one is finally in a position to see a conflictive situation more clearly so as to determine one's own role in it. One is ready for the final task of Step One in becoming a Christian conflict manager.

CHAPTER **4**

Step One, Task Three:
Determining Roles

The church officer's stomach churned. What had begun as a struggle of the governing body over the budget was becoming another round of thinly veiled personal attacks between the Bruce family and the preacher. Once again, she thought, the rest of the board was caught in the cross fire. Once again board members would try to settle things by reasoning and voting. Neither activity would resolve anything. The feuding would just go on, holding the board hostage. It wasn't the board's fight, and yet the board was being twisted like a pretzel by it. Whose fight was it, anyway?

The church officer had a good question. Becoming a Christian conflict manager involves answering that question by determining the differing ways or roles in which parties, including oneself, are related to a conflictive situation (see fig. 4.1). While one may manage a conflict from any role, one's role will determine how one will operate as a manager. One can be a combatant who instigates refereeing as a shared task with the other combatants.[1] Or one can be a referee who sets up and monitors combatants' fair fighting. In either case, one's job as a manager is to secure the needed refereeing. One's activity in the implementation of this refereeing will be different when one is a combatant from what it is when one is not. Of course, as with more traditional understandings of conflict management, one can be an outside consultant secured by combatants or other parties to serve as a designated, official referee of a conflict. What is common to any role in relation to a conflict is the necessity of establishing some way in which refereeing will occur.

44

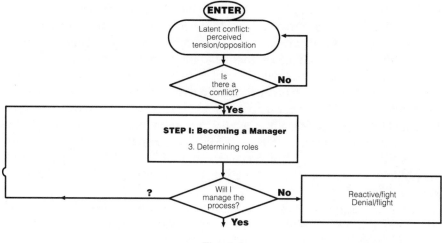

Fig. 4.1

Defining Roles in Conflictive Situations

Parties to church conflicts who are not outsiders will usually be concerned to represent more than just their own personal interests. They may represent the structural interests of the church organization housing the conflict—the interests of a committee, of staff responsibilities, of a fellowship group, of a church school class, or of a governing board.

Parties may also be representative of political interests:

- the interests of a theological enclave or faction of shared opinion, mentality, or attitude
- the interests of communal habits, unwritten rules/codes/rituals of a faith community's life, often spoken of as "the status quo"
- the interests of a particular institutional program or project
- the interests of a network of long-term friendships or allies
- the interests of larger denominational politics
- the interests of special interest groups in the neighborhood from which church members come

Although parties to church fights may appear to be acting only as individuals, they usually represent organizational or political interests greater than their own. In any case, roles in a conflict derive from how parties, individual or representative, relate to the matters at issue.

One does not choose one's role as a party to a conflict. One's role results from how one's own interests are involved in the situation. However, one does make a choice to manage a conflict's process as well as to stand for one's own interests. One's role is determined by one's interests. One's ministry of conflict management is a response to one's Christian vocation.

For example, pastors are parties to virtually every major church fight in the parish they serve. Since pastors have the highest visibility in the community, conflicting parties will often seek to draw them into or take them on in a conflict. Pastors have little choice over whether they will be parties to a conflictive situation where they are employed. But pastors always have a choice whether or not they will initiate management of a conflict's process. Pastors also often have a choice whether they will pursue their interests in the role of combatant or in another way. Even though pastors cannot choose whether they will be involved, pastors can choose how they will be involved.

In the literature on conflict management, various terms are used for parties to a conflict.[2] What is important is not the term used but clarity over the distinctive ways in which parties' primary interests and positions relate them to a conflictive situation.

Principals

A principal in a church conflict is a party whose interests—purposes, needs, desires, responsibilities, and/or commitments—are in collision with those of at least one other party. Principals are related to a conflict because they have stakes in *the conflicting differences.* It is the differences between principals that must be resolved if the conflict is to be resolved. It is their conflict. They alone can resolve their issues constructively.

When parties are principals primarily because of their institutional responsibilities, they are structural principals. When parties are principals primarily because of their status, they are cultural principals. As we have already observed, paid church staff are frequently structural principals in church conflicts. Professional staff also have high cultural status as communal authority figures. Since professional and support staff are in roles that often overlap or influence each other, it is not surprising that many church conflicts involve conflicts within church staffs or conflicts between church staff and volunteer church leaders.

Paid staff, however, are not the only structural principals in church conflicts. Volunteer chairpersons of committees and officers of governing bodies also frequently become structural principals as they fulfill their commitments in church conflicts. Their responsibilities require them to work as volunteers. They often carry a greater portion of the financial and voluntary obligations in faith communities than church staff do. Indeed, one hears of churches where volunteers frequently suffer burn-out simply from serving in conflicted situations between church staff and people in the pew. Their responsibilities require them to work with church staff, while their lay perspectives lead them to identify with church members.

When people are principals primarily because of ideological or social group memberships, they are political principals. Political principals represent special mentalities, attitudes, beliefs, or ideologies resident in faith communities and denominational systems. There are church professionals and church members whose loyalty to long-term friends and associates is even more influential with them than their own thinking or opinions. They will take a position in a conflict more out of interpersonal allegiance than out of personal conviction. Both structural and political kinds of representative principals will be constrained by interests larger than their own. Such kinds of representation in church conflicts are more the rule than the exception.

In summary, principals in church conflicts are those parties who have conflicting personal and/or representative interests at stake. It is their behaviors that generate malevolent or benevolent cycles of a conflict.

Bystanders

A bystander in a church conflict is a party whose interests—purposes, needs, desires, or responsibilities—are related to the impact of a conflict's resolution on the community or church entity housing it. Bystanders are more invested in how principals resolve their differences than in what principals' resolutions may be. Bystanders are like parties in a fishing boat in which principals get into a fight. Their primary concern is that principals' behaviors not sink the boat.

For some, the term "bystander" may sound passive. A mental picture of spectators comes to mind. This image is applicable when bystanders choose to be passive spectators. Such passivity contributes to the destructiveness of unmanaged conflicts. But this image is inappropriate when bystanders proactively choose to use their communal power to secure a conflict's management. A community of responsible bystanders can impose constraints on principals. These constraints may not resolve the issues but can prevent a win/lose resolution of the issues. A community of responsible bystanders can also reinforce constructive behaviors by the principals, thereby contributing to a win/win resolution of the issues.

Parties to church conflicts often confuse the roles of principals and bystanders. Because bystanders may have very high stakes in the effects of a conflict on the larger community, they often enter the fray in order to resolve issues by taking sides. They become, in effect, secondary principals who mistake taking sides as the way to prevent destructive resolution. Rather than taking measures as bystanders to prevent the sinking of the communal boat, their taking sides often polarizes situations, making the communal boat rock even more dangerously. The way for bystanders to pursue their interests in a conflictive situation is to intervene in the process of the conflict rather than to position themselves over the matters at issue.

Although the primary stake of a bystander is in the constructive management of a conflict, most bystanders will have very real stakes in the differences of principals involved in a conflict. Being a bystander does not mean that one has no investment in the substance of the conflict. Being a bystander simply means that one recognizes that one's investment in constructiveness outweighs one's investment in the issues or parties involved.

Most ministers and lay leaders of integrity recognize that they are called and employed to provide moral and spiritual leadership for their faith communities. Such moral and spiritual leadership is a continuing, primary interest underlying their services. Since most significant church conflicts involve moral and spiritual issues of real import, ministers may feel that choosing the role of bystander/manager is actually a way of betraying their integrity as leaders. They do not see how they can be neutral on the issues without violating their personal conscience or professional vows. Choosing their role seems to them a dilemma.

This model does not lead anyone to abandon his or her spiritual or professional interests just for the sake of managing a conflict constructively. A third alternative exists for ministers and lay leaders. They can consider other ways than being principals by which they can pursue the interests underlying their concerns: through other programs or projects or in other organizations or at another time in their ministries. The point is that when ministers and lay leaders identify their underlying interests, they may find that they will get more of them realized in noncombative ways than by pursuing them as principals. It may be that in one case their underlying commitments are best served by choosing to be a principal, while in another case these same underlying commitments will be better served by their choosing to be a bystander. Their responsibility is to recognize and make a choice rather than to assume that the only way their underlying interests can be pursued is as principals to every conflict that arises in their church community.

While often a church leader may choose between being a principal or a bystander in a conflictive situation, one does well to stay with one's choice. Jumping from one role to another in the midst of a conflict destroys trust and credibility with other parties. Either one chooses at the outset to be a bystander and to pursue one's vocational commitments in other ways, or one chooses at the outset to be a principal and to pursue one's commitments in terms of the conflict itself. Should one find oneself compelled to change one's role in the midst of a conflict's management, it is absolutely necessary that one explicitly negotiate or identify one's changing role with other parties involved.

Bystanders play a critical role in this book's model for managing church conflict. They provide a manager with the power to constrain destructive exchanges between principals. They also encourage principals' ethical proclivities toward resolving their issues constructively. It should be emphasized, however, that not every member of a faith community or church body housing a conflict will be a bystander. Many such members behave as spectators rather than bystanders; they ignore or flee from conflict rather than standing for its constructive management. When the apathy and moral irresponsibility of spectators outweigh the integrity and moral responsibility of bystanders, a conflict's constructive management is put at great risk.

Third Parties

A third party to a church conflict is an outside party whose interests—purposes, needs, desires, or responsibilities—relate only to the dynamics of a conflict. While bystanders have primary investments in the dynamics of a conflict, third parties are invested *only* in the dynamics of a conflict. This is possible because outsiders are not directly affected by either the substantive resolution or the effects of the dynamics. To pursue the fishing boat analogy, a third party is one standing on the shore giving guidance to the principals and bystanders in the boat.

People who are staff to regional and national governing bodies in connectional denominations often think of themselves as third parties because they are based outside the faith community hosting a conflict. Such thinking mistakes social location for the way one's interests relate to a conflictive situation. A regional staff person's responsibilities in a conflicted pastoral relationship may make her or him a bystander or even a principal rather than a third party. Other parties recognize such a structural or political investment. They may well distrust the church bureaucrat or regional church official who claims to be a disinterested third party simply because she or he participates in another church entity as a bystander.

People in church systems often use the term "third party" rather loosely to designate anyone who undertakes to resolve a conflict constructively, whether by process management, gathering and interpreting data, appeasement of political powers-that-be, interpersonal stress management, or formal arbitration of substantive issues. The confusion seems to arise from thinking of outsiders as experts and of conflict management as a matter of technical expertise that "fixes" differences rather than manages the process by which principals resolve their differences. Obviously, this model's use of the term is far more restricted in role definition.

Because conflictive situations in churches are often both painful and complex, it is often tempting to seek an outsider "to fix things." As the old saying goes, "If you give a person a fish, you feed that one for a day. If you teach a person to fish, you feed that one for life." The hazard is that insiders will misuse outsiders by wooing them into resolving a conflict *for* both principals and bystanders rather than *through* principals and bystanders.

Only the originating principals can truly resolve their differences. What principals and bystanders need from an outside third party is process help, not substantive solutions.

The polities of most North American church systems, however, confuse the differing roles of bystanders and third parties. These church polities make little or no explicit provision for a conflict's management at the instigation of outsiders. The usual provision is for a conflict to be arbitrated by outsiders under the guise of outsiders' political negotiation with the principals. These church polities were formed in an agrarian culture that used authoritarian ways of leading and resolving conflicts.[3] Hence, the authority of an outside person from a denomination's middle or national governing body was brought into conflicted situations in a Solomonic style. It was as if an outside church official would settle a church conflict in the same way as a parent might be expected to resolve a conflict between children. Consequently, some parties to a church conflict may still today seek from an outside authority figure the substantive resolution of their conflict. Fortunately and unfortunately, however, that day is swiftly passing in current North American church systems.

Even so, third parties can be very effective today as those who secure a conflict's management by the bystanders and principals involved. The ultimate need for an outside third party to arbitrate conflicts that insiders will not manage constructively can be a persuasive prod for insiders' management. Outsiders can also be very helpful to insiders' management of a conflict by offering process assistance and relevant information not previously possessed by insiders. Finally, in conflicted primary relationships, particularly pastoral relationships, outsiders are often required to direct a mediating process because of the emotional intensity involved. An outsider's geographical distance also facilitates his or her providing the kind of nonanxious presence that is most helpful for working through the emotional debris of conflicted relationships. In every case, however, the primary usefulness of a third party is here seen to be as process consultant rather than as authoritarian arbiter of church conflicts. Only when a conflict's constructive management fails is outside arbitration appropriate.

Arbiters

An arbiter is a party whose interests—purposes, needs, desires, or responsibilities—relate only to the conflicting differences between principals. Arbiters are needed by all parties when efforts to manage and resolve a conflict constructively fail.

As we have seen, one cannot make others fight fair. There are situations in which aggressive/manipulative principals and a community of passive bystanders combine to yield a destructive win/lose resolution or destructive irresolution of a conflict. Responsible bystanders and third parties alike are held hostage by such situations. Arbiter(s) representing a larger institutional system are needed to resolve the issues so that all those destructively affected by the situation can move on.

The resolution reached by arbiters applies primarily to the community of bystanders rather than the original principals. In effect, the arbitrated resolution liberates bystanders of goodwill to proceed with reconstructing communities that have been devastated by win/lose or lose/lose conflicts. It helps when it is made clear to bystanders that one or more of the original principals will probably withdraw from the larger community. Codependent faith communities will resist the loss of any party.

However, an inclusive church cannot compel any party to choose to participate constructively in its life. Concerned members need to recognize that recalcitrant antagonists exclude themselves from constructive community rather than the community's excluding them.

With the increasingly democratic mentalities of voluntary North American church members, arbitrated settlements of church disputes are proving less and less binding. Resolutions may be reached by outsiders, but the relationships between the original parties remain fractured, and the resolutions are often ignored. In this context, it is much more promising to allocate institutional resources and energy in efforts to manage conflicts than in efforts to arbitrate conflicts. Arbitration can be seen as the option of last resort when management efforts have failed.

Managing Conflicts in Role

This book's model for managing conflicts provides ways a principal in a conflict may also be its manager. It is like a pickup basketball game at the YMCA or on a company picnic. Players function collectively as their own referee. When a rule is in dispute, players collectively negotiate the call. Similarly, a principal in a conflict may activate other principals as a collective referee. Time will be consumed over formulating collective refereeing calls; however, time and money may be saved by not securing the services of a third party.

There is one important handicap to managing a conflict as a principal in it. Just as a coach may not play on the team being coached, a principal is not in a position to coach directly another principal. Recognition of this limitation is important because many ministers have learned to disarm their opponents by paying them a "pastoral visit." This limitation illustrates the effects of role on the way in which one may act as a conflict's manager. This limitation will be explored later in this book (see chapter 10). A second limitation on being a principal/manager relates to highly conflicted interpersonal relationships in which the emotionality of parties hazards the rational capability of any one of them. This limitation will also be explored later in this book (see chapter 12).

With these exceptions noted, principals to a conflict may be its managers as well. What distinguishes them from other principals is their knowing and choosing to address a conflictive situation's process prior to dealing with its substance. Once a principal/manager has obtained collective responsibility for a constructive process, a principal/manager may assume advocacy for her or his concerns like other principals.

For example, Keith was intensely opposed to his pastor's recommendation that the parish make a monetary gift to a neighboring congregation's program of sanctuary for illegal aliens. He knew he was not alone. Local newspaper reports about the illegality of the sanctuary program had concerned many in town. Keith was convinced that such a monetary gift would cost far more than the gift itself. His first instinct was to pull together those board members likely to support his stand and persuade them to vote negatively as a block when the board met. On second thought, however, he recognized that such a political assault on his pastor might win a battle at the cost of losing a productive pastoral relationship. He chose to contact his pastor, state that he would oppose the recommendation, and propose some ground rules for the board's debate. In making this choice, Keith became a principal/manager. He moved first to establish a responsible process before taking his stand on the issue. He not only maintained a constructive relationship between himself and his pastor, but he also worked out a compromise that provided that parish members would be solicited for personal contributions in place of a corporate contribution from the parish budget.

Often the greatest difficulty of principals who become managers lies in their abandoning their own issues in order to be "neutral" managers. A principal/manager may abandon his or her interests in exchange for other principals' cooperation. Or a principal/manager may abandon her or his interests in order to appease other principals. Whenever a principal/manager abandons his or her interests, however, a false peace results. One's interests do not dissipate. The solution is for a principal/manager to fight first for fair fighting; then to fight for his or her interests along with the other principals.

When one is both principal and manager in a conflict, others may find one's role confusing. They may expect any conflict manager to be an outsider who is neutral over the issues. Or they may distrust one's management of the process, feeling it to be a ploy for gaining psychological or political advantage regarding the issues. It is often wise at the outset of one's intervention to make explicit and to contract one's role as a principal/manager with the other principals.

Finally, should one be an outside third party, one's management may involve the somewhat awkward task of initiating contact with parties to offer one's services. In doing so, there are a number of concerns to keep in mind. First, one must make clear that one's stake is in the conflict's constructive management so that its resolution will not require outside arbitration. Second, one must undertake Step Two tasks with representatives of the community of bystanders rather than directly with the principals. Third, one will need the authorization of decision makers of the community housing the conflict if one is to participate in the community's process. When decision makers are themselves the principals, one asks for their authorization for one's work with bystanders in seeking benefits for all parties involved.

Naming the Parties to
Conflictive Situations

This book's Step One for becoming a Christian conflict manager has focused on managing oneself: one's gut theology, one's skill at being assertive, and one's clarification of one's role.

As one determines one's own role in a conflictive situation, one begins to recognize the apparent roles of other parties. One is now in a position to begin to assess a conflictive situation by distinguishing between those who are principals and those who are bystanders. Using the "Work Sheet for Appraising Conflictive Situations" (see appendix 5), one lists the names of those who appear to be the principals, representative or individual, of the matters at issue.

One begins with one's own name. Is one's stake as a manager primarily in the matters at issue or primarily in a constructive process? If the former, one lists oneself as a principal. If the latter, one does not list oneself on the work sheet.

Next one puts down the names of individuals representative of communal structures, rules, ideologies, or factions. To recognize what names to list, ask, Who among the parties seem to have a stake in these differences rather than just in how differences are dealt with? Who seem to care enough to contend for their interests? Who have track records of being principals in this context? The names of parties who come to mind in answering these questions are listed in the column headed "Principals." The names of parties whose primary concerns are with the ways principals deal with their differences are listed in the column headed "Bystanders."

In conflictive situations where people's behaviors indicate that a conflict exists in latency but has not yet been acknowledged, one lists the names of potential principals whom one would propose due to their helpfulness and influence.

A novice at conflict management may have difficulty naming the principals in a church conflict. There are a number of common psychological barriers that may get in the way. One barrier is a habit of looking only for personalities as principals rather than looking for principals who embody or represent larger communal factors or political interests. Another common barrier to naming principals is one's assumption that one can name principals only by knowing their issues rather than by observing their verbal and nonverbal behaviors, such as distancing, hostility, reticence, short spokenness, physical avoidance, tone of voice, use of emotionally loaded terms, or reluctance to make eye contact. A general guideline for distinguishing between those parties who are principals and those who are bystanders is to list no more than five parties for any one conflictive situation. For example, while there may be thirty church officers on a governing board, only three of them will be highly invested and representative of differing mentalities over a particular issue among board members. In this case, out of thirty church officers, only three principals would be named.

For example, let's return to the case mentioned at the beginning of this chapter of the chronic antagonism between the Bruce family and the preacher. In this case one might list as principals

1. the Bruce family member of highest familial status
2. the chairperson of the personnel committee
3. the minister

Or, as a second example, there may be a congregation with a total of twenty-four members. In a conflict over benevolent giving, unless the congregation has been completely polarized into warring camps, the principals will fall into one of three enclaves:

1. those who oppose any giving beyond the congregation
2. those who support giving beyond the congregation
3. those who favor selective giving beyond the congregation

Note that these presenting positions do not reveal parties' underlying interests and real issues.

Another reason one may have difficulty naming principals is because a conflict is latent. As we shall see, many congregations are in the habit of denying, masking, or suppressing conflicts. In such congregations a conflict may simmer beneath the surface for a long time without principals' identifying themselves. The only behavioral evidences will be a tense emotional climate, an occasional snide comment, or superficial conversations between members about "safe" topics like sports or the weather. One really has no idea which parties to name as principals in such a deliberately diffused situation. The occasional snide comments offer no clues about names.

In such situations one can intuit what may be some of the conflicting differences by observing the differing mentalities of members of the community. As differing mentalities come to mind, one can guess what groups or structural interests are likely to find representative spokespersons should these differences surface. One can tentatively list "potential" or "latent" principals in such a conflictive situation.

The benefit of dealing with conflictive situations that are denied or suppressed by parties is that one can choose whom one would want to propose as spokespersons if or when the conflict was surfaced. Obviously one would choose and list those parties who evidenced more constructive than destructive ways of behaving in conflicts. While one cannot choose these more constructive parties as representative principals, one can be prepared to propose them when one surfaces the conflict by naming it and proposing ground rules and procedures for its management. When proposing representative principals, one will want to be sure that they are explicitly validated and empowered by those they are to represent in the resolving process.

Sometimes one can name one or two of the principals in a conflict, while realizing that there may be others yet to surface. One can begin to assess the situation working on the basis of the two principals one has identified. If additional principals come to mind or into view, one can update one's original assessment by adding them or substituting them for others on the list.

There are also times when a number of people seem to represent a particular interest. It is not clear which of them will become the spokesperson in a conflict. One can profile the general traits of the conflicting interests as a "composite" principal to list on the work sheet for further assessment.

Perhaps the greatest barrier to naming principals lies within ourselves. We have been conditioned by Western culture to analyze and prove rather than to intuit and interpret our circumstances.[4] We have been trained to think in order to control more than to participate. We have come to believe that one should not act until one can be both objective and reasonably certain. Such training is a prescription for "analysis paralysis" in most conflictive situations. Naming principals is as much a matter of tentative intuition as of provable logic. Naming principals includes both facts and interpretation, both observations and intuitions, both one's thoughts and one's feelings. When we give ourselves permission to be intentional and accountable rather than having to be objective, we will recognize that naming principals is an inconclusive but valuable aspect of preparing to manage a conflictive situation.

Contracting with Oneself as Conflict Manager

We are now reaching the conclusion of Step One: becoming a manager. One may conceive of this step as a matter of beginning to fight fair with oneself. The step leads one into dealing with inner conflicts between one's feelings and beliefs, one's self-esteem and assertiveness, and one's own special investments and one's desire to be fair and constructive. Most people who undertake the tasks of this step continue doing them as they proceed with Steps Two and Three below. These tasks are ongoing within oneself as one manages a conflictive situation. Once one's feelings have become more positive than negative, one will want to move on to the tasks of Steps Two and Three. Often, however, when old feelings from habitual messages recur as one proceeds, one will need to revisit the first two tasks in Step One. The axiom is that only as we continue to fight fair with ourselves will we be positioned to help others fight fair.

One useful way to anchor one's inner fair fighting is to draw up a contract with oneself as a conflict manager. This contract may include one's role, resources, limitations, and intentions as a party to a conflict. For example:

> I choose to manage this conflict. I am a principal [or bystander or third party] in it. I bring to it a tendency to shame myself and to avoid making others angry. I will remember that I and my opponents are worthy loved-ones of God. I will stand for myself with them, not against them. I will continually appeal to the common sense and good faith of this community for the resources to formulate and the communal power to implement a constructive process for managing this situation.

Such a contract can keep us in touch with ourselves as conflict managers. Writing the contract down and putting it where it can be seen daily anchors us as conflict managers. We are encouraged to remember that we are both limited and responsible selves who can intervene but not alone control the conflict we face.

PART TWO

STEP TWO: APPRAISING A CONFLICTIVE SITUATION

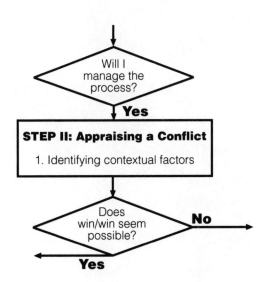

CHAPTER 5

Step Two, Task One: Identifying Contextual Factors

The second basic step in managing a conflict is to appraise a conflictive situation by examining its context and the parties to it. When appraising a conflictive situation, the focus of one's appraisal will define the target of one's interventions. One may adopt a fix-the-principals focus, assessing who is good or bad among the principals to a conflict. Or one may adopt a fix-the-issues focus, assessing what is right or wrong about the conflicting positions of the principals. Or one may incorporate both of the above by adopting a fix-the-process focus, assessing what is constructive or destructive about what is happening between principals. Interventions that focus on the principals utilize psychological and spiritual resources for managing conflicts. Interventions that focus on the issues utilize problem-solving, faith interpretive, and communication resources for managing conflicts. Interventions that focus on the process of a conflict utilize all the above resources with the addition of systemic communal resources for managing conflicts.

This model focuses on assessing and working with the process of a conflict for three reasons:

1. Every conflict has many issues, rather than "the" issue.
2. Every principal has differing perceptions that make sense from their own perspectives and interests.
3. The win/win way of resolving conflicts lies in identifying and working to combine underlying interests rather than in contesting the rightness or wrongness of the issues, per se.

This model's way of appraising conflictive situations, therefore, pursues two foci of the process of the conflict: (1) identifying contextual factors influencing all principals' behaviors (chapter 5; see fig. 5.1) and (2) assessing the fight postures of principals by weighing the balance of power between them and by discerning their apparent ethical proclivities (chapter 6). This chapter's assessment of communal factors provides a framework in which to then locate and assess the principals themselves, which is discussed in chapter 6.

Adopting a Systemic Perspective

In his essay *The Responsible Self*, H. Richard Niebuhr describes three approaches to understanding and changing social situations:

> Biology and sociology as well as psychology have taught us to regard ourselves as beings in the midst of a field of natural and social forces, acted upon and reacting, attracted and repelling. . . . It will not do to say that the older

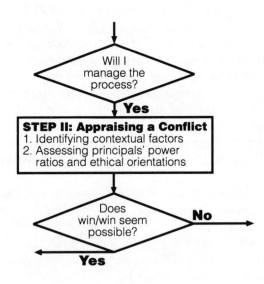

Fig. 5.1

images of the maker fixer and the citizen judge have lost their meaning in these biological, psychological, sociological, and historical analyses, . . . but the pattern of thought now is interactional. . . . Purposiveness seeks to answer the question: "What shall I do?" . . . Deontology tries to answer the moral query by asking, first of all: "What is the law and what is the first law of my life?" Responsibility, however, proceeds in every moment of decision and choice to inquire: "What is going on?"[1]

In this model, assessing a conflictive situation involves looking at what is going on in order to intervene responsibly for its constructive management.

As we have already observed, our assumptions about what is going on in a conflict strongly influence our assessments of it. For example, one may assume that the way to make a conflict constructive is to change a party's information, or psychological makeup, or beliefs. With such an individualistic assumption, one's assessment of a conflictive situation might involve investigating the particular misinformation, personality traits, or distorted beliefs operating within one or more of the parties to the conflict.

A systemic perspective on conflicts expands rather than invalidates an individualistic assumption. One is concerned with parties' interactions as well as their individualities, with parties' communal contexts as well as themselves.[2]

Individualistic Assumptions	*Systemic Assumptions*
1. Meaning is discovered. "I will investigate this situation to find out what the parties' problem is."	1. Meaning is created. "I will investigate how parties see things and help them define problems seen."
2. Parties are *only* individuals. "I will find out what makes each party tick."	2. Parties are interacting players in relationships. "I will explore what's happening among them and between them and myself."
3. Issues between parties are simple: They're either/or—either this or that, good or bad, right or wrong. "I can determine which is the one best/right/good definition of the issues."	3. Issues between parties are complex: they're both/and—both this and that, good and bad, right and wrong. "I can incorporate differing views to reach a more holistic sense of the issues."
4. Conflicts arise from a series of cause-and-effect events. "I will ask, 'WHY IS THIS HAPPENING?' to discover the causes at work."	4. Conflicts arise from patterns of reciprocating influences. "I will ask, 'WHAT'S HAPPENING?' to recognize patterns of interaction."

5. Truth is information.
"I will gather data about this situation so I can tell others how to make it right or fix it."

5. Truth is meaning.
"I will join others in this situation in experiencing the meanings of its history, context, and possibilities."

Making a systemic assessment of a conflictive situation includes looking at the contextual factors bearing on parties. For purposes of conflict management one examines three aspects of the social context bearing on the parties: communal culture, communal structure, and the dynamics of the communal environment.

Identifying Communal "Rules"

Church systems operate with both written and unwritten rules of conduct for participants. The formal rules can be found in such written documents as constitutions, organizational charts, and manuals of operation. These formal rules are known and acknowledged in the consciousness of parties to a conflict. The informal rules can only be found by observation and experience. Informal rules are often so familiar or habitual to parties that they become largely unconscious prescriptions for people in the system which will be seen by outsiders. Informal rules include unstated ways of making communal decisions and unwritten prescriptions for parties' language, dress, attitudes, ways of expressing feelings, and such matters. Informal rules create a community's emotional climate, reflect its cherished myths and symbols of meaning, and find embodiment in its status figures.[3] While formal rules create a community's structure, informal rules constitute its implicit structure and culture.

Informal rules usually have more impact than formal ones on parties' behaviors in conflictive situations. For example, a pastor who says "damn" in a quite traditional sermon on sin may well stir up a tempest of protest. The pastor has not broken a formal rule of orthodox theology or authorized belief. But this pastor has broken an informal rule about acceptable language in the pulpit. The furor arises because of the "informal" rule about communal language rather than formal standards of belief.

In communities where conflicts have been destructive, one will find either isolating or enmeshed behaviors around conflict. A communal rule of isolating prescribes that when there is a conflict, all parties should obey a "no talk" rule. Conflicts are ignored, even to the extent of isolating anyone who begins speaking about them. Isolating behaviors suggest that past conflicts have been so brutal that people quickly erect barriers to protect themselves from conflict.

Enmeshed communal rules also prevent the explicit confrontation of differences by parties. In communities where parties are emotionally merged together as a way of relating, conflicts are "stuffed," held in a chronic stage of submerged latency. Parties fight "beneath the table" because they cannot attain sufficient emotional distance to fight "above the table." Power is therefore used manipulatively to control differences rather than to surface and work through them. Finding enmeshed prescriptions for relationships in a community suggests that past conflicts have been so personally wounding that they must now be suppressed. Some key questions for observing current communal attitudes toward conflicts of enmeshment or isolation are discussed in the following text.

1. To what extent, when one takes a stand about what one believes, do others respond with their own "I believe" statements or respond argumentatively with "you" statements about your position?[24]

Church systems in which people cannot disagree without "getting in one another's hair" are emotionally enmeshed systems. Parties to conflicts are psychologically stuck to one another, as if their differing interests were clothed in Velcro. When they encounter differences, they are driven to change one another rather than accept disagreement or differentiation. Unwritten communal rules expressive of communal enmeshment are rules like these:

- Christians always take care of others.
- If you can't say something nice, don't say anything.
- Read others' minds rather than know your own.
- Caring Christians don't hurt others' feelings.
- Being kind is more Christian than being honest.

Unwritten rules for coping in communities where conflict is to be avoided, ignored, or suppressed are rules like these:

- Don't bring up things that anger others.
- Deny or discount your own feelings around others.
- Talk in generalities, not specifics.
- Talk only about noncontroversial things like the weather.
- State your own opinions indirectly as hearsay or as "people are saying."

Since these kinds of rules originated from previous communal conflicts, one's assessment of a community's present involves learning about a community's past.

2. How was this church body originally created? To what extent did it form out of the needs of the founders? To what extent was it a splinter group from another established church body?

Church systems that originated to meet positive communal purposes will tend to have unwritten communal rules that encourage direct, assertive, trustful expression of parties' differing interests. Members will be expected to be "up front" about what they want and think. The unwritten communal rules would tend to be as follows:

- Speak up and say what's on your mind.
- Accept yourself and others.
- Speak for yourself, not for others.

Church systems that originated out of protest or dissatisfaction will tend to have unwritten communal rules that encourage indirect, passive/aggressive, distrustful expression of parties' differing interests. The unwritten communal rules will tend to be as follows:

- Find out what others think before you speak.
- Always be right.
- Always look good.
- Be critical of imperfections or mistakes.

Another question that can reveal the impact of past conflicts for current communal rules about conflict is this one:

3. How have past major communal conflicts been dealt with? Have they been repressed and never really settled? Were they resolved in win/lose ways, leading losers to drop out? Were they resolved in respectful ways of working things out?

The emotional responses one may get to this question are most revealing. When parties talk with gusto about past conflicts, they reflect a cultural openness, acceptance, and accountability about communal conflicts. One may infer that the unwritten cultural rules of this community work so that

- conflicts are brought out in the open;
- conflicts are resolved in mutually acceptable ways; and
- conflicts are dealt with accountably.

Conversely, when parties avoid, ignore, or clam up over this question, one may infer that the unwritten cultural rules of this community work so that

- conflicts are denied or swept under the rug;

- conflicts are unresolved or resolved in win/lose ways; or
- conflicts are kept secret from the community as a whole.

In summary, faith communities carry unwritten rules reflective of communal inheritances from past experiences with conflict.

A sampling of some constructive communal norms or rules to seek would be as follows:

- Be real. Exercise self-control when interacting with others.
- No one here is perfect. Mistakes are human and forgivable.
- No one here is superior or inferior. Everyone is valuable.
- When differences arise, there will be no labeling and no personal attacks.
- Honesty is the best policy.
- Speak for and be yourself.
- No personalizing of issues. Address behaviors, not persons.
- Conflicts are problems to be solved, not contests to be won.

Asking questions about a community's past can reveal unwritten communal rules that encourage members' constructive or destructive behaviors whenever conflicts arise.

Identifying Communal Structure and Procedures

The explicit and implicit structure and procedures of a community also influence the ways parties exercise power in conflictive situations. For example, when access to communal information is implicitly restricted to an elitist group, an imbalance of power is created between them and others. Or when decisions are implicitly reached by caucusing on the telephone before a governing body even meets, parties will tend to discount or distrust the explicit provisions for formal governance. Structure and procedures influence parties' uses or abuses of power in conflictive situations.

Any or all of the following questions can help one assess communal patterns in the exercise of power:

1. To what extent are the founding members still in power or present in the parish, regional church body, or church agency?
2. How many different ministers or other professionals has the parish, regional church body, or church agency had? What is the rate of turnover of lay leaders in the parish, regional church body, or church

agency? What is the average length of stay in salaried positions? How
does this average compare with the denominational average length of
stay? (Note: The average longevity of pastoral relationships in North
American Protestant parishes, the Methodists excepted, is four to
five years.)

3. What has been the nature of the previous separations between professional leaders and the parish, regional church body, or church
   agency? To what extent have these separations been mutually affirmed? To what extent has the professional or the church system
   been the initiator?

4. How are people in this parish, regional church body, or church
   agency authorized to be system decision makers? Are decisions made
   in formal or informal ways? In accountable or unaccountable ways?
   In more participative or more authoritarian ways? How did such
   ways of using power come about?

Church systems whose founding members are still in power or have
disproportionate influence tend to have closed, elitist ways of making
decisions. This results in communal alienation, boredom, apathy, or re-
sentment on the part of those who are prevented from having communal
influence. Such generalized frustration and distrust fuel the fears and defensiveness of all parties when conflicts arise.

On the other hand, church systems that value and use members' resources in more open, inclusive, and accountable ways of decision making
encourage constructive behavior by all parties when conflicts arise. Parties
are more likely to be constructive when they know they can make a difference, or at least be respectfully heard and taken into account.

The length of pastoral relationships is also indicative of constructive or
destructive proclivities in the parties. Church systems or church professionals with habitually short relationships of less than three years may
have a tendency to flee or withdraw from conflicting differences over
leadership. Church systems or church professionals with habitually long
relationships of over ten years may have a tendency to deny or control in
authoritarian ways conflicting differences over leadership.

On the other hand, church systems or church professionals with habitual
relationships of from four to nine years may have abilities to deal constructively with conflicting differences. Such pastoral relationships seem to
involve collaboration rather than unilateral control by any party to the
relationship.

Observing the emotional climate between parties in a church system is a
particularly revealing way to measure the system's level of constructive-

ness or destructiveness. Church systems that do not reach closure when pastors leave evidence the kind of enmeshed and therefore controlling ways of relating to leaders that discourage healthy conflict. Rather than building professional relationships as partnerships between autonomous parties, enmeshed church systems tend to seek emotional fusion between themselves and their leaders. Moreover, pastors who come from enmeshed families of origin tend to find congregations that have expectations of enmeshed relationships with pastors. When conflicts arise, all parties tend to become emotionally reactive and controlling of each other. Healthy disagreements are neither envisioned nor realized. Rather than resolving their differences, principals tend to either appease one another or abandon one another.

The structure of a church system consists of such things as organizational lines of communication and accountability; communal ways of planning, making decisions, and evaluating performances; and communal procedures for securing, partnering with, and terminating professional staff. These aspects of the structure of a church system often occasion or support either constructive or destructive conflicts. The ways committees are appointed and made accountable to governing bodies can generate collaborative or competitive intergroup relationships. A lack of explicit, realistic job descriptions for employees or role expectations for volunteers can generate negative feelings and stress for parties. These are examples of the ways organizational structure and procedures influence parties to conflicts.

A major institutional source of conflicts is overlapping responsibilities between parties. A pastor and a church secretary may conflict because they both function as communication switchboards for the whole system. A committee chair and a treasurer may conflict because they have overlapping responsibilities in programming. A church school superintendent and a weekday kindergarten director may conflict because they do their jobs in the same physical space. A middle governing body executive and a national program staff person may conflict because they depend on each other's resources. A head of staff and an associate may conflict because their professional activities affect each other. Unclear or overlapping role descriptions put parties in conflict, regardless of their personal traits. When parties personalize these conflicts, their interactions become destructive.

Identifying Changes in
Communal Environment

Just as the human body requires oxygen, water, and food from its environment to survive, so a church body requires people, values, time, and energy to survive. Changes in the supply of these necessary institutional resources can both create church conflicts and exacerbate them. A systemic assessment of a conflictive situation includes asking questions about the state of a community's social environment:

1. What, if any, major changes have recently occurred between this community and its social environment, such as geographical relocation, completion of a new building or wing, major shifts in support staff or voluntary leadership?
2. What, if any, major changes have recently occurred within the social environment supporting this community, such as economic change, ethnic population change, social class population change, zoning change, or larger denominational change?
3. What is the church system's reputation in these environmental and denominational contexts?

Major changes within a community's supporting environment can generate conflicts within church bodies. The greater the scope and significance of the change, the greater the emotional insecurity and intensity among church parties who are affected by these changes. The more rapid the rate of social change, the greater the risks of confusion, inaccurate information, and anxiety between church parties to conflict. In both respects, social changes within or without church bodies can generate destructive conflicts over shrinking resources.

A person who is starving to death is more likely to steal, lie, or attack others for food than one who has enough to eat. Similarly, a church system that lacks adequate information, funding, or participants to continue current operations is a church system in which conflicts are more likely to become win/lose struggles for survival. A church system that is losing such resources as money, volunteer work hours, communal self-esteem, or status in the larger community is "put on edge" emotionally. Parties to conflicts within that system are more likely to displace and act out system tensions and fears on one another.

Significant social changes in the social environments of church bodies also generate destructive conflicts within them. Often a congregation may scapegoat its leaders for declining membership that is due to a changing environment rather than to the leadership. Conversely, a minister may manipulate a board for salary increases in light of membership growth that is due not to the minister's performance but to an expanding and prospering environmental base. When parties in conflicts generated by changes outside church systems personalize the issues within systems, violence is done to the facts as well as to the parties themselves.

Assessing the Contextual Factors
Influencing Parties

Appraising a conflict involves both logical and intuitive ways of thinking. Because of the relational and contextual focus of a systemic perspective on conflictive situations, the intuitive way of assessing them is primary.

At the end of the previous chapter the "Work Sheet for Appraising Conflictive Situations" (found in appendix 5) was introduced. The first column of this work sheet provides space for listing what the manager considers to be key communal rules, key communal structures, and key environmental circumstances influencing all parties to a conflictive situation. These key rules, structures, and/or environmental circumstances are listed in abbreviated ways in the first column of the work sheet, headed "contextual factors." When communal rules, communal structures, and environmental circumstances together seem to afford an overall positive influence on parties' fight styles, a rating of +1 is made. When such contextual factors seem to afford a balance between positive and negative influences on parties' fight styles, a rating of 0 is made. And when these contextual factors seem to afford an overall negative influence on parties' fight styles, a rating of −1 is made.

Often, managers balk at this point. They may feel insecure because they cannot prove that the factors they select are objective or provable influences. Managers feel uncomfortable about the subjectivity of their own perceptions. They may have learned in a scientific culture dominated by logical criteria of analysis that intuitive ways of thinking are invalid and untrustworthy. On the other hand, their unscientific perceptions will in fact influence how they perceive and respond to a conflictive situation. The best insurance is not the logical texture of their perceptions but the productivity of responses based on their hypothetical perceptions. What is accurate in their intuitions will be self-validating; what is not will be revised. The issue is not acceptable provability but acceptable risk.

An Illustration of Completing
the First Column of the Work Sheet

Jim was dismayed. In the middle of the governing body's meeting, he had just learned that the actual number of members was 294 rather than the 430 reported on the church information form he had studied when he was considering accepting this church's call. This was a difference of over 130 persons, 32 percent less. No wonder the church was having such a struggle to pledge the minimal congregational budget. Why had they lied about their membership? What was going on? Something was fishy, and that suggested a hidden conflict.

The next day Jim pulled out a copy of the "Work Sheet for Appraising Conflictive Situations" (see appendix 5). Jim did not know enough yet to even guess who the principals to this latent conflict were, but as he reviewed questions about contextual factors, he began to recognize some seemingly destructive circumstances. He took note on the work sheet of some of the following traits he had observed or intuited about his new communal charge (see fig. 5.2):

Key Communal Rules
- Love this church or leave it, just like we did when we left old First to start this congregation thirty years ago.
- If you can't say something nice about this congregation, don't say anything.
- Don't bring up issues over which some members might leave.
- At church functions, only talk about safe topics like sports and the weather.
- Things were best when we had Dr. Saint as pastor.

Key Communal Structures
- The older founding members control by keeping information privileged. Decisions are made by phone, not in meetings.
- No one but the secretary knows about cash flow.

Key Environmental Circumstances
- Ebenezer Church (nearby congregation of the same denomination) is completing a major building program and is attracting young families.
- Young families are coming to this neighborhood from out of state to buy the older homes being vacated by retirees.

As Jim reflected on these contextual factors, he intuited a cumulatively negative bias of -1. All members of his congregation were influenced by factors that discouraged the expression of honest differences, and limited access to reliable communal information prevented leadership by any who had not been around for at least five years. Overall the congregation seemed to be stuck emotionally back in the days of Dr. Saint. "No won-

Contextual Factors	Principals	Power Assets Personal (✓)	Role (✓)	Ratio H/M/L	Ethical Proclivities Dirty Fight	Fair Fight	Rating DF/FF/BF
A. Key Communal Rules — Love us or leave us — Be nice, don't upset others — Don't bring up controversial issues (Rules suggest shamed community with a no-talk rule)							
B. Key Communal Structures — charter members in elitist network for making communal decisions — support staff control financial information							
C. Key Environmental Circumstances — Ebenezer's new appeal — Out-of-staters buying nearby homes							
Overall +/- = <u>-1</u> (+1/0/-1)							

Fig. 5.2: Work Sheet for Appraising Conflictive Situations

der," Jim said to himself, "they deceived me and probably themselves about their declining membership. Just the two factors of the no-negative-talk rule and Ebenezer's recent growth explain the misrepresentation of current membership."

Jim was beginning to understand his conflicted congregation in a constructive, systemic way. Rather than focusing immediately on theological differences about social issues, Jim was recognizing communal traditions, habits of operation, and rules about conflict and negative feelings that made sense of the situation. He felt less betrayed and more insightful. He would now test with some leaders his perception of the influence of these key contextual factors, thereby opening up a nonjudgmental conversation about matters heretofore unmentionable. He was beginning to think in terms of what was happening in his congregation that explained the misrepresentation of facts rather than who was to be blamed and shamed for the misrepresentation of facts. He was on track with the first task in this model's way of appraising a conflictive situation.

CHAPTER 6

Step Two, Task Two: Assessing the Principals

The governing body had asked the senior and associate pastors to leave while the church officers discussed salary increases for them. When the two ministers came back into the meeting room, there was awkward silence. It was now after 10:30 P.M. A member of the board announced that they had approved the senior pastor's salary increase as requested. He then turned to the associate and said, "Alex, we all like you and think you've done a good job here. But we need to cut the budget some place, and we've decided we can't afford two pastors. So since you have come more recently than Tom, we voted to eliminate your position and to ask you to seek relocation during these next twelve months."

Church officer Jerry thought that the basic issue was feminism because he felt that Alex had incited the latent antagonism of board members toward women pastors when he recently married a clergywoman. Church officer Ruth thought that the basic issue was social activism and that board members had made a masked protest against Alex's advocacy for a congregational pledge of funds to a ministry with migrant agri-workers. Vice-chair Pat thought that the basic issue was financial, reflecting the drop in congregational giving from $274,000 to $237,000, and that older board members on fixed incomes feared the pressures of inflationary costs in a rapidly growing community. Senior pastor Tom thought that the basic issue was leadership. Such action by the board without his presence was a protest of an enclave of old charter member types against his change-oriented leadership and vision. In reality, each party's definition of the issue had validity. They were all at least partly correct, but only partly correct.

Many of us have the habit in conflictive situations of understanding them by deciding what the basic issue is rather than by assessing who the principals are. Having decided what the basic issue is, we formulate what we think is the right solution and begin working for its adoption. Such activity plunges us into power struggles with others whose own definitions of and solutions to the basic issue clash with our own.

For this reason, this model's prescription for managing a conflict leaves the issues to the principals to handle. The manager's job is to assess the principals rather than define their issues. Having considered contextual factors bearing on all parties, we now assess a conflict's principals in two respects: the approximate balance of power between them and the apparent ethical proclivities motivating them (see fig. 6.1).

Naming the Primary Principals

As part of Step One for preparing oneself to manage a conflictive situation, we were asked to distinguish between those parties who have a primary stake in the issues and those who have a primary stake in how parties behave. Principals were described as those whose primary investments are in *what* the resolution of issues may be. Bystanders were described as those whose primary investments are in *how* the resolution of issues occurs, destructively or constructively.

Bystanders are those whose church community is affected by principals' behaviors. In many church conflicts the problem is not that bystanders do not care, but that they are provided no way of acting on their interests other than by taking sides between the principals. In effect, bystanders think that if they do not take sides on the issues then they will not be able to affect principals' behaviors. Ironically, when bystanders take sides on the issues, the effect is to polarize the situation, thereby exacerbating the threat to the whole.

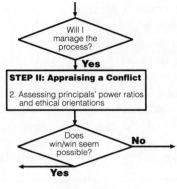

Fig. 6.1

When determining whether one is a principal/manager or a bystander/ manager, we made a provisional list of all apparent principals. Now the manager selects from the provisional list no less than two nor more than five primary principals. The names of these principals are entered in the work sheet column for principals. Usually these principals will be spokespersons who embody the interests of larger groups or structures: political alliances, attitudinal factions, persons with structurally mandated responsibilities, and/or enclaves of particular theological concerns.

Let us see how senior pastor Tom used this model. First, he placed within brackets his own assessment of the issue so that he could begin his assessment of the situation in order to manage it as a principal/manager.

Tom recognized that by virtue of his role as senior pastor, he was unquestionably a primary principal in this situation. He quickly thought of Pat as another primary principal. Pat was the sole proprietor of a men's clothing store. He was used to running a business, not participating with others in shared decision making. Six months after he became a church officer, Pat had begun to attack Tom for the way Tom was running the church. He assumed that Tom should run the church the same way Pat ran his business—that the governing body was just a formality. After his second year on the board, Pat was elected vice-chair of the board and thereby chair of its executive committee. After being named chairperson, Pat said he "was going to get this church to be what it should be." Tom began to work on assessing the principals in light of contextual factors he had already entered in the first column of the work sheet.

Understanding Power

"Every encounter, whether friendly or hostile, whether benevolent or indifferent, is in some way, unconsciously or consciously, a struggle of power with power," observed Paul Tillich.[1] As we have seen, conflict involves the use of power in the same way that commerce involves the use of money. The power of a principal is that party's ability to influence other principals. Goldhamer and Shils state that "a person may be said to have power to the extent that s/he influences the behavior of others in accordance with her/his own intentions."[2] Amitai Etzioni describes three kinds of power principals may use in conflictive situations: (1) coercive (physical, force-based forms of power), (2) utilitarian (economic or remunerative forms of power), and (3) normative (persuasive, manipulative, or suggestive forms of power).[3] Principals may possess these kinds of power personally or by means of their organizational role or communal status.[4]

For example, one principal to a church conflict may be an older gentleman whose primary power resides in his name, Harry Payne of the Payne

Contextual Factors	Principals	Power Assets Personal (✓)	Role (✓)	Ratio H/M/L	Ethical Proclivities Dirty Fight	Fair Fight	Rating DF/FF/BF
A. Key Communal Rules	Tom (senior pastor)						
B. Key Communal Structures	Pat (chair, executive committee)						
C. Key Environmental Circumstances	Fred (vice-chair of governing board)						
Overall +/- = ___ (+1/0/-1)	Alex (associate pastor)						

Fig. 6.2: Work Sheet for Appraising Conflictive Situations

Memorial Church. As the current male head of the Payne clan, Harry possesses communal status and hierarchical dominance among at least one third of the church's one hundred members. A second principal in this church conflict may be the Rules, a young couple who not only represent the first young couple to join the church in years but also provide the largest current annual pledge due to their dual income and occupational connections. The Rules possess utilitarian kinds of power: money and the ability to secure new, young members. A third principal in this conflict may be the pastor, who possesses normative kinds of power—both pastoral authority and persuasive preaching. None of these principals possess coercive power. However, they all have potential access to coercive legal power that resides in the civil laws governing the congregation's environment.

Understanding and Assessing Power Balances
Between Principals

Whatever normative and utilitarian kinds of power principals possess, they are derived from a combination of their traits and role assets. These kinds of power are listed in the respective columns for power assets on the work sheet. The following catalogue of the kinds of power principals may possess serves as a checklist for one's awareness.

Personal Traits
- physical traits: sex, size, age, race, appearance/appeal, health, energy level
- aptitudes: articulation, charisma, memory capabilities, storytelling, the communicative arts
- institutional skills: planning, chairing, problem solving, debating, data processing, leading groups, computer/technical expertise, financial/budgeting, programming, evaluating, administering
- professional resources: educational credentials, professional credentials, attributed knowledge/skills of professional expertise, reputation/stature among professional colleagues
- socializing capabilities: hosting/entertaining, communication skills, elitist connections
- social status: family status/name; socioeconomic class and connections
- social possessions: money, longevity in community, knowledge of communal operations and culture, political alliances and relationships

Role Assets

- from employed or elective positions in the system housing the conflict: access to communal or institutional information, communication channels, rules, politics, status, funds, decision-making processes, leaders and authorities
- from employed or elective positions in the larger context of the system housing the conflict: access to communal or institutional social status, economic resources, educational position, denominational influence, civic or legal processes directly bearing on principals

Many Christians think that power is itself evil. However, power can be used assertively and creatively as well as selfishly and corruptly. Power is evil only when it is exercised for evil purpose or destructively. Power is a moral good when it is exercised assertively in accountable, straightforward, and respectful ways with others. This model's way of assessing the principals in a conflict also addresses the predominant ways principals appear to use their power, what we call the ethical proclivities to power *within* them.

In conflicts, power per se is meaningless. The meaning of power lies in its relative usefulness.[5] The impact of power in conflictive situations depends on the usefulness of that form of power both in context and in relative balance with the power of other principals.

For example, if a principal, and/or those she represents, has enough money to pursue her interests, another principal's money will have relatively little influence. But if a principal, and/or those she represents, is desperate for money, another principal's money will have considerable influence. Similarly, if a principal, and/or those he represents, has political church connections effective enough to help him get his way, another principal's political status will have relatively little influence. But if a principal, and/or those he represents, has few political connections, another principal's political status will have considerable impact. The usefulness of power is relative.

The usefulness of power is also contextual. An upper-class principal may be automatically influential in a suburban church community but not in an inner-city one. An educated minister may have status in a congregation of professionals but less status in a congregation of union members. The rules, structures, and resources of church systems housing a conflict may enhance or neutralize the usefulness of principals' power assets. In a congregation that has a "no talk" rule, an assertive principal is likely to be shunned. In a congregation that has a "speak up" rule, the same principal may be highly respected.

Therefore, the manager reviews the impact of each principal's power assets in light of other principals' assets and of contextual factors bearing on all principals' assets. First, those assets that remain useful or are enhanced by these contexts are marked with a check mark on the work sheet. Second, the manager intuits the relative balance of power between each principal's marked assets. Those assets with checks are ranked in the aggregate as having relatively "high," "moderate," or "low" salience in relation to the aggregated assets of the other principals. This rating is recorded in the ratio column of the work sheet. On occasion, all principals may have high, or moderate, or low rankings. Often, however, the relative power between principals will be unbalanced so that one may have a high power rating while others have moderate or low power ratings. In any case, the relative balance of power between principals will be of key significance when choosing as manager which strategies to use in managing the conflictive situation one is appraising.

At this point Tom began to backtrack. The first blank column on the work sheet directed his attention to the contextual factors bearing on all parties. He began recalling the history of his parish to bring to mind its key system traits. He added them to his work sheet. Tom returned to listing and rating each principal's power assets. He checked the key forms of usable power each principal had been exercising. As he did so, he recognized that while Alex had the most to gain or lose as a principal, he had very little usable power in this situation (see fig. 6.3).

Formulating a Christian Ethic of Fair and Dirty Fighting

All human behavior is value laden. How principals fight reflects their primary values: in what or whom they trust. Fighting fair and fighting dirty are activities that express a principal's confession of faith.

Secular models for managing conflict assume that the major constructive value that principals bring into conflicts is enlightened self-interest.[6] A Christian ethic for principals' behavior augments the concept of enlightened self-interest with Christian beliefs about human fulfillment. Human fulfillment is seen as knowing and enjoying God. From a Christian perspective true self-interest in conflictive situations consists in *approximating* God's justice, grace, compassion, and peace for all parties, including oneself. A New Testament way of speaking for such inclusive fulfillment is the ethical appeal to "speak the truth in love." As we previously stated, this model finds four behavioral criteria required to speak the truth in love in conflicts: assertiveness, accountability, respectfulness, and inclusiveness of a larger common good.

In conflicts, even approximate truthfulness is difficult. Principals' self-deceit is often cunning and destructive. As Sissela Bok observes,

Contextual Factors	Principals	Power Assets Personal (✓)	Power Assets Role (✓)	Ratio H/M/L	Ethical Proclivities Dirty Fight	Ethical Proclivities Fair Fight	Rating DF/FF/BF
A. Key Communal Rules = –1 • Ethnic German culture • Money is what we fight over • Budget is to control vs. resource • Elect critics in order to appease • Win/lose history = "winners stay, losers leave"	Tom (senior pastor)	• Intelligence • Attractive ✓• Physical health ✓• Trustful & self-worth ✓• 17 years positive pastoral track record ✓• Knowledge of cm. model	• Respected as minister ✓• Authority as head of staff • Parliamentarian ✓• Info switchboard • Denom. status	H			
B. Key Communal Structures = +1 • Extended family system • Majority of non-German members • Increasingly participative decision making • Productive committee system	Pat (chair, executive committee)	✓• Lifelong member ✓• Extended family connects • Traditional moral convictions • Successful businessman • Controlling personality	✓• Chair exec. comm. • Control of money info ✓• Status with old-timers' enclave & theological traditionalists	M			
C. Key Environmental Circumstances = +1 • Influx of non-German members since WWII • Rapid communal growth • New position of assoc. pastor • Den. ord. of women pastors	Fred (vice-chair of governing board)	• Lifelong member • Wisdom • Sense of humor ✓• Age — 60s ✓• Serenity ✓• Spirituality	• Highest lay office • Veteran church officer ✓• Senior statesman status ✓• Trusted politically	H			
Overall +/– = ±1 (+1/0/–1)	Alex (associate pastor)	• Youth • Creative • Fun loving ✓• Skilled • Open • Enthusiasm • Attractive wife	• Loved by youth • Gratitude of parents • #2 on staff team • Strong seminary recommendations	L			

Fig. 6.3: Work Sheet for Appraising Conflictive Situations

The moral question of whether you are lying or not is not settled by establishing the truth or falsity of what you say. In order to settle this question, we must know whether you *intend your statement to mislead.* . . . When we undertake to deceive others intentionally, we communicate messages meant to mislead them, meant to make them believe what we ourselves do not believe. We can do so through gesture, through disguise, by means of action or inaction, even through silence. . . . Deception then, is the larger category, and lying forms part of it.[7]

What is so destructive about deception, Bok goes on to say, is that deceiving others leads increasingly to deceiving oneself. Her prescription for overcoming such deception with truthfulness requires a larger accountability to others. She continues:

Justification must involve more than . . . untested personal steps of reasoning. Such justification requires an audience: it may be directed to God, or a court of law, or one's peers, or one's own conscience; but in ethics it is most appropriately aimed, not at any one individual or audience, but rather at "reasonable persons" in general.[8]

In the context of this book, the bystanders of the faith community housing the conflict are held to be the "reasonable persons." Accountability to this larger community of bystanders is required as a critical behavioral standard of a Christian ethic of "speaking the truth in love."

We have also already observed that Christian perspectives on love in the context of a conflict are respectfulness and inclusiveness rather than sentimentality or intimacy. This awareness is of special importance in the individualistic North American culture, which tends to glorify individual rights at public expense. As Arthur Lange and Patricia Jakubowski observe,

When rights are overly stressed . . . some people become "rights conscious" and start overreacting to every violation of their rights. It is as though they have come to believe that other people *must* treat them fairly and that it is a personal affront and an *unforgivable outrage* when other people are unfair. Instead of focusing on their own goals, taking into consideration some aspects of the other person's situation, and determining how they could possibly assert themselves in the unfair situation, these individuals solely focus on the misdeed of the other person and the injustice of it all.[9]

Personal gain at the expense of a larger common good misses the mark of a Christian ethic of justice in conflicts.

Douglas Sturm further develops such Christian understanding of speaking the truth in love as respectful inclusion of all parties' interests in conflictive situations:

The individual's political duty is not merely to respect the rights of other individuals. It is to contribute to the common good, the good of the polity.

Rights are not ends in themselves. They are requisites to creative symbiosis.
. . . To act in the public good is not to deny the individuality of persons or
associations, but it is to reject the indifference to others of individualism. It is
to accept the obligation of being a gift to the entire community of being.[10]

This respectful inclusiveness reflects Paul Tillich's grounding of the principle of justice in the intrinsic claim of everyone to be considered a person.[11]
From a Christian perspective, both respectfulness and inclusiveness are behavioral standards of a Christian specification of Fair Fighting in conflicts.

What emerges from this and the earlier discussion of a Christian ethic
for fight behaviors in conflicts is the following set of standards. All principals to a conflict will

- share responsibility for and control of their behaviors;
- respect and assert their own intrinsic worth;
- act accountably with each other and bystanders; and
- seek a good that approximates a more universal good.

Based upon these axioms, we derive a Christian specification of Fair and
Dirty Fighting in conflicts, against which to assess each principal's apparent ethical orientation.

Fair Fight Behaviors	*Dirty Fight Behaviors*
1. Struggling for shared control with others	1. Struggling for singular control over others
2. Seeking a common good for partisan interests	2. Seeking a partisan good at common expense
3. Acting assertively to respect self and others	3. Acting aggressively or manipulatively to violate self and others
4. Behaving accountably with principals and bystanders	4. Behaving deceptively with principals and bystanders

Assessing Principals' Ethical Proclivities

Although a Christian ethic for church conflicts can be clearly articu-
lated, it is not so clearly observable in oneself or others. A biblical perspective recognizes that all parties to a conflict harbor within them both an
intrinsic goodness and a compulsive sinfulness: both Fair Fight and Dirty
Fight proclivities. This is reflected in Paul's exasperated outburst about
himself: "For I do not the good I want, but the evil I do not want is what I
do" (Rom. 7:19—itself a revealing description of the experience of shame-
based persons who seek to be responsible with others).

Principals in a conflict bring to it both fair and dirty fight behavioral proclivities, both grace-ful and shame-ful ways of behaving. The task of the manager is to discern which kind of behavior appears to be currently predominant. Discerning principals' ethical proclivities involves remembering and observing the relative balance in their behaviors between seeking to control and sharing control; acting assertively or acting with passivity or aggressively; and behaving accountably to or deceptively with a larger community of bystanders.

No one fights perfectly fair. No one is totally unfair. Principals' ethical proclivities will reflect which part of their humanity is currently dominant: their God-given capacity for creative community or their humanly created woundedness from experiences of sin and shame in a meantime world. Assessing principals' ethical proclivities is not a spiritual judgment undertaken to reckon their eternal destiny. Such judgment belongs to God alone. It is a provisional assessment in order to determine whether principals' current behavioral tendencies point toward probable constructive or destructive exchanges.

The manager now completes the work sheet for appraising conflicts by listing perceived fair and dirty fight *behaviors* of principals and by rating the apparent predominance between them within each principal. The predominance of ethical proclivities is designated as DF (dirty fight), BF (balanced fight), or FF (fair fight). DF proclivities toward patterns of controlling, deceptive, partisan, and aggressive/manipulative behaviors are compared with FF proclivities toward patterns of collaborative, accountable, inclusive, and assertive behaviors. These patterns reflect how each principal is at "her best" or "her worst." The manager compares these constructive and destructive behavioral patterns in light of both their apparent intensity and frequency. Whereas power ratios were derived by looking *up and down* the work sheet to compare principals' aggregate power assets, ethical orientation ratings are derived by looking *across* columns to compare the fair and dirty fight proclivities of each principal independently.

When ranking principals' ethical proclivities, contextual factors are now taken into account. When the cumulative import of contextual factors is negative, they are seen as enhancing parties' DF ethical proclivities and/or reducing parties' FF ethical proclivities. Thus when a manager finds it a close call between rating a principal as FF or BF, BF or DF, a negative contextual rating will tip the scales toward the more destructive rating. Similarly, a positive contextual rating will tip the scales toward the more constructive rating. For example, communities with histories of controlling leaders will reinforce the controlling tendencies of principals, while communities in which leaders have used power in participatory ways will reinforce the collaborative tendencies of principals. Church systems that make decisions without lines of communication to the larger body will reinforce nonaccountable behaviors by principals; communities with such lines of communication will reinforce accountable behaviors by principals.

In light of principals' proclivities and the contextual factors bearing on them, the manager rates (not ranks) each principal's predominant ethical proclivity by characterizing it as dirty fight (DF), fair fight (FF), or balanced fight (BF). A rating of DF means that it is probable at this point that a principal will fight dirty. A rating of FF means that it is probable at this point that a principal will fight fairly. A rating of BF means that it is ambiguous at this point whether a principal will fight dirty or fair. The manager's completion of ethical proclivity ratings for each principal completes the appraisal of a conflict for the purpose of managing it.

For example, Tom began to work on the apparent ethical proclivities of the principals. He scrutinized himself. He began dredging up all his shortcomings, not knowing which ones to list. Then he remembered that his task was not to judge his total being but just to assess how his current behavior with these principals had been assertive or manipulative, deceitful or accountable, partisan or inclusive, controlling or collaborative. As he became clear about his own behavioral orientation, he began to see more clearly the ethical proclivities of the remaining principals (see fig. 6.4).

Common Difficulties When Using
This Model of Appraising Conflicts

The novice using this model often experiences certain difficulties. When one begins to appraise a conflict, one may have difficulties in naming any principals or in naming too many principals. Difficulties in naming principals usually arise because one is thinking of principals only in personal terms rather than as players whose roles place them in conflict with others. One may also have difficulties because of defining principals in terms of the issues rather than in terms of their observable behaviors. Difficulties in naming too many principals (over five) usually arise because one thinks of principals only in individual terms rather than as players who embody the interests of larger groups, factions, or socioeconomic enclaves in a community.

When one begins to assess the ethical proclivities of principals, one may have difficulty with the seeming spiritual arrogance or harshness of it. Such difficulties arise because one begins judging players' characters rather than assessing their behaviors. Difficulties may also arise because one forgets the distinction between guilt-based wrong-doing, for which players can make responsible amends, and shame-based wrong-being, for which play-

Contextual Factors	Principals	Power Assets		Ratio H/M/L	Ethical Proclivities		Rating DF/FF/BF
		Personal (✓)	Role (✓)		Dirty Fight	Fair Fight	
A. Key Communal Rules = −1 • Ethnic German culture • Money is what we fight over • Budget is to control vs. resource • Elect critics in order to appease • Win/lose history = "winners stay, losers leave"	Tom (senior pastor)	• Intelligence • Attractive • Physical health ✓• Trustful & self-worth ✓• 17 years positive pastoral track record ✓• Knowledge of cm. model	• Respected as minister ✓• Authority as head of staff • Parliamentarian ✓• Info switchboard • Denominational status	H	✓• Being nice vs. being honest • Avoid conflict • Swallow negative feelings • Avoid hurting others	• I messages ✓• Own feelings ✓• Share info and power ✓• Admit mistakes	FF
B. Key Communal Structures = +1 • Extended family system • Majority of non-German members • Increasingly participative decision making • Productive committee systems	Pat (chair, executive committee)	✓• Lifelong member ✓• Extended family connects • Traditional moral convictions • Successful businessman • Controlling personality	✓• Chair exec. comm. • Control of money info ✓• Status with old-timers' enclave & theological traditionalists	M	• Blaming others • Judges differing beliefs ✓• Runs exec. comm. by controlling floor and info ✓• Gossips ✓• Dogmatic over church administration	• Loyal to church ✓• Honest re $ • Humorous perspective ✓• Admits mistakes when losing	DF
C. Key Environmental Circumstances = +1 • Influx of non-German member since WWII • Rapid communal growth • New position of assoc. pastor • Den. ord. of women pastors	Fred (vice-chair of governing board)	• Lifelong member • Wisdom • Sense of humor ✓• Age — 60s • Serenity • Spirituality	• Highest lay office • Veteran church officer ✓• Senior statesman status ✓• Trusted politically	H	• Denies problems • Mind-reads others without checking • One-on-one deals • Adapts own position to fit others'	✓• Good of church comes first • I messages ✓• Negotiates differences ✓• Keeps word	FF
Overall +/− = +1 (+1/0/−1)	Alex (associate pastor)	• Youth • Creative • Fun loving ✓• Skilled • Open • Enthusiasm • Attractive wife	• Loved by youth • Gratitude of parents • #2 on staff team • Strong seminary recommendations	L	• Self effacing ✓• Hero child script • Submissive to "superiors"	✓✓• Faces problems ✓• Thinks for self ✓• Shares info ✓• Cooperates	FF

Fig. 6.4: Work Sheet for Appraising Conflictive Situations

ers need healing before they can make responsible amends. Caring managers can be vulnerable to a spiritual naïveté that is due to their own denial of the power of evil in human experience and behavior.

Conscientious managers may be feeling some resistance at this point to this seemingly cold, arbitrarily subjective, unsubstantiated way of assessing principals' morality. Some may feel incompetent. Others may feel insecure. Still others may feel ashamed. One or more of the following observations may help deal with one's emotional resistance.

What one puts on the work sheet is clearly subjective and interpretive. As we have seen, a systemic understanding of reality recognizes the validity of both subjectivity and objectivity in human knowing. Putting before us what we already know about a conflictive situation yields two immediate benefits: (1) We become conscious and accountable for the perceptions that have and will inform our actions in the situation, and (2) we consciously assess the behavioral evidence that confirms or modifies our initial interpretative responses to the situation. We become more accountable and thoughtful about our interpretations of reality. In so doing, we also discover what we do not know and therefore which of our current perceptions we might want to test with another trusted observer.

It also helps to remember that our purpose in appraising conflictive situations is to cope with them responsibly rather than to play God in them. Recognizing contextual factors discourages our blaming parties or personalizing issues. Recognizing power ratios alerts us to the hazard of triggering shame on the part of relatively powerless players. Recognizing particular expressions of fair and dirty fight behaviors informs us about what specific dirty fight behaviors to constrain and to what specific fair fight behaviors to appeal when making our interventions to manage the conflictive situation.

Finally, one can understand that one's appraisal of a conflictive situation is provisional. It is still no more than a single frame from a moving picture. It changes as we work with a situation. It is a working hypothesis rather than an ironclad prediction. It informs us of where we are in beginning to manage a situation rather than of what we shall find when we finish managing it.

Clearly, no human being can judge his or her own soul correctly, much less a whole conflictive situation. God alone has the wisdom and compassion to judge all of us. Our task is to do the footwork so that God can do the headwork of realizing good news out of the threatening circumstances of a conflictive situation. The outcome of Step Two is the generation of information on which one can base a plan to manage a conflict. Having managed ourselves and appraised our situation, we can proceed to plan how we shall manage it.

PART THREE

STEP THREE:
MANAGING CONFLICTS

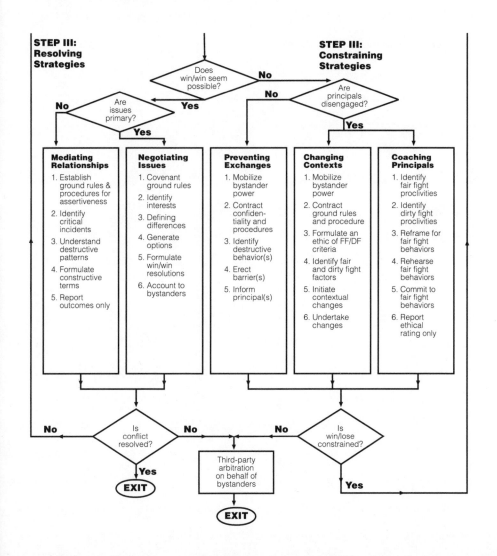

CHAPTER 7

Step Three:
Managing Conflicts

Managing conflicts is a ministry of reconciliation. We do not do the reconciling. God does. We do the preparatory work for God's reconciling activity among parties to church conflicts.

> For the love of Christ urges us on, because we are convinced that one has died for all. . . . And he died for all, so that those who live might live no longer for themselves, but for him who died and was raised for them. . . . So if anyone is in Christ, there is a new creation; everything old has passed away; see, everything has become new! All this is from God, who reconciled us to himself through Christ, and has given us the ministry of reconciliation. (2 Cor. 5:14–19)

Managing conflicts is a critical need of our times. As Rensis and Jane Likert have observed about American life,

> Win-lose, in one form or another, appears to be the prevailing strategy for resolving conflicts. Confrontation, nonnegotiable demands, and ultimatums have become the order of the day as the way to deal with deep-seated differences. One party marshals all its forces to compel the other party to do what the first has decided it wants.[1]

In no social institution is the need for constructive ways of dealing with differing convictions greater than in mainline North American church systems that are struggling today with massive and rapid social change. Virulent conflicts over issues of human sexuality alone have more than filled the plates of church members and leaders with conflict. We will discuss this further in the final chapter of this book.

The preparatory work we do for God's reconciliation in conflicts consists of making process interventions. We minister by choosing, proposing, contracting, and implementing strategic interventions that either constrain win/lose resolutions or secure win/win resolutions. The goal of our ministry is God's reconciliation. We may not always be able to attain win/win wholeness on this side of the grave. Therefore, the exercise of our ministry in a meantime world involves constraining human brokenness as well as realizing human wholeness. Managing conflicts means acting intentionally as responsible selves rather than as controlling selves to affect the dynamics of conflict.

Managing conflicts also requires considerable assertiveness by the manager. While managers cannot make parties become responsible bystanders or principals in conflictive situations, managers must assertively propose, contract for, and monitor these parties' constructive processes. Proposing, contracting, and enforcing processes provide a safe context and a sane procedure whereby bystanders can constrain destructive principals or principals can resolve their issues constructively. Unless a manager fights with parties for fair fighting, the benefits of a conflict's management cannot be realized. Moreover, by fighting assertively for clear and credible processes, a manager also models for bystanders or principals how they can exercise power assertively as well. Managing conflicts is a proactive rather than a passive activity. It involves using power assertively to block others' nonassertive uses of power. A manager must fight intensely over process if all parties are to fight assertively over issues.

For example, one might propose two behavioral ground rules and the procedures of problem solving to principals, for a win/win negotiating process. Initially, all agree to one's process proposals. But within minutes one of the principals ignores a behavioral ground rule, while another principal keeps restating his position in shrill tones. The manager's credibility as a process manager is at risk. She will want to intervene assertively in such a way as this: "We have agreed not to label one another. We have also agreed to move from stating our positions into exploring interests underlying them. Principal A, please say what you said without labeling. Principal B, we have heard your position; please tell us now about your underlying interests." Should principals continue to ignore the manager's intervention, she will want to intervene again, this time confronting the principals *as a group* with the necessity of meaning and keeping the process agreements they have made. Should the principals as a group still ignore the manager's assertions, she will probably want to abort the whole process, adjourning the meeting until further notice. One cannot manage a conflict with credibility unless and until one assertively enlists all parties in saying what they mean and meaning what they say. In this model, such credibility begins over process agreements. Until they are meant and followed, there will be little chance of credibility between principals or over their issues. Assertiveness is the road to credibility in win/win conflict resolution.

Using Communal Power to Manage Conflicts

The assertive power of managers to manage a conflict is derived from mobilizing the common sense and good faith of a larger community of bystanders. Bystander-power is exercised by a manager to secure constructive behavior by principals or constructive disengagement between principals. One's mobilization of bystanders serves notice that the larger community has a stake in the impact of principals' behavior. In effect, the conflict manager channels the larger community's interest in securing constructive control of conflictive interactions within its communal boundaries.

Win/lose conflicts are costly to social systems housing them. When principals engage in win/lose power struggles, they use communal resources as weapons. Cashing in political IOUs, manipulating privileged information, polarizing the community's population, and/or using communal funds covertly—these are but a few of the common ways in which win/lose conflicts can wound or even break apart a larger community. Distrust, resentments, and diverted expenditures of time sap the energy and well-being of the larger system. Bystanders have an urgent investment in preventing costs of win/lose conflicts within their midst.

However, when principals engage in a win/win resolution of their differences, communities have much to gain. A common good of justice strengthens communal bonds and accountability. Productive partnerships are built through honest, creative give and take. Truthfulness and accountability, in turn, increase trust among all members. Emotional energy is harnessed for creative activity. Diversity is safeguarded, and cohesion is broadened in scope and thereby made more stable. Bystanders have a big stake in reaping communal benefits from win/win resolutions of conflicts within their bounds.

When a conflict's assessment portends win/win combat, one designs ways principals can collaborate in working through their differences respectfully and accountably. In resolving strategies of conflict management, principals achieve shared control over their interactions so that they can exercise self-control in seeking a common good. On the other hand, when a conflict's assessment portends win/lose or lose/lose combat, principals are constrained by communal controls that interrupt and/or block their destructive behaviors.

For example, church officers A and B are getting angry with each other in a church school class over the topic of abortion. As their angry feelings toward each other intensify, they begin labeling each other, broadening the nature and scope of the issues between them while verbally abusing each other. At some point, another member of the class interrupts their verbal power struggle by firmly addressing the teacher. "In my opinion, what's going on here is generating more heat than light. For the sake of us all, I move that this class recess for this morning, and that you formulate some ground rules to propose for further class discussion when we reconvene next Sunday."

Or again, rumors are flying among church members that the recent vote to raise money to renovate the church school facility is leading three social-justice–minded families to consider moving their church membership elsewhere. Fear, blame, anxiety, confusion, and guilt mount among members, and these emotions are directed toward the pastor as blame or as pleas for rescue. Her phone is ringing off the hook as various parishioners request, demand, or advise her of actions to prevent the three families from leaving. In response, she expresses appreciation for her callers' concerns and asserts that she will meet with the governing body's executive committee to explore what, if any, congregational initiatives might be undertaken with the families.

As long as we think that our ability to manage conflicts depends on our power to control others or solve their difficulties, we will usually feel powerless in conflictive situations. Deep down we know we do not have the power or wisdom to fix conflicts for others. Once we recognize our ability to access the power of all parties for shared control and collaborative wisdom, our anxiety begins to feel more like assurance. We begin to manage rather than be managed by conflictive situations. The contextual power and sanity of a community is greater than our own or any single principal's power and goodness.

One's power to manage a conflict is more political than personal: It does not consist in expending one's own resources but in activating communal resources. One appeals to the power of principals to resolve their issues. Failing that, one appeals to the power of bystanders to constrain the principals from win/lose interactions. Thus in the examples cited above, the class member who calls on the chairperson to intervene in the shouting match is actually mobilizing and focusing the power of the class to set limits on and provide directives for the behavior of officers A and B. Similarly, the pastor who calls a meeting of the executive committee to deal with disaffected members is securing the wisdom and accountability of communal leaders as a group to determine how to manage the anger and anxiety of those threatening to jump ship.

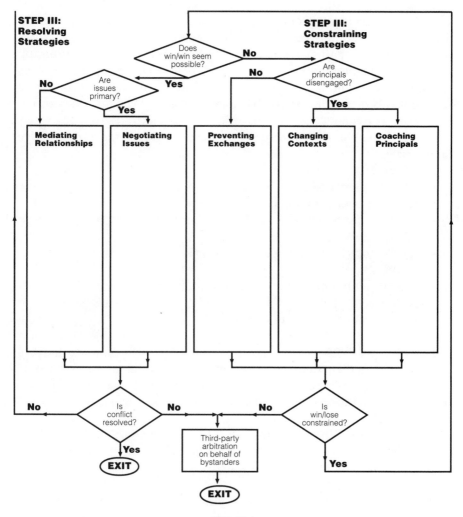

Fig. 7.1

Recognizing Limitations on
Managing Conflicts Constructively

There are congregations and social systems where the community of bystanders is characterized by shame and bad faith rather than grace and good faith. When a manager offers such communities the opportunity to use their power for constructive behaviors, they forsake their own communal good, often blaming or even scapegoating the would-be conflict manager.[2] Members resist becoming bystanders by taking a stand for constructive management. Members remain what might be called spectators. The author has experienced such a congregation. In outward appearances he remained their pastor. But the reality was that his pastoral relationship with this faith community was terminated. Following worship services, he spoke to no one, and no one spoke to him. Neither he nor they could find the means to manage their conflict constructively. He could not partner with them as bystanders.

As we have seen, such congregations manifest the marks of destructive family systems:

- collective denial of pain and conflict
- preservation of communal secrets at all costs
- preference for a deceitful calmness rather than honest struggles about reality
- maintenance of a false security through rigid roles or authoritarian control
- collective numbing of emotions and intuition
- resistance to challenges of the status quo by rejecting, labeling, or excluding anyone who seeks change

Destructive church systems can extinguish the opportunity to manage conflicts within them constructively. No individual alone can overcome such destructive communal dynamics. A responsible manager can offer a dysfunctional faith community the opportunity to change its communal attitudes and rules, but a manager cannot compel that community to choose to change. When a community of bystanders says no to constructive conflict management, one's last recourse is to secure a conflict's arbitration by outsiders (note the alternative of arbitration on the flowchart) (see fig. 7.1).

Arbitration rarely (if ever) resolves differences between the original parties. It only resolves differences on behalf of those who have been held hostage by its chronic destructiveness.

More common than the bad faith of a community is a lack of trust by managers of a community. Faith communities often harbor a few destructive characters, but few faith communities are predominantly destructive in character. The strategic question for a manager who fears his or her community is whether its history of destructive conflict has been due to a lack of constructive conflict management or to a communal rejection of constructive conflict management. Often the histories of communities with destructive conflicts reflect a lack of informed leadership rather than a lack of communal good faith. The only way to know the predominant ethical orientation of a community is to risk appealing to its good faith in support of one's constructive interventions.

Using the Model

Three intervening strategies are provided to constrain the destructive behaviors of principals: (1) *Preventing Exchanges* between principals, (2) *Changing Contexts* bearing on principals, and (3) *Coaching Principals* for fair fighting commitments (see fig. 7.1).

Two intervening strategies are provided to serve the constructive resolution of differences by principals: (1) *Negotiating Issues* between principals and (2) *Mediating Relationships* among principals (see fig. 7.1).

Managing conflicts involves controlling their dynamics. American white male culture has habitually understood and exercised power as a means of unilateral control.[3] For this reason, "managing" a conflict sounds to many like manipulating or controlling it. In this book's model, managing signifies establishing shared control over situations rather than unilateral control over its issues or principals.

While the goal of conflict management is a win/win resolution, one chooses among intervening strategies in light of one's assessment of a conflictive situation. When the power ratio between principals is unbalanced and the ethical orientations of principals are negative, one intervenes first with constraining strategies. Resolving strategies are undertaken only after efforts have been made to change contextual factors, and/or the power and ethical orientations of principals portend a win/win resolution as a real possibility.

For example, a conflict erupts in a committee meeting. Negative feelings are escalating, while the principals seem only to restate their differences with greater intensity. The manager calls for a five-minute break. During the break the manager recognizes the committee's track record of repressing conflicts, the imbalance of power between two of the three principals, and the chronic behavior of interrupting players. When the committee reconvenes, the manager proposes that the matter be put on hold for at least one month (Preventing Exchanges Strategy), during which time the chair might work with the manager to secure missing information and propose a process for committee discussion in light of it (Negotiating Issues Strategy). The manager figures that during this cooling off period she might attempt a Coaching Principals Strategy for more assertiveness by one of the principals, and a Coaching Principals Strategy with the chair to plan procedures for the committee's anticipated conversation at its next meeting. Once the manager has the results of these interventions, she will know whether to proceed with a Negotiating Issues Strategy for resolution or a Changing Contexts Strategy for the committee as a whole.

One can imagine conflictive situations requiring both constraining and resolving strategies. In church systems in which the overall import of contextual factors is assessed to be 0, signifying a balance of positive and negative influences, a manager is likely to intervene with one constraining strategy, followed by a resolving strategy. In church systems in which the overall import of contextual factors is assessed to be −1, signifying more negative than positive influences, a manager is likely to intervene with two or more constraining strategies, in hopes of opening the way for a resolving strategy. In church systems in which the overall import of contextual factors is assessed to be +1, signifying more positive than negative influences, a manager is likely to intervene immediately with a resolving strategy.

This model for managing conflicts provides ways one can change one's chosen strategic intervention midstream. In the example just offered, the manager's proposal to postpone further consideration might be met with a principal's counterproposal that a ground rule against interruption be adopted and that all members of the committee share what they see to be the issues (first stages of a Negotiating Issues Strategy). The manager's assessment of that principal's ethical orientation would immediately change, and so would the plan of management. The manager might then suggest that a second ground rule against personalizing the issues be added and that the committee agree to extend its discussion to the next meeting should it go longer than another half hour. The model instructs a manager to engage in a continuing assessment of conflictive situations in order to update planned interventions as the effects of interventions change situations. The model also instructs managers to abort planned interventions when they are not succeeding. Flexibility and responsiveness are required in managing the surprising dynamics of conflicts.

One begins a strategy by citing actual experiences or circumstances that the strategy seeks to address. For example, when proposing a Coaching Principals Strategy, one might say, "You seemed upset to me last night, and I wondered if you'd like to talk in confidence about what's going on with you?" Or when proposing a Mediating Relationships Strategy, one might say, "You folks don't seem to be hearing each other at all right now. Let's bracket the matter at this point and talk about your relationship itself." Or when beginning a Preventing Exchanges Strategy, one might say, "Last week I was upset when I heard what X said about my friend, Y. I can no longer go through with the appearances of working with X in this church. Will you cooperate with me in setting up some barriers between me and X so that the good of the church is safeguarded?" A manager initiates intervening strategies by citing the needs for a strategy rather than naming the strategy itself.

Managing the process of a conflict requires assertiveness. One is proactive. One fights for fair fighting. While seeking to control other parties unilaterally is destructive, assertively demanding shared control with other parties is both constructive and essential. Generally speaking, until parties to a conflict exercise assertiveness for constructive process, they will not behave assertively over their issues.

One exits this model of constructive conflict management only through principals' win/win resolution of their issues or by institutionally binding arbitration of their issues. Christian realism recognizes that there can be dilemmas between conflicting "goods" that cannot be resolved, and that there is a powerless divine love that does not force people to be responsible parties. Christian realism therefore accepts the need for arbitration when principals cannot or will not resolve or live constructively with their issues. An applied ethic of conflict management holds that one should first seek to manage conflictive situations with the original parties before choosing a process of arbitration.

Choosing Among the Five Strategies

Choosing strategies for managing conflictive situations is more an intuitive art than a purely logical process. No amount of appraisal can eliminate the risk factor in managing conflicts. Appraising a conflict yields probabilities, not predictions. As one strategy is commenced, it may become clear that it is unworkable. Managers learn how to read the early warning signs. They may abort the remaining procedures of a strategy and switch to another strategy they now see to be more fitting. In other words, the failure of a strategy leads one to perceive power ratios or ethical orientations differently from one's previous appraisal. With these differences in mind, one chooses a strategy befitting them. Once one grasps the basic concept of deriving strategies from the findings of one's ongoing appraisal, one will manage conflicts with flexibility and agility.

This model for managing conflicts involves an ongoing process of updating one's ratings of power ratios and ethical orientation as one restrategizes constructive ways to cope with a changing situation. This is similar to the way an effective physician deals with an ailing patient. Just as a physician first asks a patient a series of questions about the patient's symptoms, a manager asks a series of questions to appraise a conflict's context and principals. Just as a physician then prescribes medication in light of his or her diagnosis, a manager proposes strategies in light of his or her appraisal. And just as an effective physician may reevaluate the diagnosis in light of a patient's response to a prescription, so a manager may update the appraisal of a conflict in light of parties' responses to process interventions.

Dealing with the Emotional Dimension
of Intervening

Intervening in conflictive situations entangles one in emotional triangles within and between the parties. Edwin H. Friedman describes emotional triangles in this way:

> An emotional triangle is formed by any three persons or issues. . . . The basic law of emotional triangles is that when any two parties of a system become uncomfortable with one another, they will "triangle in" or focus upon a third person, or issue, as a way of stabilizing their own relationship with one another. A person may be said to be "triangled" if he or she gets caught in the middle as the focus of such an unresolved issue. Conversely, when individuals try to change the relationship of two others (two people, or a person and his or her symptom or belief), they "triangle" themselves into that relationship (and often stabilize the very situation they are trying to change).[4]

Friedman goes on to derive a number of basic propositions that we have adapted for managers who intervene in conflictive situations:

1. The emotional relationship of any two actors to a conflict's issues is kept in balance by the way a third actor relates to each of them or to their relationship. When a given situation is stuck, therefore, there is probably a manager or issue that is part of the homeostasis.
2. If one is the manager in an emotional triangle, it is generally not possible to bring change to the relationship or to the other two actors by trying to change their relationship directly or by trying to resolve their issues directly.
3. Attempts to directly change the relationship of the other two sides of the conflict are not only generally ineffective, but also often yield the opposite result, having principals in a conflict unite against the intervening outsider or bystander as the "problem" or the "one to be blamed" for the principals' conflict with each other.
4. We can only change a conflictive situation to which we belong. Therefore, the way to bring change is to maintain a well defined relationship with each party to the conflict, and to avoid the responsibility for their relationship with each other.[5]

All the intervening strategies for managing conflicts carry the threat of emotional triangulation of the manager by the other parties. By the same token, all intervening strategies also bear the change benefits of emotional detriangulation by the manager with the parties. The key to escaping the threat and reaping these benefits is for the manager to stick with the process. When a manager seeks to change the relationship(s) between principals in a Mediating Strategy by proposing a *solution* to their difficulties, principals tend to project their emotional difficulties with each other onto the intruding manager, collaborating to scapegoat the manager rather than dealing with their relationship. Conversely, when a manager intervenes in a Mediating Strategy as a nonanxious presence who offers a *process* whereby principals can deal with their troubled relationship(s), principals are confronted with the option of dealing with their conflicted relationship themselves. Similarly, when a manager seeks to fix the inner conflicts of a principal (Coaching Principals Strategy) or fix the issues between principals (Negotiating Issues Strategy) by proposing a *solution for* them, principals tend to place the responsibility for making such solutions work on the manager rather than on themselves. A destructive emotional dependence or counterdependence between manager and principal(s) is created. Conversely, when a manager intervenes in coaching and negotiating strategies as a nonanxious presence who offers processes whereby principals can take responsibility for asserting themselves and working through their issues, principals are more likely to accept autonomous responsibility for reconciling their relationship themselves. The way to be a transforming presence in conflictive situations is to be an assertive process consultant rather than an expert who rescues the parties from their pain and differences.

Managing in Role

Many theories of conflict management require a relatively objective third party to be manager. As was indicated in chapter 4 about recognizing one's role, this model distinguishes between third parties and third-party functions. This model holds that third-party functions are essential for a conflict's management. But in this model, third-party functions are lodged in the tasks to be undertaken by any party to a conflict. The model provides that these tasks must be undertaken prior to, but not to the exclusion of, one's role as a principal. In this model one can be both a manager and a principal in a conflictive situation as long as one performs third-party functions *before* acting on behalf of one's interests as a principal. There are, however, two critical exceptions to the concept of being a principal/manager.

The first exception is that a principal/manager cannot undertake a coaching strategy directly with another principal. Coaching one's opponent leads either to abandoning one's own issues or to manipulating one's opponent under the guise of counseling him or her. When one is a principal/manager, one can deputize another party to attempt a coaching strategy on one's behalf, but one cannot coach one's opponent directly. This principle will be thoroughly discussed in chapter 10, which discusses the Coaching Principals Strategy.

The second exception involves managing a Mediating Relationships Strategy. It is often almost impossible to remain in the role of a manager when one is a principal to a prolonged, conflicted relationship. Principals in conflicted relationships may manage a Mediating Strategy between them for a while. But when difficulties persist and emotional issues between them are not being resolved, principals will find it almost impossible to continue to be managers of the conflict. In many conflicted relationships, principals will require another person to serve as a third party to mediate a conflicted relationship (see chapter 12).

Using a Reframing Process in Conflictive Situations

Obviously, the need for change is embedded in conflictive situations. Principals will want to change their circumstances or change their opponents in order to satisfy their interests. Bystanders and managers will want to change the behaviors or interests of principals to enhance a larger common good. This model of managing conflicts assumes two theological positions about human change: (1) Morally responsible people can participate in changing themselves, but they cannot make others change, and (2) morally responsible people can participate in changing circumstances that influence parties, but they cannot manipulate parties by doing so behind their backs.

A reframing process achieves change by affirming what parties perceive and believe while changing how parties interpret what they perceive and believe.[6] The concept is that the meanings parties make of their situations and experiences are anchored in the assumptions and thoughts that they bring as a framework to their situations and experiences. For example, one may interpret another's being angry to mean that one has done wrong. Or one may interpret another's being angry to mean that the other has done wrong. Or one may interpret another's being angry to mean that the other is being responsibly assertive with and trusting of one. The meaning one makes of another's behavior is anchored in the assumption one uses to frame that person's behavior. Parties' mental contexts generate their interpretations.

A reframing process changes the meaning of situations by changing the assumptions or contexts parties use in making meaning. A reframing process takes one's situation, lifts it out of an old context of interpretation, and places it in a new context that gives it different or new meanings on which to act. For example, one may describe a "small and struggling" congregation as a "caring and tenacious" congregation. Or a party may observe, "We run off our minister every three years," while one may comment in response, "Well, your ministers seem to have been so attractive that you've lost them in less than four years."[7]

Reframing a thought changes a party's consciousness in the same way that changing the frame on a picture changes the appearance of the picture. The same reality looks, feels, or sounds different to the party, not because it has changed but because the party's interpretative frame of understanding has changed. With new meanings parties are motivated for new behaviors. Their behaviors change, and consequently they make changes in their circumstances.

Reframing is positively oriented. It consists in claiming more what is right with people than what is wrong with them. It aims to invite rather than to persuade people to change. It seeks to affirm where people are and offer them new perspectives, rather than to confront them over where they are and criticize their perspectives. It asks people more about what they want and what they are for than about what they do not want and what they oppose. Reframing focuses more on moving people through the present into a future than on rejecting the present because of the past. In Christian terms, reframing is rooted more in a consciousness of the goodness of our creation than a consciousness of our sinfulness.

With reframing, one experiences oneself more as a worthy child rather than a broken work of God. In this model, one seeks to realize needed changes in conflictive situations by reframing rather than remaking the parties to a conflict.

Reframing also provides parties with responsible choices about what they will make of their situations and experiences. While reframing can be used manipulatively to trick parties into seeing things differently, the reframing process used in this model presents parties with deliberate choices for them to make in interpreting things. Responsible Christian behavior is more a matter of choice than of duty. While finite parties cannot create or change circumstances as if they were God, they can choose to interpret the meanings of circumstances from God's revealing perspectives.

Flowing with the Model

Conflicts are dynamic rather than static realities. Managing conflicts involves flowing with what is going on rather than rigidly sticking with one's original assessment or planned interventions. On the one hand, a manager needs to stick with the model so that at any time she or he knows which strategy or step of the model is being pursued. On the other hand, a manager needs to move with the model, flowing from a third-step intervention back to reassess a second-step assessment of the situation or a first-step recovery of oneself as a manager (see appendix 1). To jump out of the model because of resistance or confusion simply increases one's confusion. To get stuck in any one step of the model because of one's emotional rigidity or perfectionism simply puts one in a reactive and controlling position as manager.

Often managers will experience the need to abort a strategic intervention before completing it. In seeking to secure behavioral ground rules for a Mediating Relationships Strategy, principals may refuse to cooperate, at which point a manager would stop the meeting, dismissing the principals and following the flowchart back to a second-step reassessment of the principals. Or when seeking to formulate new communal fair fight rules in a Changing Contexts Strategy, bystanders may prove unwilling or unable to override a prevailing "be nice rule" to talk honestly about their community's habits of dirty fighting. In such circumstances a manager would stop the conversation, observe what the prevailing rule seems to be, and invite parties either to override it and proceed or continue to accept it and end their conversation. Or in seeking to mobilize bystanders to cooperate in a Preventing Exchanges Strategy, a manager may begin to be scapegoated by bystanders' discomfort. Rather than working with the manager to erect barriers between destructive principals, bystanders are blaming the manager for not fixing the problems and feelings of the principals. With such a turn of events, a manager would abort the remaining tasks of the Preventing Exchanges Strategy and might follow the flowchart back to the first step of management of self before a second-step reappraisal of the situation. Or finally, in pursuing a coaching strategy for oneself as principal/manager or bystander/manager, one may come to see that an unconstrained, chronic destructive conflict is proving to be both unmanageable and too costly to be tolerated any longer. Rather than following the flowchart back to the first or second steps, a manager would seek third-party arbitration. Strategic interventions are to be pursued unless or until they prove unfeasible, at which point this model directs managers to abandon the particular strategy by following the flowchart rather than forsaking it. Flexibility and accountability, not intractability or rightness, are the traits of effective conflict management. Managing conflicts involves coping with, rather than controlling, what is going on.

Finally, we have already stated that this model uses a flowchart because of the dynamic nature of conflicts and their management. One is never finished with any step in the model until one exits from the whole process shown in the flowchart by resolving or arbitrating a conflict. The purpose of this book's model is to guide us in going with the flow of intentional, Christian management of a conflict rather than going with the flow of malevolent, irresponsible reactions to a conflict.

Common Difficulties with Using
This Model

When one undertakes strategic interventions, difficulties may arise for a number of reasons:

- trying compulsively to control parties rather than control the process
- seeking to change others by persuasively rescuing or judging them rather than by reframing their realities
- failing to trust others in coaching them or to trust a deputy to coach them on behalf of fair fighting
- attempting to deal with substantive differences without first securing behavioral ground rules
- failing to contract with others the procedures of a strategy before proceeding into it
- failing to follow the prescribed procedures beyond the first or second task
- failing to flow through the three steps repeatedly as a conflictive situation and the results of efforts to manage it keep changing

Such difficulties are not fatal to the management of a conflict. Parties to a conflict are resilient. When a mistake is made, one can assertively disengage from the difficulty by recognizing what is going on and either rethinking one's strategy or redoing one's implementation of the strategy. No party to a conflict is perfect, and no conflict is managed perfectly. Difficulties can be and will be experienced and repaired as one manages church conflicts. When managing church conflicts, as with the rest of one's life, one learns to trust God and trust the process.

Step Three/Constraining Strategies: Preventing Exchanges

A staff person from the denomination's regional office had been invited by the Springfield Church governing board to attend their meeting. The meeting was called to receive the sudden resignation of their pastor, who had been with them only one year. Board members had heard complaints about how the minister had gossiped about members, was arrogant, and was never in the church office. The regional representative knew that the minister had received these criticisms and had been making changes, including installing call-forwarding to his home so he could be reached while taking care of his children. Suddenly, however, he was leaving. The regional director knew that this minister was not the major problem. This pastor was but the latest in a succession of ministers who had been wounded by this congregation. The regional staff person vowed to herself that this time the deeper problems of this destructive, ninety-six member congregation would be identified and confronted before another minister would be permitted to be called and mauled.

Because many people tend to deny or ignore conflicts until their dynamics have become destructive, one's first intervention to manage a conflict will often be one of preventing virtually all exchanges between principals (see fig. 8.1). The most common situations in which one may choose to use a Preventing Exchanges Strategy are when (1) principals are engaged in increasingly destructive combat, (2) one is ambushed by destructively attacking principal(s), or (3) one seeks the time and space to assess a conflictive situation that seems to be emerging.

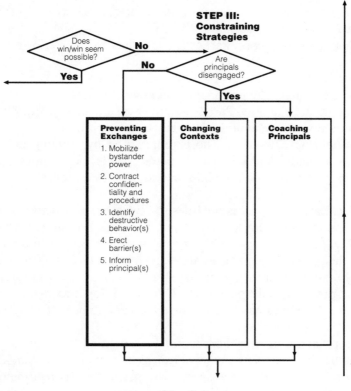

Fig. 8.1

Blocking Destructive Exchanges

Although a Preventing Exchanges Strategy erects barriers to constrain virtually all exchanges between principals, the kinds of behavior one targets are their dirty fight behaviors. We have already defined these behaviors as verbal or nonverbal exchanges that are exclusively partisan, consciously or unconsciously deceitful, and aggressive, manipulative, or otherwise disrespectful of others. Rensis and Jane Likert list common examples of these kinds of destructive behaviors in win/lose cycles of conflict:

1. Enemy-making behaviors: Parties close ranks against each other as the "enemy."
2. Hierarchically controlling behaviors: Parties seek as leaders to monopolize and exercise power as control over others.
3. Polarizing behaviors: Parties' exchanges permit less and less time or place for discovering additional options.
4. Repressing behaviors: Parties' all-or-nothing thinking leads them

to interrupt, ignore, discount, or deny the complexity or diversity of perspectives in a situation.

5. Judgmental behaviors: Parties judge others to be inferior or inadequate people.
6. Violating behaviors: Parties' language, body movements and/or tone of voice violates the personal boundaries of others.
7. Adversarial behaviors: Parties ignore or invalidate what they have in common with one another. We/they language is used.
8. Caricaturing behaviors: Those represented by winning principals speak of and relate to them as heroes; while those represented by losing principals speak of and relate to them as traitors.[1]

There will always be occasional destructive exchanges between principals in even the most constructive conflicts. Since no one is perfect, no principal will behave in perfectly constructive ways. But when a manager observes that two or more parties are behaving in *increasingly* destructive ways with one another, a preventing strategy is needed to interrupt the escalating spiral of a malevolent cycle. One has to stop dirty fighting before there can be the emotional space and time needed to begin fair fighting in its place.

One stops destructive exchanges not by obtaining the consent of the principals but by exercising the power of bystanders to erect barriers between the principals. Often managers try to persuade dirty fighting parties to stop being destructive. Ironically, dirty fighting parties are the least likely parties to cooperate in this. Managers are usually powerless to constrain dirty fighting parties by persuasion. A preventing strategy is needed when dirty fighting parties will not consent to fight fair. When a preventing strategy is needed to interrupt a malevolent cycle of conflict, it must be based on the consent of bystanders rather than the cooperation of principals. The manager's power to constrain destructive exchanges lies in mobilizing the interests of bystanders to erect structural barriers between the principals. Once bystander power has been mobilized to erect such barriers, one may then seek to work with principals by coaching them or to work around principals by changing contextual factors influencing them.

A preventing strategy not only depends on the power of bystanders but also is morally accountable to bystanders. Being accountable to bystanders requires a manager to distinguish between truthfulness as candor and truthfulness as disclosure. A metaphor may help us recognize this distinction. People wear clothes because no one can tolerate being naked in public. Wearing clothes, however, is not a denial of the body that is clothed. It is simply a way of honestly acknowledging one's body without disclosing it. Similarly, one may be accountable to bystanders by acknowledging that one has information without disclosing it. Just as one may unclothe in an intimate, committed relationship with another, one may disclose information only when and where it is appropriate in conflictive situations. In conflictive situations, one is ethically required to exercise accountable candor rather than accountable disclosure with bystanders.

Being candid with bystanders involves informing them about the consequences or effects of privileged information, rather than the privileged information itself. A manager shares with bystanders her or his assessment of the conflictive behaviors of principals rather than information about their issues or wrongdoing. One's assessment is given in order to provide a rationale for enlisting bystanders' power in erecting fitting barriers, rather than to embroil bystanders in principals' business.

Finally, one needs to remember that there are governing boards, church bodies, and other faith communities in which the majority of members choose to deny or flee from conflict as spectators rather than to assume their collective responsibility as moral bystanders. In a Preventing Exchanges or Changing Contexts Strategy, such irresponsible behavior by the majority of members makes it impossible for a single manager to constrain principals' destructive behaviors. As we shall see in chapter 10, a manager's rebuff by spectators leads one to pursue a self-coaching strategy as one's only remaining constructive option.

Remembering Faith Meanings for a Preventing Strategy

When one proposes a preventing strategy, one often encounters qualms of conscientious resistance from some bystanders or even from within oneself. The thoughts behind such feelings might be any of the following:

- This feels unfair—like we're ganging up on principal X behind her back.
- This feels manipulative—like we're forcing fellow members to change by threatening to exclude them.
- This feels arrogant—like we're talking about others' faults while ignoring our own.
- This feels dangerous—like the manager is giving us only part of the picture—the part that supports his proposed intervention.
- This feels un-Christian—Jesus cares about every individual. We have no right to erect barriers against anyone.

When the manager or bystanders have these kinds of thoughts, it is time to go back to Step One of this model and update parties' operating gut theologies again. Just as a manager will want to regularly update gut theologies in the way outlined in Step One, so a manager will want to work with other parties to a conflict for their regularly updating their gut theologies.

At first, it may seem contradictory that a ministry of reconciliation in conflictive situations might include a strategy of erecting barriers between principals. This apparent contradiction is like the apparent contradiction of a loving Jesus coldly calling Peter a viper or angrily overturning the vending tables at the Temple. What seems a contradiction is actually the paradox of what has been called "tough love."

We have already observed that we live in a meantime world in which the evil results of human sin bring out the dirty fight capacities of all parties to a conflict. We have also recognized the difference between the wrongdoing of a guilty sinner and the wrong-being of a compulsive, shame-based sinner. The ethical meaning of a preventing strategy is that it is a necessary, lesser evil in a meantime world. A preventing strategy not only protects bystanders from the evil effects of dirty fighting but also protects principals from themselves. What is being rejected and constrained is the destructive behavior of principals, not the principals themselves.[2] What is being protected from destruction is the inherent goodness of both principals and bystanders. Erecting barriers against dirty fight behaviors provides a way for all parties to explore fair fight alternatives. A preventing strategy provides guilty wrongdoers the opportunity to repent and shame-based wrongdoers the chance to begin to heal as well. A preventing strategy opens the way for God's grace to be claimed by responsible parties who choose to accept it.

The tough love of a preventing strategy is both tough and loving. It is tough because it mobilizes communal resources to set barriers that block parties' behaviors without their consent. It is also tough because dirty fighting parties usually interpret a preventing strategy as a personal attack on themselves rather than as a constraint on their behavior. But a preventing strategy is also loving because it gives parties a chance to claim the love and justice of God for themselves and with others.

In summary, a preventing strategy involves caring enough about all parties to fight for the realization of God's image in them. It affirms each party's created goodness. Because reconciliation is the prescribed goal of a Christian ethic of conflict management, a preventing strategy is not the only intervention a Christian manager makes in managing a conflictive situation. As the flowchart of the model indicates, once the principals have been disengaged, a manager will further intervene to coach principals or change contextual factors so that a constructive resolution for the well being of all may be pursued.

One final ethical concern in using a preventing strategy may arise in a scrupulous manager's conscience. One may question whether one is using a preventing strategy as a noble way to suppress all conflict, or even as a way of winning over others by using a disguising righteousness to overcome one's opponents for one's own egotistical interests.

The moral safeguard against a manager's misuse or self-deceiving use of a preventing strategy rests in the required accountability of a manager to a community of bystanders. By submitting one's own perceptions of dirty fighting and one's own constraining proposals to the communal scrutiny of others, one is protected from moral self-deception or grandiosity. When the *collective* judgment of a community of bystanders recognizes the justice and common good to be approximated by preventing specific dirty fight behaviors, a manager's own ethical concerns are met.[3]

Interrupting a Malevolent Cycle

One often must institute a preventing strategy "on the spot." Enemy-making, controlling, polarizing, repressing, judgmental, violating, and/or adversarial exchanges are increasing, and there is time for neither a manager's assessment nor communal consultation.

One erects a provisional barrier by interrupting the proceedings: calling a break, adjourning a meeting, ending a phone call, or refusing to interact further. Such interruptions are temporary. They afford the opportunity to assess the need for and consult with self or others about erecting more long-term, structural kinds of barriers between principals.

Provisional barriers can be erected because everyone has the power of saying no. In situations other than physical entrapment, any parties to a conflict have the power to assert their boundaries: to stand up for their right to stop being party to destructive exchanges. Such behavior would be a case of flight behavior if one were simply quitting a conflict without further assessment and consultation for its management. But asserting one's right to interrupt destructive exchanges in order to pursue management of the conflict is a matter of responsible choice rather than irresponsible flight.

Often principals in an escalating malevolent round will withdraw of their own accord. Typically they realize that the benefits of winning are not worth the increasing emotional and political costs they are incurring. They disengage from one another, but without accountability. In such circumstances a manager may intervene immediately with a Coaching and/or Changing Contexts Strategy to secure a benevolent cycle. Rather than just letting sleeping dogs lie, managers seize the opportunity afforded by the mutual flight of dirty fighting principals to initiate Coaching or Changing Contexts strategies. Otherwise, the pressures of dissatisfaction will build between principals until their dirty fighting erupts again.

In summary, when one's experience of a conflictive situation evidences negative contextual factors, unbalanced power ratios, and dirty fight ethical orientations, and principals are in a round of increasingly destructive exchanges, a preventing strategy is instituted as quickly as possible.

Implementing a
Preventing Exchanges Strategy

Once destructive exchanges have been provisionally interrupted by a manager's separation of principals or by principals' own temporary withdrawal from one another, one may proceed with the following stages of a preventing strategy (see fig. 8.1 on p. 104 above). Like stacking children's blocks, the achievement of each stage depends on the productive completion of the stage immediately preceding it.

Mobilize Bystander Power

The first stage of a preventing strategy is to mobilize and channel the power of the bystanders whose community is housing the conflict. This is done by candidly informing bystanders about their own interest in securing the conflict's constructive management. Discussion of the issues or of the moral character of the principals is specifically banned in this initiative. Such discussion would simply be a way of mobilizing bystanders to take sides between or against the principals, a polarizing of the community hosting the conflict. Moreover, such discussion would fuel rather than interrupt the malevolent cycle. Rather than involving bystanders in the issues or personalities of the conflict, the manager involves bystanders in the management of a conflict's process by candidly describing destructive behaviors that should be blocked.

For example, a manager might begin a preventing strategy by calling a meeting of a governing board or a special gathering of influential communal leaders. Unless the manager also happens to be a principal, no principal would be included in this conversation. Having secured from the bystanders a contract of strict confidentiality, the manager might speak along the following lines:

> I believe that no one wins from dirty fighting. I wish to speak candidly with you about a destructive conflict. I will not tell you my understanding of the issues. Nor will I share with you privileged information about the principals. I don't want you to take sides. I do want you to empower the conflict's management by working with me to erect barriers to parties' increasingly destructive exchanges.
>
> Will you join me in using the structures and processes of this community to stop dirty fight exchanges, which are putting us all increasingly at risk, spiritually, financially, and emotionally?

Because the final power in church fights to constrain dirty fighting principals consists in setting limits on their behaviors rather than curbing or changing their malevolent intentions, this stage of contracting the tasks of a preventing strategy with bystanders is critical. A manager needs more than the assent of the bystanders. A manager needs the cooperative exercise of communal power represented by the bystanders. Bystanders must agree to proceed with these tasks if the tasks are to be really achieved. Should the bystanders resist the manager's request for their cooperation in preventing destructive exchanges, the manager aborts this strategy, dropping down on the flowchart through the remaining stages of this strategy to decide whether to seek third-party arbitration or just a continuation of the provisional disengagement of principals while the manager explores alternative strategies.

In summary, one begins a preventing strategy by asserting what one sees to be the basic interest of the bystanders in securing their power for constructive management of the situation. Rather than beginning by disclosing privileged information or even risking stating one's own perceptions of the situation, one simply asserts one's understanding of the need to mobilize communal power for constructiveness in the situation.

Contract Confidentiality and Procedures

Confidentiality is absolutely essential in a Preventing Exchanges Strategy. We have already spoken of the distinction between truth as candor and truth as disclosure. Before any party to a preventing strategy can be honest with sensitive information about one or more principals, she or he must be absolutely sure that such information will not be shared with anyone outside the process. An explicit contract of confidentiality will be made with each individual present. Such a contract might read as follows: "I promise that nothing that is said by anyone in this process will ever be shared by me with any outsider in any way." The manager will want to ask each participant to make an explicit commitment to such a statement of confidentiality before proceeding with any discussion of any principal's behavior.

The next task in a preventing strategy is for the manager to outline and contract the remaining tasks that participants will undertake in this strategy. Participants will need to understand and agree to participate in these tasks. Otherwise, one can find oneself as manager in the unproductive position of being the only participant who speaks honestly about difficulties in the situation and ways to address them. Bystanders in a preventing strategy will participate in sharing sensitive information rather than simply be present as observers.

The tasks one describes and contracts with them involve how they will scrutinize the manager's perceptions as well as share their own perceptions of the conflictive situation:

- statement of the manager's perception of specific destructive behaviors to be constrained
- cooperative scrutiny of the manager's perceptions
- joint identification of specific destructive behaviors to be constrained
- joint formulation and implementation of communal barriers to block these behaviors
- joint advisement of principals of communal action taken

Identify Destructive Behavior(s)

The kinds of behaviors one lists to be blocked can be illustrated as follows:

- character assaults on party A by party B, especially in telephone conversations/gossip
- physical and verbal violations of party B by party A in the fellowship hall last Sunday
- misrepresentations by party A to bystander F in the parking lot about what party B has said/done
- threats by party B to withhold giving and to call a gathering of sympathizers to request party A's communal rebuke

Our job is not to take sides or judge the moral character of these principals nor the righteousness of their issues. Our job is to block further exchanges between them so as to buy the time and space to work for a constructive resolution of their differences.

Once the manager has listed the kinds of destructive behaviors to be blocked, bystanders become involved in sharing their observations and information to validate or invalidate, reduce or expand, this list, until they achieve consensus on the major specific behaviors to be blocked.

Erect Barriers

This task consists of the manager and bystanders consulting over the particular structural, procedural, or normative kinds of institutional elements that can be utilized as barriers to specified destructive behaviors. The purpose of structural barriers is to establish institutional conditions that maintain disengagement between dirty fighting principals. Efforts to change the principals themselves are undertaken in other constraining strategies of Coaching or Changing Contexts.

The following are possible ways a manager and bystanders can erect barriers against destructive exchanges:

Use Position Descriptions
- changes in principals' assigned tasks or duties
- changes in principals' access to organizational funds or other physical resources
- changes in principals' lines of supervision, consultation, or accountability
- changes in the criteria and processes for principals' performance evaluation

Use Group Memberships
- changes in principals' membership on boards or committees
- changes in principals' authorized access to governing boards or work groups

Use Lines of Communication
- changes that limit or exclude principals' participation in lines of communication about communal funds, personnel, or policy concerns
- changes in procedures for gathering and verifying information used by communal members

Use Organizational Procedures
- changes in the dockets of meetings that involve principals
- changes in the norms of meetings that involve principals

Use Time Frames or Space Arrangements
- changes of deadlines for deciding or implementing matters in which principals are involved
- changes in the location or frequency of meetings in which principals are involved

Use Institutional Policies
- changes that require use of verifiable data in formal decision making
- changes in procedures for communication and accountability by decision makers to the community as a whole

The manager and bystanders review such a list of possible barriers, choosing one to three changes that would most effectively block destructive exchanges between principals in the conflictive situation.

For example, in the illustration presented above, the manager identified four specific kinds of dirty fighting between parties A and B: character defamation, physical and emotional violations of personal space in the fellowship hall, misrepresentations of facts to bystanders, and threats of financial and political boycott. A manager and bystanders might consider the following kinds of barriers to block these behaviors.

In regard to character defamation and misrepresentation of fact by one or more of the principals, a potential barrier might be a letter advising the whole community to refuse to receive or pass on further hearsay from any principal in this dispute. Another barrier might be to adopt a policy of accepting from all parties *only* reports of wrongs independently validated by at least two bystanders who have communal credibility.

In regard to violating the physical and emotional space of one of the principals, a potential barrier might be to advise principals not to engage each other over their differences at communal functions and to instruct principal A's associates to use an answering machine to screen out telephone conversations from principal B. Another barrier might be to state in writing to principal B at what times or in what places principal A would be willing to communicate at all.

In regard to threats of financial and political boycott, a barrier might be to compose a written statement to all members of the community reaffirming the spiritual basis of giving and citing the procedural, legal, and communal requirements applicable to any formal consideration of charges against any party.

Once the manager and bystanders have formulated and established one to three barriers to block destructive exchanges between principals, their final task is to jointly communicate their action to the principals.

Inform Principal(s)

A preventing strategy undertaken by bystanders is respectfully communicated in the name of the community to the principals. Often the most effective way to inform principals of barriers erected to prevent their destructive exchanges is a private, compassionate, written communication. Information about barriers that does not require general communal awareness is communicated only to the principals. Information about barriers that does require general communal awareness is communicated with candor, but without disclosing privileged information about the principals or their issues. Every effort is made to respect the integrity and privacy of principals and to affirm their responsibility to resolve their issues. Care is taken not to embarrass the principals or inflame the community by publicly disclosing any privileged information. The axiom that guides communication with principals about barriers is this: The community's only legitimate interest in their conflict is that it be managed constructively. The principals' issues are not the community's business.

The outcome of a preventing strategy is the cessation of destructive exchanges, not the cessation of hostile feelings or the resolution of conflicting differences. Communal limits on principals' destructive behaviors are accompanied by communal respect and affirmation of principals' inherent worth and dignity. Care is taken that in blocking behaviors, principals are not shamed. A conflict is not kept secret, but neither are its substantive issues divulged. The distinction between a public record of the interest of bystanders and public protection of the privacy of bystanders is carefully maintained.

Those who intervene with a Preventing Exchanges Strategy often experience dirty fight responses from one or more principals. Typically such responses are accusations by one or more principals that communal barriers to destructive exchanges are actually expressions of communal rejection, betrayal, exclusion, or punishment of them. A shame-based principal tends to blame the community as victimizer rather than respect the community as its responsible member. Should such distorted responses occur, communal representatives assertively and compassionately assert the distinction between principals' behaviors and principals' inherent, God-given worth. Such assertive behavior by communal leaders will model the assertive respectfulness and compassion all parties can adopt as principals.

An Illustration
of a Preventing Exchanges Strategy

The pastoral candidate was in his thirties. Toward the conclusion of his conversation with the search committee, committee members had agreed, without debate or dissent, that the church secretary for twenty of the twenty-four years of the congregation's history had to be terminated. No reasons were given. It was simply observed that she was in declining health and was approaching the retirement age of sixty-five. The candidate requested that, since he had neither knowledge nor prior involvement, the matter be settled prior to his arrival as new pastor. The committee agreed to this request.

Within two weeks, the congregation extended him a call to be their pastor. During the following weeks the pastor made weekly visits to preach and provide crisis pastoral care while he was being cleared to receive and accept the congregation's call. On each weekend visit the incoming pastor made it a point to confer with professional staff regarding immediate pastoral concerns without meeting in any way with the church secretary.

On his first full day of work as new pastor, he was greeted in the church office by the nonterminated church secretary. She immediately confronted him: "Why did you try to have me fired?"

He paused and then said, "I didn't."

"Well," she demanded, "am I or am I not your secretary?"

Feeling sorely pressed, the pastor responded, "Well, I don't know. I guess we both need to find that out."

"Well, we'll see about that," she said as she stood and left the room.

What ensued for the next two months was an increasingly malevolent cycle of conflict. The pastor and the church secretary became increasingly distrustful, hurt, angry, and destructive with each other. Gossip swirled through the congregation. The pastoral honeymoon ended before it had hardly begun. The search committee seemed to evaporate in thin air. The conflict was increasingly costly to all parties, both their present circumstances and the promise of their future together. Clearly, neither principal was winning, and all parties were losing.

By the third month, the pastor felt like resigning, an action that would severely wound both the congregation and himself. He did not know how to assess the situation responsibly. He did know that something had to change. Finally, while reading a book on managing conflicts he stumbled on the concept of erecting barriers to block destructive exchanges between antagonists.[4] He saw in such an intervention the chance to stop destructive exchanges without having to determine who was primarily to blame, much less settle the mushrooming differences between them. He formulated two barriers: a change in position description and a change in an organizational line of communication and accountability. First, he decided that the woman would continue to be the church's secretary, but not his secretary. He would take care of his own secretarial needs. Second, he decided to propose that the governing board, rather than himself, serve as the church secretary's immediate and final supervisor. As pastor he would work alongside her, but not in partnership with her.

Having formulated these barriers, he informed her of them and then informed the governing body of them. The church secretary affirmed his formulation of her position, indicating that she would be glad to be his secretary as well. He declined. Neither formulation was challenged by the governing body. Had he known more about the tasks of a preventing strategy, he would have conferred first with the governing body, seeking joint action with them in formulating and erecting these barriers. However, by informing them of his formulations, he provided them at least an opportunity to scrutinize his thinking before validating his proposed structural and procedural changes. Within another three months he proposed to the governing board a third barrier between himself and the church's secretary. This third barrier consisted in his securing a second telephone line with no extensions for his sole use.

Although these barriers against destructive exchanges between pastor and church secretary did not resolve their issues, they provided a way for both of them to coexist with respect. Their malevolent cycle was interrupted. Triggers for additional malevolent cycles were eliminated by separating their work responsibilities. Gradually pastor and church secretary were able to rechannel their energies from struggling with each other to practicing their respective ministries with the congregation. The destructive costs of their conflict were substantially reduced, even though their issues were not resolved. Rather than further polarizing the congregation, the disengagement between pastor and church secretary defused the conflict for the congregation. Pastor and church secretary were not reconciled, but they did come to respect each other. Moreover, the suspension of their destructive exchanges opened the way for progress toward healing other wounds in this chronically conflicted congregation. Indeed, in hindsight it became clear that the pastor/secretary conflict had been but a symptomatic expression of larger communal conflicts.

In Conclusion

A preventing strategy is undertaken when two or more principals are engaged in increasingly destructive exchanges that are damaging the larger community. In conflictive situations where dirty fighting principals do not disengage themselves or where dirty fighting principals only withdraw temporarily to reengage at more costly levels of destructiveness, a preventing strategy is required to cut the costs for both principals and their faith community. Once dirty fighting principals have been disengaged due to the erection of barriers between them, a manager can explore additional interventions to constrain the destructiveness of the situation: interventions to change contexts or coach principals for constructive resolution of the conflict.

CHAPTER 9

Step Three/Constraining Strategies: Changing Contextual Factors

When exchanges between principals are disengaged by mutual withdrawal or blocked by barriers, a manager is free to undertake strategies that address destructiveness in the situation. The two strategies are (1) to change contextual factors that are destructively influencing principals' behaviors (Changing Contexts Strategy) and (2) to change predominating traits within principals that are destructively shaping their behaviors (Coaching Principals Strategy, see chapter 10). The common goal of both the Changing Contexts and the Coaching Principals strategies is to reorient principals so that they will be ready and willing to resolve their differences constructively.

In Step Two of appraising a conflictive situation, the manager was asked to list some key contextual factors bearing positively or negatively on parties in the situation (see chapter 5). These factors consist of influences on all parties from a larger community's implicit or explicit rules and structures as well as any key changes in that community's environmental circumstances. A Changing Contexts Strategy (see fig. 9.1) involves all spectators willing to become bystanders in a process of recognizing, assessing, and changing contextual factors so that their influence on parties will promote fair rather than dirty fight behaviors. The purpose of this strategy is to change principals' behaviors indirectly.

Changing Principals' Behaviors
Indirectly

Christians are in the habit of trying to change others by direct persuasion. We preach sermons, teach church school classes, or engage in direc-

Fig. 9.1

tive kinds of pastoral counseling. Often such direct efforts at influencing others have positive effects. But when one is dealing with destructively oriented principals, such efforts at direct influence fail. Direct persuasion is often ineffective with shame-based parties. Their shame distorts all incoming messages. They put malevolent interpretations on benevolent intentions. Rather than limit ourselves to direct change efforts only, we may also undertake indirect change efforts. Indirect ways of changing others involve changing contextual factors bearing on all parties, including the principals.

Strategies of indirect change are called second-order change. Second-order change is more promising as a way of constraining destructive parties in conflicts because, unlike direct efforts of change, indirect change does not depend on the cooperation or even the consent of the principals themselves. Changing contextual factors depends on the cooperation of the larger community of bystanders. Moreover, indirect efforts of change have the advantage of encouraging principals to change without incurring "face" issues. Principals are incorporated by rather than singled out by changes in contextual rules, structures, and responses to environmental conditions. Principals are neither identified nor confronted by such changes unless they choose to resist them.

In the case of second-order change, principals are given opportunities to change in response to changed circumstances bearing on them rather than in response to others' direct efforts to change them. Principals are often more likely to choose to change themselves in response to changed conditions rather than in response to any personalized request or demand of other principals.

Efforts to make the United States a smokeless society provide a good case in point. For most of the twentieth century, North American culture interpreted smoking as socially desirable. Personal sophistication, emancipation, popularity, and even sex appeal were culturally attributed to smoking. Through advertising, smoking behavior was sold indirectly in these terms. Structurally, the smoking habit was supplied by an array of marketing outlets from cigarette machines to supermarkets. Finally, the profound stress that has accompanied the massive technological, economic, and political change of the twentieth century served to motivate people's cravings for the emotional relief of using nicotine. Thus key cultural rules, institutional structures, and environmental circumstances all operated as positive contextual factors supporting an obviously self-destructive behavior. The destructive effect of these contextual factors was so great that many smokers continued to smoke even against their own powerful instincts for survival. Smokers kept smoking while knowing that they were risking death and shortening their lives. Information about the effects of smoking was making little difference.

However, in the 1980s the contextual factors about smoking in North American culture began to change. The nation's Surgeon General called smoking an addiction rather than just a dirty habit. Public media began to portray smoking as physically unattractive and socially offensive. Socially desirable traits like sophistication, emancipation, popularity, and sex appeal began to be attributed to healthy eating and physical exercise rather than to smoking. Meditation and exercise were promoted as ways of coping with stress. Corporate and other institutional structures were changed. Smoking was increasingly prohibited on airline flights and in almost all public buildings. Many hospitals became smoke-free buildings. Restaurants were required to provide nonsmoking sections. Taxes on cigarettes were increased, and many cigarette machines were removed, impeding the marketability of cigarettes.

As these changes in contextual factors about smoking occurred, smokers found themselves increasingly beleaguered. They were often isolated from others socially, they were increasingly penalized financially, and their motives were subject to reorientation. Many more of them began to choose to stop smoking. After decades of failing to change smokers by direct persuasion, American society began to change smokers indirectly. Similarly, a

Changing Contexts Strategy seeks to change the destructive behaviors of principals by reorienting cultural meanings and institutional structures for constructive behavior.

Remembering Faith Meanings for a
Changing Communal Contexts Strategy

Many humanistic models for managing conflict reflect an individualistic mentality that is deeply embedded in the North American culture.[1] Such individualistic models focus on the principals as if they were autonomous players in conflictive situations. While this book's model concurs with American individualism's emphasis on the necessity of principals' exercising moral choice and responsibility in conflicts, the model also concurs with the biblical emphasis on communal sources, claims, and contexts of principals' awareness and behavior in conflicts. As Joseph Haroutunian would have put it in the nonsexist language of our times,

> The Bible constrains us to modify the general religious notion that a spirit enters an individual and causes some sort of ecstatic exhibition. God's business is not with certain individuals as such, and God's Spirit does not enter anyone for one's private benefit. God's business is with God's people, and with God's servants the rulers and prophets and priests for God's people's sake, for the sake of their life together as a covenanted people.[2]

In this model's concepts of parties' behaviors in conflicts, the "habits of the American heart" are wedded to the perspectives of biblical anthropology. An American appreciation of persons' rights is joined with a Christian appreciation of human ends. Rather than just dealing with principals as autonomous individuals, this model deals with principals as subjects both shaped by and shaping larger social influences in their families, their work groups, and their religious communities. Principals' moral behaviors in conflicts are seen as deriving from both personal proclivities and these larger contextual circumstances.

A Christian ethic of conflict management also includes a Changing Contexts Strategy because of the usefulness of indirect change when direct change efforts are blocked. One may not make principals choose to fight fair, but by changing one or more contextual factors one may make it much easier for principals to choose to fight fair. By increasing principals' conscious awareness of how they have been unconsciously influenced by destructive contextual habits of behavior or of interpretation of the past, one enhances principals' options for conscious, intentional behavior in the present. Understanding arises where there may have been inappropriate or unfinished feelings of guilt or shame. Changes in contextual factors can cultivate changes in principals' mentalities toward increased self-valuing, accountability, and dignity.

From a Christian perspective another negative consequence of American individualism is unbalanced attention to individual rights and dignity at the expense of communal rights and individual responsibility. The value of individual rights is often not linked with the values of communal nurture and wholeness. Indeed, individualist parties to a conflict may actually think of any indirect way of changing principals as manipulation rather than responsible activity.

Second-order change, however, is no more manipulative than first-order change. Efforts to influence others are not inherently manipulative of others. Any order of change is manipulative when it is undertaken deceptively, seeking to bypass or subjugate persons' moral choices and responsibility. Interventions to change contexts bearing on principals are not undertaken or implemented behind principals' backs. Indeed, a Changing Contexts Strategy requires an open participation of all parties and a public process of community-wide decision making. All parties, including the principals, will be consciously informed about and make choices in response to changes in communal rules, structures, or responses to the environment.

Unlike a Preventing Exchanges Strategy, in which bystanders often work with privileged information, a Changing Contexts Strategy involves working with public information in inclusive ways.

When Changing Contextual Factors
Surfaces a New Conflict

As with a Preventing Exchanges Strategy, a Changing Contexts Strategy is undertaken with representatives of a community of bystanders. However, unlike a preventing strategy, a Changing Contexts Strategy will include principals as members of that community of bystanders. For this reason, what is begun as a nonadversarial process of reflection about and change of communal conditions can trigger additional conflicts between principals who see their power assets threatened or between latent principals hitherto unidentified. Some bystanders may declare themselves or reveal themselves to be principals in yet another emerging conflict.

One may respond to such a development in at least one of two ways. One may publicly recognize the emerging conflict and propose that the Changing Contextual Factors process be suspended until principals have worked to resolve their conflict constructively. Or one may publicly recognize the emerging conflict and propose that its principals pursue their differences separately from the Changing Contextual Factors process. The first alternative is fitting when the emerging principals together possess a large proportion of the total of communal power. In most cases, the second alternative is much to be preferred. Often, when a few principals possess the bulk of communal power, it is because most bystanders have not claimed their potential exercise of communal power. Indeed, a Changing Contextual Factors process may itself have activated the communal power of bystanders so that principals who previously possessed a large measure of communal power no longer do.

Whichever procedure one proposes, it is necessary that one make public the fact that a conflict has surfaced and that one challenge the community of bystanders to choose which procedure is to be followed. Either way, one will be making a clear distinction between the problem-solving character of a communal process of Changing Contextual Factors and the combative character of a conflictive contest initiated by self-declared principals.

Sometimes one's public identification of an emerging conflict and one's proposal of a procedure that distinguishes it from the Changing Contextual Factors process will have the effect of offering emergent principals the opportunity to reclaim their role as bystanders, thereby restoring their conflict to latency.

Implementing the Tasks of a Changing
Contexts Strategy

As the flowchart of the three steps for managing church conflicts shows, a manager chooses a Changing Contexts Strategy when (1) win/win efforts to resolve differences seem improbable because of negative contextual factors, power ratios, and ethical orientations; (2) the principals are disengaged or barriers have been erected between them; and (3) a Step Two appraisal of contextual factors indicates that some communal rules and/or structures are biasing all parties toward dirty fighting.

Mobilize Bystander Power

While a Preventing Exchanges Strategy is undertaken only with bystanders, a Changing Contexts Strategy (see fig. 9.1 on page 118) is undertaken primarily with bystanders. In either case the power to make constructive changes in communal structures or culture resides in the community as a whole. While a Preventing Exchanges Strategy is undertaken because escalating, destructive exchanges are occurring, a Changing Contexts Strategy may be undertaken while conflicts are only incipient or in a latent stage of apparent tranquility.

There are many occasions in the life of faith communities that can serve as fitting communal moments in which to initiate a Changing Contexts

Strategy for constructive conflict. Such occasions include the regular meetings or special retreats of governing bodies, communal birthday celebrations, liturgical celebrations of Christian festivals in the church year, or the beginnings and endings of pastoral relationships. These occasions provide an opportunity for bystanders to take inventory of positive and negative patterns within their communal behavior and environmental circumstances: communal gut theologies, communal attitudes toward differences, communal memories and interpretations of constructive or destructive conflict, communal ways of using or abusing power in communal life. Should one's Step Two assessment of contextual factors reveal destructive communal structures or rules of behavior, one might propose a communal event for presenting one's observations for communal response. Should the Step Two assessment of principals' behaviors in a conflict suggest that a larger communal distrust or dishonesty is one source of principals' behaviors, one might initiate communal discourse over what past events or circumstances might have occasioned such a negative emotional climate. If the Step Two assessment of principals' attitudes in a conflict exposes an unwritten communal rule about being nice at all costs, one might propose a communal inquiry into what are the unwritten rules in general that unconsciously inform parties to communal conflicts. Should the Step Two assessment of principals' behaviors in a conflict give evidence that major communal decisions are being made behind closed doors in privileged, unaccountable ways, one might surface and test such a perception by instituting an anonymous, random sampling of members' perceptions and evaluations of how communal decisions are made. Or should the Step Two assessment of all parties' behaviors around conflicts reflect a communal belief that all conflict is sinful, one might propose a community-wide Lenten study of a Christian theology of power, suffering, and redemption through conflict. In each case, one would initiate a Changing Contexts Strategy by proposing that a community focus on rules, structures, or environmental change(s) that appear in one's own mind to encourage destructive behavior or discourage constructive behavior of any parties to a communal conflict.

Contract Ground Rules and Procedure

Because contextual factors already seem to be supporting dirty fight behaviors by all parties, some of the bystanders' habits of behaviors with regard to differences will most likely need to be curbed by constructive ground rules. Fighting dirty for fair fight communal rules and structures is contradictory. Sometimes just the formulation of some fair fight ground rules may in itself increase participants' awareness of some habitual unhelpful communal ways of thinking and communicating. Almost certainly the explicit provision of behavioral ground rules will contrast with the usually implicit character of communal rules of behavior. The second task of a Changing Contexts Strategy is for a manager to propose and contract with bystanders behavioral ground rules and a procedure for becoming conscious of and more responsible about the ethical effects of communal cultural habits and structural arrangements.

The proposed behavioral ground rules need to be short and simple if they are to be practiced. Managers will want to propose no more than two or three ground rules. The primary focus of ground rules for a Changing Contexts process is to safeguard participants' respectfulness and assertiveness over their differing subjective experiences and assessments of communal ways of operating. Unless and until participants find the way to differ without getting into aggressive or manipulative power struggles with one another, they will not be in a position to make constructive changes in their community's unspoken behavioral rules or informal and formal structures. Here are examples of some behavioral ground rules that focus on constructive ways of surfacing and working with differing perspectives:

- No labeling of persons or groups who disagree.
- No attacks on current or past communal leaders.
- Propose what change you want rather than just harping on what you don't like.
- Talk about specifics, not in generalities.
- Respect and explore subjectively differing experiences of the same circumstance or event.
- Assess factors by recognizing their benefits and costs rather than by judging them all good or all bad.

As behavioral ground rules for examining contextual factors are formulated and contracted with participants, these rules should be written and posted for continuing visibility and use by all. Making behavioral ground rules visible keeps them psychologically current and accessible for enforcement or revision by participants as a whole.

A manager next proposes and contracts the order of procedure prescribed as the remaining steps of this intervention. One should remind the participants that the primary focus of inquiry and ethical assessment is on contextual factors and traits rather than on communal members or leaders. One should also clarify with bystanders the distinction between working with differences as dissonance and fighting over differences as conflict. Dissonance is both necessary and valuable in a Changing Contexts Strategy. Conflict is not.

If bystanders are to participate productively in a Changing Contexts

Strategy, they need to subscribe explicitly to the ordered sequence of steps for their reflection, debate, and decision making. As with a Preventing Exchanges Strategy, a manager will want to secure bystander agreement to engage in these steps of interaction rather than passively to observe the manager's own work with these steps.

Formulate a Communal Ethic
of Fair and Dirty Fight Criteria

A critical task in a Changing Contexts process is for participants to determine what shall be their *community's* behavioral standards of fair and dirty fighting. This task is central for forming a communal context that encourages or discourages constructive management of all conflicts. The manager will want to explore participant's own opinions about what should be morally prescribed for the behaviors of parties to communal conflicts—whether participants subscribe or not to this book's prescription of an ethic of respectfulness, accountability, assertiveness, and inclusiveness for all parties to church conflicts. Until participants agree on a shared ethic, they cannot proceed to engage coherently in shared assessments of the moral significance of current communal rules and structures.

Managers will also want to be alert to the opportunity this task often presents for thinking theologically as Christians about the meanings of conflict, the church, humanness, love, and grace in participants' experiences. The emotional climate that works best is one of sharing rather than disputing participants' own faith understandings and commitments in conflicts. Often one is able to encourage participants in recognizing and updating both personal and communal gut theologies of conflict. Participants can be encouraged to take time to communicate their spiritual journeys during this part of a Changing Contexts process. While the focus of the strategy is on communal matters, the heart of the process is the participants' own ethical awareness and responsible choice making. It is this part of the Changing Contexts process that welcomes personal sharing rather than impersonal assessment of contextual factors.

After determining their community's ethical criteria for fair and dirty fighting, bystanders can then proceed with the additional tasks of identifying and evaluating the fair and dirty fight influences of communal rules, structures, and environmental circumstances. A manager might stimulate bystanders in undertaking these steps by sharing some of his or her own observations and assessments made in a Step Two appraisal of a conflictive situation. But a manager's sharing should seek to stimulate rather than substitute for participant's own recognition and moral assessment of communal rules, structures, and/or environmental changes.

If is often helpful to lead participants in considering contextual factors in the categories of spoken/unspoken communal rules, written and unwritten communal structures and procedures, and changes in the community's environment that seem to have helped or hindered constructive attitudes and behavior by communal members. Participants can brainstorm (without disputation) what they consider to be significant factors in these categories. Then participants can return to this list and assess how each factor may be primarily dirty fight (DF), fair fight (FF), or mixed in impact on communal members.

Initiate Contextual Changes

When bystanders have identified the ethical import of key communal contextual factors, they then formulate and establish changes in these contextual factors that support fair fighting behavior. Such changes may involve the formulation and adoption of new communal "positions" of prescribed ethical behaviors for all members when conflicts arise. Such changes may involve a charter of faith challenges about how to surface and work through differences between members. Such changes may involve the formulation and adoption of new communal "policies" about how emerging differences over communal activities are to be communicated, channeled, and debated in communal life. Whatever changes are made, they need to be formulated as explicit recommendations to the governing body of the faith community for action and response. Specific contextual changes rather than vague communal intentions are the desired outcomes of a Changing Contexts intervention.

We have already discussed how faith communities, like families of origin, have emotional habits and prescriptions of behavior for all members. These communal factors are communicated primarily by behavior, often even without conscious awareness. In order to stimulate bystanders' awareness, a manager might review with them this sampling of rules and messages supporting dirty fighting:

- Christians don't fight.
- Judge others.
- Defend God at all costs.
- Pastoral leaders are always right (always wrong).
- If you can't say something nice, don't say anything.
- Being Christlike means sacrificing yourself.
- Be right at all costs.
- Good Christians don't compromise; compromise is selling out.
- Don't rock the boat.
- Be perfect.
- It's never been done that way.

A sampling of unwritten communal rules and messages that support fair fight behaviors is

- Confront differences openly.
- Speak up for yourself.
- Take responsibility for your feelings.
- Christians fight fair.
- Be accountable.
- You win when all win.
- Explore differences.
- Everyone is valuable.
- Don't personalize differences.
- To keep up with Jesus, keep changing.

These are but a few examples of the kinds of unspoken rules and messages that people learn from faith communities to which they belong. Communal rules and messages are put in simple, ordinary kinds of speech.

To further illustrate, here are some communal rules and procedures considered by a Lutheran congregation in order to enhance constructive conflicts in the community:

- Gather as much information as possible from as many sources as possible.
- Stick with conflict resolution efforts to the end. Hang in there.
- Learn when to call "time out" to allow for a "cooling down" period.
- Don't make snap judgments about those whose behavior annoys you.
- Admit your mistakes and limitations.
- When the body has reached a consensus, do your best to be part of it rather than to resist it.[3]

Communal structures also have great impact on the behaviors of parties in conflictive situations. Authoritarian structures are absolutist. They eliminate any give and take between the authority and others.[4] They vest authority in the role incumbent without rationale for or consent by those governed. Authoritarian communal structures thereby protect or mask a lack of accountability by leaders. Authoritarian structures usually breed a general alienation, apathy, or passivity in a faith community. Principals are supported in behaving secretively or unaccountably. Differences are resolved secretly. Power is exercised as control of others. Conflicts are repressed until they explode.

On the other hand, legitimate authority is accountable and nurturing of shared power and values between authorized leaders and followers. Legitimate moral authority provides security, trust, and coherence in social groups. Conflicts that arise are to be resolved through the service, not control, of authorities in groups. Authorities model the exercise of power in assertive and accountable, rather than unilateral and arbitrary, ways.

Hierarchical communal structures also tend to engender dirty fighting. Hierarchical structures arrange parties in a descending order of privilege as well as responsibility. Such a gradation of status and privilege between parties tends to lead to the use of power by those at the top for the maintenance of the structural arrangement itself. Substantive issues are often consciously and even unconsciously formulated to suit the benefits and purposes of those at the top. Hierarchical good is thus often sought at the expense of community-wide good. When conflicts arise, principals at higher positions on the ladder may strive above all else to control those below them rather than resolve differences for the benefit of all.

On the other hand, collegial structures usually breed an emotional climate of power sharing and collaboration to deal with differences. Respect for the integrity of all parties tends to circumvent power plays by any one party.

Finally, an awareness of how environmental circumstances have shaped the conditions of a community can often provide participants with more balanced perspectives about the circumstances bearing upon principals' conflictive issues and behaviors. These larger perspectives can reframe all parties' awareness in ways that prevent personalizing of issues and assigning blame for situations beyond any single principal's control or intention. For example, rather than members' blaming the minister or a minister's blaming members for declining church membership, participants may recognize that much larger and more complex social forces are at work. Issues of "face" are eased by such realizations. The blaming that goes with shame stops. The complexity of most conflicting differences is recognized in place of simplistic thinking about any one party's particular strengths and weaknesses. The way is opened psychologically for parties to invest their energy in discovering creative responses to changing environmental circumstances rather than in scapegoating their enemies.

Undertake Communal Changes

As the final task in this intervention, bystanders through their governing body formulate and undertake ways of communicating and undertaking with all parties the changes made in communal rules, structures, or responses to the environment.

Like a social vaccination, specific changes in contextual factors must be "taken" if they are to work. Real social changes are communicated in deed as well as in words. To be sure, the writing of communal rules, structures, and procedures is often in itself a significant change in a community's context. But the bottom line of changes chosen through a Changing

Contexts process is their implementation in the daily operations of the community. Changes in contextual factors also require the continuing communication and attention of all members of a community. A community's contextual rules and structures are usually habitual, deeply embedded ways of thinking, feeling, and behaving in communal roles. People do not make such changes simply by cognitive assent. People make such changes by practicing them over time. The community of bystanders is encouraged to post changed behavioral rules in a very visible place in meeting rooms and class rooms. A governing body is encouraged to regularly include in bulletin inserts or newsletters the description of communal structures and procedures for dealing with conflicts. In short, until and unless the changes in contextual factors are repeatedly practiced, they will not be credible or effective. Managers will want to do all they can to ensure that changes will not be announced only to be quickly ignored or soon forgotten.

An Illustration of a Changing
Contexts Strategy

Jan had become pastor of Bethany Church. Bethany was laboring under heavy financial debt from constructing its sanctuary and dining/fellowship hall buildings. In one of the first meetings of the governing body Jan attended as pastor, a request was made to permit the annual church craft fair to take place in the sanctuary building because it had more space than could be had in the recently completed dining/fellowship hall. Discussion was as sharply edged as a razor and as taut as a high-voltage wire. A vote was taken. A bare majority vote gave permission.

When the decision was communicated within the congregation, considerable opposition was voiced. This opposition, however, did not request a review of the decision. The fair was held in the sanctuary space but was poorly attended and produced meager financial benefit. When the sound of controversy had subsided, an emotional climate of tension and suppressed feelings seemed to remain. The unity of the congregation seemed crucial as the problem of managing its debts remained unsolved.

Although the immediate conflict seemed to be over, Jan observed the same kind of emotional intensity and restrained debate in subsequent meetings of the board. The newly completed fellowship hall seemed to be generating more discomfort than enthusiasm. Jan began to surmise that there was more to the whole situation than met the eye. Some communal rule or structure was inhibiting open debate and constructive negotiation of differences between members in general. She decided to undertake a Changing Contexts Strategy before another conflict further endangered the whole enterprise.

Jan proposed a weekend retreat of church leaders to tell the story of the congregation's decision to relocate and build its current plant. She proposed that since the retreat's focus was on past history, the goal of the retreat would be to get out differing understandings and concerns about what had happened without having to reach any agreements among participants. She stated that the following ground rules should be contracted with anyone who came:

1. We will speak only for ourselves, not for others.
2. We may challenge perceptions but not motives.
3. We will permit no personal attacks.
4. Feelings will be acknowledged, but not acted out.

The retreat was voted. A planning committee was appointed to determine who should be invited and to select who might be asked to give their eyewitness accounts of the history.

The retreat turned out to be well attended. Three eye witnesses gave their accounts of the decision to relocate and the decisions about the building. Although a few members had left the congregation over the decision to relocate, the major troubles began around the building of the dining/fellowship hall.

Some highlights of this story about the buildings began to illumine the current dis-ease of board meetings. Bethany's decision over its first building had been difficult and lengthy. But once the decision had been made, the congregation had closed ranks and supported it. Bethany had gone $200,000 in debt with this building. As originally planned, this building had a large room for use as both a sanctuary and a fellowship hall. The plan was that future expansion would involve the building of a dining/fellowship hall and the furbishing of the large hall exclusively as worship space. The compromise was that holy space would not always be used for dining/fellowship activities as well.

During the first building's construction, however, a small group had come forward to push again for the immediate construction of the proposed fellowship hall as well. Their proposal was accepted by the board with virtually no discussion. The skids seemed to have been greased behind the scenes. Many in the congregation were angered and dismayed by the board decision. The additional dining/fellowship hall, however, was built, further exacerbating a mounting congregational debt.

Obviously, the seemingly innocent request to have the annual craft fair in the sanctuary had been fraught with the emotional baggage of unresolved animosities between those who had sought and those who opposed building the fellowship hall itself. The request had simply triggered another masked round of combat between these unreconciled factions. Moreover, the board's way of responding to the requested space for the craft fair was also familiar. It was almost a replay of the way the board had made the decision to build the fellowship hall: abruptly and secretively.

Jan was not the only participant on whom these understandings began to dawn. At one point the animosity over the decision to build the fellowship hall began to erupt. Jan quickly intervened, pointing to the ground rules she had posted on newsprint. Rather than stopping the exchanges, she simply directed participants to share their feelings without acting them out. After about thirty minutes of tense exchanges, a participant observed that while the decision to build the fellowship hall was over, feelings about the way the board had acted were not over.

This observation turned out to be a turning point. Participants began to talk about their hurt with the secret politics of the decision and their distrust of the board since. An emotional climate of caring began to displace defensiveness. By the end of the retreat, participants unanimously indicated their desire that the board appoint a special group to formulate some new rules for board discussion and for board consultation with the whole community when considering major communal decisions. Without an explicit assessment of contextual factors contributing to dirty fighting in board meetings, those at the retreat had completed the major tasks of a Changing Contexts Strategy. In the board meetings that followed the retreat, new procedures and rules were enacted, and the community began to heal.

In Conclusion

A Changing Contexts Strategy seeks to change parties to a destructive conflict indirectly. It is concerned directly with communal contexts and only indirectly with principals' issues or ethical orientations. It does not resolve conflicts, but it may be of major consequence in opening the way for principals to resolve their conflict constructively. As communities of faith change, members are given the choice to change as well.

CHAPTER 10

Step Three/Constraining Strategies: Coaching Principals

Of all this model's strategies for intervening in conflictive situations, a coaching strategy of working individually with principals will seem the most familiar to ministers and laity. The scenario goes like this. The telephone of the pastor or lay leader rings. The caller reports that party A is upset. The caller's message is simple: "You'd better get over there and take care of this situation before it gets worse." Now the pastor or lay leader, like Daniel in the lion's den, goes to see party A to "minister" to them by listening, cajoling, arguing, apologizing, or praying them out of being upset/angry/offended/hurt. Such "ministering" may involve allowing party A to ventilate feelings until she or he is drained of the motivation to pursue matters further. Or such "ministering" may involve one's appeasing party A by absorbing feelings until she or he begins to feel heard or appreciated again. Or one may reason with party A by giving information or insights to make the party think more clearly. One may even attempt to rescue party A by finding a solution acceptable to the party and negotiating it with others through shuttle diplomacy. In any case, the pastor or lay leader's "ministering" creates an emotional triangle in which one takes primary responsibility for another's conflict.[1] Such habitual ways of reacting to troubled parties in conflicts do not work for long. They are neither practical nor ethically responsible. In place of such anxious, reactive ways of solving others' problems, this model prescribes a Coaching Principals Strategy (see fig. 10.1).

Coaching for Principals' Self-Change

A Coaching Principals Strategy is an intervention that addresses conflicts within principals rather than between them. It is the only strategy in

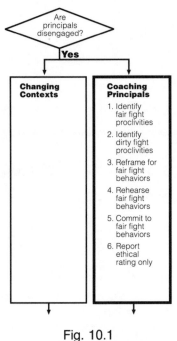

Fig. 10.1

this model that is nonadversarial. The manager does not "take on" a principal to make him or her change. One does not seek to confront, cajole, beg, persuade, reason, or convict principals so that they will change. The manager invites, accompanies, and coaches principals to consider how they might get what they really want in constructive, responsible ways. What changes is not the interests of the principals but the ways they choose to understand and pursue their interests.

Whatever principals' interests may be in a conflictive situation, a Coaching Principals Strategy involves a manager in teaming with principals for them to fight fairly with themselves. The conviction underlying a coaching strategy is that until a principal fights fairly with self, a principal (whether an individual or a group) will not fight fairly with others.

A coaching intervention is a one-on-one dialogue or one-on-group caucus that is strictly off the record. It occurs outside the presence of any other principals or bystanders. A manager guides a principal in coming to recognize, respect, and affirm what about the principal is worthy, godly, and conducive to fair fighting. The manager engages in directive listening. Directive listening is a more directive, but still open-ended, form of active listening. By directive listening a manager guides a principal to focus on what is right along with what is wrong about themselves; what they do rather than can't do; what is hopeful rather than hopeless about their circumstances. From a Christian perspective, a coach's directive listening leads a principal to discuss God in the principal's conflict.

A coaching strategy may be undertaken only by a bystander. No principal can coach another principal in this way. Principals who are constructive enough to coach each other are in a position to be constructive enough to resolve their issues with each other. When a principal seeks to coach another principal, one of them will either abandon his or her own interests in supporting the other or manipulate the other by deceptively cloaking his or her interests in terms of the other's welfare. For such reasons alone, no manager who is a principal can undertake a coaching strategy directly with another principal. The way for a manager/principal to undertake a Coaching Principals Strategy is to do so indirectly by deputizing a bystander to do the coaching. This will be described below.

Coaching principals involves honestly affirming them as God's loved ones. People change by being validated as inherently worthwhile, lovable, capable, imperfect, and responsible selves. They do not change by being invalidated as inherently worthless, disgusting, helpless, defective, or irresponsible selves. What dirty fighting parties to a conflict need to change is not their created worth but the wounded, rebellious, sinful, frightened, or controlling ways they have learned to seek to be of worth.

Finally, a coaching strategy is therapeutic, but it is not therapy. Life itself is therapeutic because it requires of us processes of growth and change as long as we are alive. Therapy is needed when a party is unable for whatever emotional or physical reason to participate in the therapeutic processes of being alive. Coaching is applicable when a party is undertaking the spiritual and emotional journey involved in these therapeutic processes.

In a coaching process one may encounter not only resistance but also incapacity. Should one encounter in a coaching process a party's incapacity to change, one will want to abort the strategy and formulate an intervention to refer the party to therapy. The general rule of thumb is that until one encounters a party's incapacity to work with the necessary changes of being alive, one assumes that a party can cope with the emotional pain and struggle of working with internal conflicts.

Coaching principals involves assertiveness, not persuasion. Arguing or trying to persuade a principal to receive one's input is counterproductive. Such efforts to make another change usually reflect codependent behavior aimed at rescuing others rather than interdependent behavior aimed at equipping others. Coaching principals involves the self-assertiveness of being a "nonanxious presence" to a principal's inner struggles without getting hooked into such inner struggles. The coach must consistently assert his or her own personal boundaries and limitations. When a principal seeks to get a coach to fix things for him, her, or them, an effective coach will restate and reassert his or her basic limitations and terms for helping the principal help himself, herself, or themselves.

Remembering Faith Meanings for a Coaching Strategy

We have already observed that a basic faith conviction underlying a coaching strategy is that no principal can or will fight fairly with others until that one fights fairly with self. We love others as we love ourselves. Loving others begins with loving ourselves. Respecting others begins with self-respect. Trusting others begins with self-trust. We love others as we love ourselves. For Christians such self-love and self-trust are not necessarily learned human capacities in a meantime world. Self-love and self-respect are seen as gifts from a gracious God who restores within us the capacity to accept forgiveness and learn to respect and value ourselves as God respects and values us. As John put it,

> Beloved, let us love one another, because love is from God; everyone who loves is born of God and knows God. Whoever does not love does not know God, for God is love. . . . In this is love, not that we loved God but that he loved us and sent his Son to be the atoning sacrifice for our sins. (1 John 4:7–10)

Implementing a Coaching Principals Strategy involves affirming as Christians the essential, created goodness of a principal's humanity for which God's Son died. The sinfulness of a principal's humanity is not ignored or discounted. However, a principal's dirty fight traits are addressed only within the framework of being a loved one of God. When a principal regains awareness of his, her, or their essential fair fight traits, she, he, or they will constructively deal with learned dirty fight traits. The spiritual birthright of any principal is to become a responsible self.

This Christian belief in the essential worth of and gracious gift of God's re-creation for any principal also safeguards us from the danger of sentimentalizing how one is caring of a principal. When one sees another human being in spiritual or emotional pain, one may feel anxious as well as empathetic. The anxiety arises from one's own pain over the other's pain. One is tempted to resolve the other's pain in order to relieve one's own pain. This is often how enmeshed relationships originate. Caring is turned into protecting or rescuing another from pain or loss.

Christians believe that Jesus saves; we do not do it. Whatever the focus of a coaching process, one works *with* principals, not *for* them. One helps principals help themselves by discovering choices in God's providence that they, and they alone, can make. As in coaching players in a sport, coaching principals for fair fighting helps them do their own fighting. The players, not the coach, practice for and carry out the plays of the game.

Milton Mayeroff's definition of caring as helping the other to grow makes clear what a coaching relationship is about:

> To care for another person, I must be able to understand the other and that one's world as if I were inside it. . . . Instead of merely looking at the other in a detached way from outside, as if the other were a specimen, I must be able to be *with* the other in that one's world, . . . In being with the other, I do not lose myself. . . . Seeing the other's world as it appears to that one does not mean having the other's reactions to it, and thus I am able to help the other in that one's world: something the other is unable to do for him/herself.[2]

Coaching principals involves this kind of caring. By standing with principals a coach helps them learn how to stand up for themselves in fair fight ways.

Finally, a Coaching Principals Strategy reflects the Christian understanding that being human involves harboring both fair and dirty fight proclivities. As James, the reputed brother of Jesus, put it when describing principals in primitive church fights,

> From the same mouth come blessing and cursing. . . . Who is wise and understanding among you? Show by your good life that your works are done with gentleness born of wisdom. But if you have bitter envy and selfish ambition in your hearts, do not be boastful and false to the truth. Such wisdom does not come down from above, but is earthly, unspiritual, devilish. For where there is envy and selfish ambition, there will also be disorder and wickedness of every kind. But the wisdom from above is first pure, then peaceable, gentle, willing to yield, full of mercy and good fruits, without a trace of partiality or hypocrisy. And a harvest of righteousness is sown in peace for those who make peace. Those conflicts and disputes among you, where do they come from? Do they not come from your cravings that are at war within you? (James 3:10a, 13–18; 4:1)

Should one assume that a principal's character will be completely constructive or destructive, a coaching strategy would be irrelevant. One coaches principals because one assumes that within them are power struggles between the proclivities of their created goodness and those of their learned sinfulness. Re-creation is the aim of coaching: an aim that trusts God's recreating Spirit to inter-dwell exchanges between coach and principal.

Deputizing Bystanders as Coaches

We have already observed that because a coaching strategy involves being present in nonadversarial ways to a principal's inner conflicts, a manager/principal is ineligible to undertake this strategy with another principal. Only a bystander can undertake coaching with a principal. This is why, early in this chapter, the caricatures of "ministering" to a troubled principal were deemed both unworkable and unethical. When a manager/ principal sees the need for a Coaching Principals Strategy for self or another principal, she or he may initiate it by securing or deputizing a bystander to undertake it.

A manager/principal may feel penalized by this limitation on one's eligibility to implement a coaching strategy with others. Many pastors and some lay leaders are in the habit of thinking that they are the primary coaches for a faith community. They pay lip service to the idea of the priesthood of all believers, but they often behave as if they are the only fully capable priests in town. Pastors or lay leaders, manager/principals, who are confronted with the intrinsic necessity for another to undertake a coaching strategy on their behalf may also encounter for the first time the reality of a Christian understanding of the corporate dimension of exercising Christ's ministry.

In almost all faith communities there are bystanders who have proven to be trusted colleagues of pastors and others. Such people are trusted because they evidence the kinds of respectfulness and fairness toward self and others that is sought in a coaching strategy. With modest training in the skills of active listening, trustworthy bystanders may often be in a better position than a pastor to carry out a coaching strategy, even when the pastor is a bystander/manager rather than a principal/manager.

A bystander deputized to coach a principal must have a clear view of the specific purpose and the strict confidentiality of this undertaking. Often lay leaders think that being asked to do something *by* the pastor means doing it *for* the pastor. Such an assumption distorts both the appropriate character and outcome of a coaching strategy. When a pastor or other manager/ principal deputizes a bystander for a coaching strategy, the deputized coach is being asked to act only on behalf of and only for the sake of the community of bystanders. A deputized coach is representative of the community's concern for fair fighting rather than of *any principal's* issues or interests.

Second, a deputized coach is accountable to a manager *only* about the outcome of the strategy. This outcome is the deputized coach's assessment of a principal's readiness, or lack of readiness, to behave constructively. All information about the principal's interests or issues is kept in complete confidence by the deputized coach.

In summary, when a manager/principal recruits a bystander to undertake a Coaching Principals Strategy with another principal, the following axioms are to be made clear:

- The deputized coach is not to represent, report, or advocate in any way the manager/principal's interests or issues in the coaching process.
- The deputized coach is to keep in complete confidence any information shared about the principal's interests and issues.
- The deputized coach will report back to the manager/principal *only* the coach's perception of the principal's fair or dirty fight rating as the outcome of the coaching process.

These agreements are critical for safeguarding the good faith of the manager/principal, the deputized coach, and the principal being coached.

Securing Coaching for Oneself as Manager

We have already described at length in Step One the necessity for a manager to stay in touch with his or her own feelings, gut theology, and role in a conflictive situation. Often one can benefit as a manager from securing a coaching strategy for such purposes for oneself. While one's work in Step One of this model involves self-talk about these matters, one's work in a coaching process involves talking with another party about these matters.

Self-coaching is different from self-talk. Self-talk can occur in front of a mirror. Self-coaching requires the participation of another human being. Many church leaders, especially pastors, resist seeking to be coached by another. They may think of coaching as an admission of inadequacy. Or they may think of coaching as risking a vulnerability they fear. Two heads are usually better than one, however, especially when it comes to the emotional subjectivity of one's inner messages in conflictive situations. One is usually on much firmer ground when one's self-reflection is balanced by feedback from another's perspective. Many times a manager will want to secure a coaching process with someone else for at least a portion of that manager's Step One work.

Even though one may not be a principal when managing, the procedures of a Coaching Principals Strategy described below are applicable to oneself when one is the subject of a coaching process. Remember, no principal is qualified to be one's coach when one is a manager. One will want to contract with a bystander or a third party to be one's coach. One will also want to share with one's coach the concepts and procedures of this process, described below. In a conflictive situation one seeks coaching, not therapy and not being rescued. Often one's peers are better equipped than professional therapists or consultants to be one's coach.

The usefulness of a coaching process lies primarily in the procedures rather than in the coach.

Implementing a
Coaching Principals Strategy

As the flowchart of the book's model for managing conflicts indicates, a manager chooses a Coaching Principals Strategy for self or other principals when (1) win/win efforts to resolve differences seem unlikely to work because of dubious contextual factors, power ratios, and/or ethical orientations, (2) the principals are disengaged by default or by barriers erected between them, and (3) an assessment of a principal's ethical orientations identifies specific dirty fight proclivities that might be addressed and redressed by a coaching process.

Identify Fair Fight Proclivities

One's first task with a principal is to listen actively for fair fight proclivities manifested by the principal (see fig. 10.1, p. 133). Coaching begins by interviewing a principal about his or her commitments and actions that can be honestly affirmed in a Christian perspective. Such fair fight proclivities will be a principal's deeds or interests expressive of accountable, assertive, respectful, and/or inclusive ways of dealing with self and others. As examples of such fair fight behaviors arise in the conversation, the coach underlines and emphasizes them with positive feedback. In so doing, the coach joins psychologically with the principal in identifying what is good and redeemed about the principal. One allies oneself with the fair fight aspects of the principal's character and interests. Should a principal focus obsessively only on what is sinful, wrong, or bad about himself, herself, themselves, or others, one can probe with the principal for the good reasons underlying such destructive traits. The point of actively listening for the fair fight proclivities of a principal is not to deny the dirty fight proclivities but to reframe them in light of God's grace and humanity's universal created goodness. As a coach works with a principal to identify and ally with what is worthy about the principal, a coach and principal establish a partnership in which to identify and change what are broken or sinful parts of the principal.

In summary, a Coaching Principals Strategy is directive and proactive, not just reactive or reflective. Based on the coach's previous or current observations of the principal, one actively listens for the other's honorable proclivities, offering affirmation of the principal. One seeks to team with a principal to invoke his, her, or their most constructive inner parts before addressing the principal's destructive parts.

Identify Dirty Fight Proclivities

The second task in coaching principals is to partner with them in identifying and changing what is destructive in their attitudes, perceptions, and behaviors. A coach listens for and names a principal's behaviors that express deceitful, aggressive or manipulative, violating, or partisan ways of operating with self and others. A critical task in the process of recognizing such dirty fight proclivities is to guard against shaming. A coach intervenes whenever a principal's work with these dirty fight proclivities crosses the line from guilt over wrong-doing to shame over wrong-being. Coaching requires making this clarification, often repeatedly.

For example, when exploring a principal's manipulation of others, a principal may begin talking about himself or herself in hateful or ugly ways: "I'm really lousy" or "I'm really a bastard" or "I must be pretty sick to have acted that way." The coach's response is to accept the wrongness of the action and refuse to accept the wrongness of the person: "Well, it was a lousy thing to do, but you're not lousy for admitting it or having done it" or "Honesty is true honor," or "Acting destructively does not mean that one is basically destructive," or "Since you're not a bad person, you must have had some good interests in acting so destructively." Each time a principal experiences the distinction between experiencing guilt rather than shaming self, a principal grows toward being able to repent of dirty fighting and choose fair fighting.

The following are examples of the kinds of topics of conversation that might develop when identifying a principal's dirty fight proclivities:

- updating a principal's gut theology that is preventing his or her constructive assertion of self, such as learning not to play victim, blame others, make enemies, or discount positive feedback
- dispelling a principal's unexamined, unconscious fears from previous life experiences now past—for example, fearing physical harm from adult confrontation with others because of the experience of physical abuse as a child
- appropriating new, strange, or different ways of thinking or seeing things as a principal, such as learning to accept change without losing self, learning that God does not need to be defended, learning that to compromise is not to betray
- identifying and mobilizing a principal's unrecognized forms of power for assertive use with others
- recognizing and breaking free from a principal's forms of distorted thinking, such as all-or-nothing ways of thinking, either/or ways of thinking, overgeneralizations in thinking, negative mental filtering that picks up only the negative aspects of people or situations, losing

realistic perspective by catastrophizing one's perceptions, putting simplistic labels on self or others in one's thinking, turning substantive
differences into personal attacks, and other ways of thinking in distorted ways[3]
- understanding and practicing assertiveness as the way to express a
  principal's feelings, rights, perceptions, and needs[4]
- increasing the principal's skills in such activities as active listening,
  brainstorming, group interactions, interpersonal communication, and
  problem solving

Reframe for Fair Fight Behaviors

The purpose of jointly identifying a principal's dirty fight proclivities is
to explore how they might be transformed. The goal of a Coaching Principals Strategy is to *uncover* what legitimate human needs and interests
underlie a principal's dirty fight behaviors so that with them one can
discover constructive ways the principal's needs and interests can now
be pursued. One way of distinguishing between a principal's legitimate
interests underlying destructive behaviors is to reframe a principal's self-
understanding and awareness. This change process is called "reframing."

The way people behave results from the meaning they make of their
circumstances or themselves. These contexts of meaning are like the
frames around a painting. As long as the frame is the same, the picture will
look the same. As Richard Bandler and John Grinder observe, "The heart
of reframing is the recognition that behavior can become detached from
the outcome it is supposed to achieve."[5]

The process of reframing involves changing the framework of meaning
that a principal habitually places around self or situations. The self or
circumstances may be the same, but changing one's framework of meaning
changes the way one wants to behave about them. To put it in ordinary
language, changing the way a principal sees things or self changes the way a
principal will respond to things or to self. A reframing process takes a
principal's current circumstances or being, lifts them out of the principal's
habitual context of understanding and meaning, and puts them into a new
context for understanding and meaning.

As an example, the story is told of a person who made exaggerated
demands on family members for neatness around the house. He interpreted their failure to meet his standards of neatness to mean that they did
not respect him. This was the habitual context of assumption with which
he framed the meaning of their behavior for himself. When he was offered
a new context of assumption—that their behaviors showed how much they
valued and trusted sharing life in his house—his feelings and behaviors
changed. He stopped seeking to manipulate them with his victim stance
and chose to negotiate with them mutually acceptable standards of neat-

ness all would maintain. The situation remained the same, but the framework of assumptions of the principal about its meaning changed. Fair fight behavior followed.

A coach may use such a process of reframing the way a principal sees self, others, the circumstances, or the issues in a conflictive situation. Distorted ways of interpreting and responding to things learned in childhood or from other periods of a principal's life can be identified. An alternative way of seeing the same thing can be offered. Principals may then make a conscious choice between which framework of meaning they wish to adopt as the basis of their behavior in the conflict. Old habitual assumptions are reexamined in light of current information and awareness. Principals are given a new lease on life. Or in faith language, principals are given the opportunity to see their life situation from rebirthed perspectives.

These examples illustrate what is at the core of a Coaching Principals Strategy: not to change persons but to help persons change themselves by new ways of perceiving and understanding who they are and what their interests are as loved ones of God. One validates the legitimacy of their beings, lifting their goodness out of habitual dirty fight frames of reference or perspective and putting that goodness in fair fight frames of reference or perspective. That is why a coaching process can be understood as collaborating with principals to fight fairly with themselves.

Rehearse Fair Fight Behaviors

Learning new information requires thought. Learning new behaviors requires practice. In the same way that a pianist will practice for a recital or that an actress will rehearse for a play, a coach works with a principal to try out and rehearse new ways of pursuing their interests constructively. This is the next task of a Coaching Principals Strategy.

To rehearse, a coach and a principal set up a scene or situation to which the principal is to respond in fair fight ways. This scene might be a telephone conversation, the onset of a meeting, a home visit, the formulation of a letter, or some other way of interacting with other principals in the conflict. The manager coaches the principal in composing how she or he will act or what she or he will say in that situation. Then the principal rehearses this planned behavior, checking to see how it feels and how it works to behave in such a way. This kind of planning and rehearsing of behavior goes on until the principal is ready to participate in a real-life process of win/win resolution of their interests.

Commit to Fair Fight Behaviors

The final task of a Coaching Principals Strategy is for a principal to commit to fight fair in the specific conflictive situation. This commitment is not sought until a principal has rehearsed what such fair fighting might be. The commitment is to act differently rather than simply intend to act differently. The commitment is not to fight fair perfectly, but to fight fair consistently in light of whatever additional coaching may be required. This commitment is made to the coach, not to other principals. It is a one-on-one commitment. The results of this commitment will involve the principal in covenanting responsible ground rules of behavior and procedure with other parties when they come together to resolve their issues.

Report Ethical Rating Only

Coaching principals requires the protection and confidentiality of privacy with privileged information. Whether as manager one is a bystander reporting to other principals the outcome of a coaching process or one is a principal receiving a report from a deputized coaching process, *only* an assessment of any changes in the principal's ethical orientation rating is to be disclosed. It is critical that all parties understand and strictly adhere to this restriction on what can be disclosed to others about the outcome of a Coaching Principals Strategy.

An Illustration of a
Coaching Principals Strategy

The property committee had been meeting for an hour. The pastor had proposed that for doctrinal reasons the altar given as a memorial to Mrs. Margaret Rainer's brother be replaced by a free-standing Communion table on the same level as the pews. Mrs. Rainer was agitated. Suddenly she stood up and angrily left the room. Remaining committee members were distraught. The chairperson proposed that they postpone further conversation about the pastor's proposal until their next meeting. Members left quickly.

Within an hour the pastor's phone rang. Allen, a leading church officer, had already heard of the Rainer blowup. "Jack," he said to the minister, "I appreciate your theological point of view, but your enemy making of the Rainers is not helping yourself or anyone else. I strongly suggest that you wait a day and then get yourself over to Margaret's house and make peace."

Jack was angry. "Look, this is unfair and uncalled for," he replied. "I didn't make an enemy. Margaret is the one who made an enemy out of me. Get off my back." He hung up. Shortly he began to feel uncomfortable with himself. An hour later he had cooled off enough to see the need to manage rather than be managed by this situation. He got out his work sheet and began to assess things.

As Jack reflected on Margaret's ethical orientation, he became aware of a number of things. She had considerable fair fight proclivities: she had been loyal to the minority when, eleven years ago, a majority of the congregation had tried to pull out of the denomination. Obviously, she was not afraid to stand up for her convictions. It also seemed obvious that she cared about what her pastor thought. He had also heard that she had a good sense of humor and would let go of differences once they had been resolved responsibly.

On the other hand, Margaret also had dirty fight proclivities. She was not above using anger to manipulate. She could be dogmatic. She obviously had personalized the issue in this conflict. And she clearly had already tolerated, if not fueled, spreading gossip about her walkout. Allen was right about one thing. The gossip mill was already operating big time.

Jack called Allen back. "First," he said, "I'm sorry I blew off. I agree that something needs to be done before this situation gets blown out of proportion." Jack then explained that he wanted to fight fairly with Margaret but that he was unwilling to go over to her house and back off from his own convictions in order to smooth troubled waters. "What I propose," said Jack, "is that someone who is spiritually wise, discreet, and respected by both myself and Margaret sit down and work with her to take me on constructively. Who would you suggest I approach for such coaching?"

At first, Allen didn't understand. "Look, Jack; this is between you and Margaret. No fair sending someone to fight for you."

"I'm not," replied Jack. "I'll fight for myself, but I want this to be a fair fight on the issues. I don't want the issues to get lost in my being pastoral toward Margaret. I'm just asking for someone to go on general behalf of the congregation to work as Margaret's friend and confidant as she sorts out her interests and how to represent them constructively. I'm asking for a coach, not a referee, much less a substitute combatant."

Allen named a couple of people as possible coaches. Jack called Jane and asked her to meet him for breakfast the next morning. At that time, Jack described a Coaching Principals Strategy. Jack shared his first impressions of Margaret's fair and dirty fight proclivities. He emphasized that he wanted to know nothing from Jane's coaching with Margaret except whether Jane thought Margaret was ready to work through differences constructively with him. It was agreed.

Jane called Margaret that morning. "I've heard about the meeting yesterday. I care about you and Jack. I wonder if you'd be willing to talk with me about where you are in all this. It would be strictly off the record, and I promise not to take sides."

There was silence. Then Margaret said in an angry voice, "Oh, I don't know what to do! Well, *yes*. I guess I do need some advice."

Jane and Margaret met at Jane's home that evening. Jane had arranged for no interruptions. First she talked with Margaret about her affection and respect for her. They shared memories about the agony of the congregation's division eleven years ago. They agreed that all of them had been frightened of conflict in the congregation ever since then.

Margaret was distressed over having lost her composure at the meeting. She did not want to cause a fracas. Jane suggested that maybe now was a good time for the congregation to begin to learn how to work through differences constructively rather than burying them for fear of another painful schism. Margaret agreed.

For the next two hours the women focused on Margaret's feelings and her tendency in conflicts to personalize issues, especially church issues. Margaret remembered her father's suppressed grief over her brother's premature death in the Korean conflict and how the altar later had seemed to symbolize his having given up his son to God's will, just as Abraham had been tested with Isaac. Dammed up tears of anger were shed for her father's convoluted ways of covering up and failing to work through his grief and guilt over his son's death. The women agreed that Jack's issues had nothing to do with either the tragic death of Margaret's brother nor her father's failure to do healthy grief work. It was also agreed that Margaret might want to propose a ground rule at the next committee meeting proposing that others not mistake her anger as an attack on anyone present, including Jack. Finally, the women worked together to formulate what Margaret's legitimate interests were. The next day, Jane called Jack and said, "Margaret is ready to deal with you for a win/win at the next meeting of the property committee."

"Thanks," he said. He then called Allen and asked him for a coaching session for himself!

Using a Coaching Strategy
as the Constructive Option of Last Resort

There are situations in a meantime world when the common sense and good faith of a faith community are not predominant. In church fights, there are faith communities whose members choose to remain irresponsible spectators rather than responsible bystanders. There are faith communities that choose to appease a rich member's power plays rather than accept communal responsibility to honor fairness and honesty. Leaders get blamed and made the scapegoat for a pastor's own unresolved family conflicts. Pastors or other managers get violated by shame-based members whom the rest of the community refuses to challenge or constrain.

There are church systems in which members are enmeshed in layers of intertwined differences so that anything that arises becomes another round in a chronic, decades-old, malevolent power struggle between factions. Such congregations are highly reactive emotionally, so that when anyone says what he or she believes or thinks, someone will be quick to tell that person what's wrong with what he or she believes or thinks. One cannot be oneself without finding oneself facing another's disapproval. Pastoral relationships die after a honeymoon because none of the parties to them have the emotional space to be both different and connected at the same time.

There are marriages in which the unresolved emotional issues of partners from their own families of origin dissolve their bonding and subvert their vows. Rather than reframing the terms of their relationship in non-adversarial mediation, they must finally turn to legal arbitration of a settlement.

When the common sense and good faith of a larger community of bystanders are lacking, constructive management of church conflicts becomes virtually impossible. One cannot make a community change its mentality any more than one can make an individual change his or her mind. One cannot make a congregation's governing body set limits on crazy-making behaviors among members. One cannot make spouses or parents and children work things out responsibly with each other.

In such circumstances, a manager will want to choose a Coaching Principals Strategy for himself or herself as the constructive intervention of last resort, but *only* after other reasonable interventions have been attempted. It is neither Christian nor responsible for one to be victim of spectators' choices not to seek a conflict's constructive management. Indeed, one's own emotional death is likely to provide precisely the distraction the community seeks in order to maintain its continuing deceitfulness and denial of unresolved communal pain and shame. Speaking the truth in love may mean naming the pain and shame of the community of spectators and modeling a nonblaming way of assertively refusing to be its next sacrificial lamb. Such assertive, nonblaming truthfulness affords both the manager and the community opportunities to change their ways.

The faith understanding underlying this matter is that every Christian community or manager is called by a risen Lord to seek to live through rather than die from destructive conflict. On this side of the grave, parties to a conflict can at least take responsibility for themselves, repent of their part in the destructiveness, and learn not to repeat their mistakes again. Of course, there are evil situations in which parties get killed emotionally or even physically. But such deaths should be due to evil forces beyond one's control rather than to shameful forces within one's soul. When all other strategies to resolve or constrain a conflict are not sustained by the good faith of a community of bystanders, we can choose life even if we cannot ensure it. That is part of the good news we receive from the one who died for us so that we can live with others constructively.

In Conclusion

A Coaching Principals Strategy is different from what is often undertaken by pastors or lay leaders as the "counseling" of principals to a conflict. The coaching process is nonadversarial. It addresses conflicts within a principal rather than between the principal and the coach. The coaching process is focused. While such coaching may initially involve ventilation of feelings or a respectful acceptance of the principal's issues or complaints, the core of the process involves a directive kind of listening on the coach's part that explores and responds to the dirty fight proclivities and/or needed fair fight skills and resources of the principal. A coaching process is privileged. Other than the coach's own appraisal of the ethical rating of the principal as a result of the process, nothing of what is shared in the process can be reported to others. Coaching principals is a private matter undertaken for a public good.

CHAPTER **11**

Step Three/Resolving Strategies: Negotiating Issues

Church conflicts do not end until contested differences are resolved. These matters may be resolved in a win/lose way, a lose/lose way, or a win/win way. The goal of a Christian ethic of conflict management is to prevent any form of resolution other than a win/win resolution. When the accumulated impact of contextual factors, power imbalances, and dirty fight orientations signifies that a win/lose or lose/lose resolution is likely, one intervenes with constraining strategies to interrupt the malevolent cycle and change the destructive circumstances (see chapters 8, 9, and 10).

When one's appraisal of contextual and principals' factors suggests that a win/win resolution is possible, one will undertake either or both of two resolving strategies: (1) a Negotiating Issues Strategy for reconciling substantive differences between principals and (2) a Mediating Relationships Strategy for reconciling disrupted or difficult relations between principals. Both the Negotiating Issues and the Mediating Relationships strategies direct principals through a benevolent cycle of conflict (see fig. 11.1).

Resolving strategies replace the win/lose dynamics of a malevolent cycle of conflict with the win/win dynamics of a benevolent cycle. Resolving strategies trigger into the open the conflicting differences that have been or are currently in a latent stage. In contrast to the malevolent cycle triggered by the substantive differences themselves, resolving strategies trigger engagement by raising matters of process: by proposing and negotiating fitting behavioral ground rules and procedures. What follows are escalating understandings of principals' interests rather than power struggles over principals' positions. Then in the third stage of the cycle, resolving strategies direct principals in a process of creatively collaborating to formulate solutions that meet all parties' interests rather than a malevolent process of

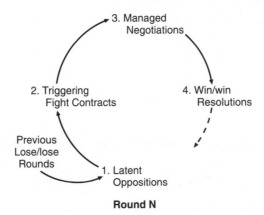

Fig. 11.1: The Benevolent Cycle
(Fair Fighting)

enforcing one party's interests at the expense of others'. The creativity that arises in this third stage derives from the interaction of the previously dissociated interests and perspectives of the principals. In the final stage of the cycle, resolving strategies provide for principals' resolutions to be accountable to a larger communal good for review by relevant bystanders. What is ethically required at the least is that principals' resolutions not be at the expense of a larger common good. As a safeguard, bystanders are provided with a procedure for challenging any solution that they deem to be at their expense.

Choosing Between Negotiating and Mediating Strategies

As the flowchart indicates, a manager initiates resolving strategies when the overall effects of contextual, power, and ethical factors are positive for principals' win/win behavior.

When win/win outcomes seem possible, a manager chooses between negotiating and mediating processes in light of which of these dimensions to any conflict seems to be the predominant focus of contention: principals' substantive differences or their relational difficulties (see fig. 11.2).

All social conflicts involve both a substantive dimension and a relational dimension. As Roger Fisher and William Ury observe,

> Every principal wants to reach an agreement that satisfies his or her substantive interests. That is why one negotiates. Beyond that, a principal also has an interest in his or her relationship with the other side. . . . Most negotiations take place in the context of an ongoing relationship where it is important to carry on each negotiation in a way that will help rather than hinder future

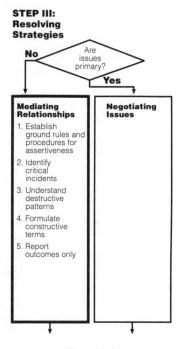

Fig. 11.2

relations and future negotiations. . . . Dealing with a substantive problem and maintaining a good working relationship need not be conflicting goals if the parties are committed and psychologically prepared to treat each separately on its own legitimate merits.[1]

In this model, processes for reconciling substantive differences and relational difficulties are not only distinguished but treated in different strategies. Two distinctive strategies are suggested because of the special difficulties involved in the dynamics of church conflicts. First, the intense emotional quality of religious commitments makes parties to church conflicts especially vulnerable to personalizing their differences. Second, the purpose of voluntary church systems—to build community among all parties—tends to seduce parties into reducing significant substantive differences of mission to being no more than concerns for the maintenance, repair, or building of harmonious communal relationships. For both reasons, this model provides two process interventions for reconciling church conflicts. One strategy focuses on resolving substantive differences. The other strategy focuses on resolving relational difficulties. When differences of viewpoint, belief, or commitment between principals predominate in a conflictive situation, a Negotiating Issues Strategy is the intervention of choice. When difficulties or alienation in the relationship between principals predominates in a conflictive situation, a Mediating Relationships Strategy is the intervention of choice.

Often church conflicts continue for years without conscious or informed efforts to manage them. As malevolent cycles accumulate, substantive differences and distressed relationships become intertwined. In such cases, both negotiating and mediating strategies are needed to realize a win/win resolution. First, a mediating process is undertaken to restore basic respectfulness, trust, accountability, and communication between the principals. Then a negotiating process is undertaken to deal with the substantive issues.

As we have repeatedly observed, many faith communities are emotionally enmeshed. Parties' personal boundaries overlap. Parties do not know how to disagree without compulsively trying to change or control one another. In communities with such enmeshed communal rules and attitudes, a church fight that begins over substantive differences about program or budget soon becomes a fight over who are principals' friends and enemies. Differences over substance quickly become disruptions of relationships. Paradoxically, in such situations it is often appropriate to pursue a negotiating strategy rather than a mediating strategy. The effort is to disentangle parties emotionally by directing them through a process of substantive differentiation.

As a general rule, a manager of church conflicts is encouraged to quickly address church conflicts as substantive issues for negotiation, before they become interpersonal issues of alienation requiring mediation. Such practice reflects an ecclesiology that seeks respectfulness rather than closeness as the criterion of Christian community. Rather than reinforce a communal tendency toward emotional enmeshment to cover up conflict, one initiates negotiating processes that keep principals at arms' length with one another. Only when efforts to deal with church conflicts as substantive matters fail should a mediating strategy be considered, and such mediating activity is a privileged rather than public process.

In summary, a Negotiating Issues Strategy is used when principals' differences consist primarily of conflicting interests. A Mediating Relationships Strategy is used only when principals' differences have come to consist primarily of disrupted relationships. The primary way to resolve communal church conflict is through negotiating interests rather than remediating relationships.

Understanding the Negotiating Process

For many Christians the word "negotiating" has a ring about it of expediency or pragmatism in place of conviction or integrity. Negotiating sounds more like selling out than remaining loyal to one's deepest faith commitments.

In a Christian ethic of conflict management the process of negotiation signifies a way by which principals incorporate their differing faith commitments into becoming part of a larger communal wholeness. Wholeness rather than partisanship or expediency is the goal. For such a process to occur, one must understand three basic concepts when undertaking a Negotiating Issues Strategy.

The first concept is that one must lead the principals in fighting for fair fighting before leading them in a process of negotiating. The concept is that unless and until the principals pool their power in establishing shared controls for self-control, they will not pool their power to negotiate in good faith. By the same token, when principals experience a commonality of shared controls over their behaviors, they begin to experience one another as trustworthy, and they become less anxious and defensive with one another. Negotiating issues involves political behavior before there can be rational behavior. A negotiating strategy does not eliminate the risks of dirty fighting, but it does significantly reduce them.

Initiating a negotiating process by addressing principals' behaviors is less threatening than immediately addressing principals' interests. There is less egoistic risk involved in fighting over process than is involved in fighting over substantive matters. As principals work to formulate key behavioral ground rules, they also test one another's readiness and commitment for responsible interaction. Should it become evident that only a minority of the principals have subscribed to the ground rules or that a majority of principals have subscribed in words only, one can abort the process rather than have it break down over principals' substantive differences. If it is evident that principals will not deal honorably over their ground rules, it is self-evident that principals will not deal honorably over their conflicting interests. Initial efforts to fight for fair fighting both reinforce the fair fight proclivities of the principals and serve as barriers against the dirty fight traits of the principals.

A second basic concept of a Negotiating Strategy is the distinction between what Fisher and Ury have called "positional" versus "principled" negotiation.[2] In positional negotiations, parties state and advocate their positions on the issues: whose position is right or wrong, godly or demonic, wise or foolish. In principled negotiations, parties state and advocate their underlying interests, needs, or desires—the hopes and concerns that inform any position they may be holding. Ironically, many Christians tend to confuse taking a position with standing for a principle or belief. Once parties to a church conflict grasp the idea that their faith commitments or moral standards are best advocated as matters underlying their positions rather than equivalent to their positions, the way is opened for constructive negotiation of their differences without betraying their fundamental commitments.

The mystery of achieving win/win resolutions of differences is not really a mystery at all. The key to win/win resolution of differences is making this distinction between principals' interests/needs/values/commitments and their partisan assumptions or perceptions of the solution that meets their interests. At its core, win/win negotiating involves communicating about principals' underlying interests and then collaborating to create solutions that take all parties' interests into account.

For example, two women are quarreling in a library.[3] One wants the window open, and the other wants it closed. Enter the librarian, who asks one why she wants the window open. "To get fresh air" is the reply. He asks the other why she wants it closed; "To avoid the draft," she says. The librarian then opens a window in the next room. Both women's interests are served.

Or again, this French fable illustrates the creative problem solving possible when principals' interests rather than positions are identified:[4] An old Arab was at the point of death. He called his three sons into his chamber to tell them how he wanted to divide his possessions. He said to the eldest that his part would be a half and to the second that his part would be a third. As for the youngest, his part would be a ninth of all his father's goods.

After a time, the father died. The three brothers met to divide their father's property. At first there seemed to be no problem among them, but soon, when it came to dividing the camels left by the father, the sons were very perplexed. There were seventeen camels; it was impossible to divide seventeen by two, three, or nine without cutting some of the animals into pieces.

The sons did not want to kill the camels, and they wanted to obey the instructions of their father. Therefore, they consulted an old dervish. It appears that this dervish was respected by everyone because of his wisdom.

The dervish was very sympathetic and intelligent. He wanted to help the three sons find a solution to their rather complex problem. The next day he arrived at their house and asked to examine the camels. He lined up the camels in front of him and added his own camel to the line next to the others.

"Listen to me," he said. "Now there are eighteen camels. Let each one take his part!"

The eldest took nine of them (half of eighteen). The second son took six (a third of eighteen), and the youngest took two (a ninth of eighteen). The sons were very content. Then the dervish remounted his camel and left, leaving the three sons intrigued.

The mystery of win/win negotiations lies in the creativity of resolving principals' differences by incorporating them in a greater whole. Even when a creative way is not found in this process to incorporate principals' differences, parties know that their interests have been validated and respected. Then solutions that meet only part of their interests are much more acceptable than solutions that appear to ignore their interests. The constructiveness of a negotiating process rests on paying careful attention to interests that are assertively communicated.

A third basic concept that is critical to a Negotiating Issues Strategy is that Christian esteem of the larger common good that we have emphasized repeatedly in this book. A Christian ethic for constructive conflict requires a balancing of larger interests with partisan interests. A Christian ethic of fair fighting conceives of resolving principals' interests as parts of rather than existing at the expense of the interests of a larger community of bystanders. It is this effort to formulate win/win resolutions that respect the interests of a larger community that augments a humanistic ethic of principals' rights.

Remembering Faith Meanings for a
Negotiating Issues Strategy

A Negotiating Issues Strategy is rooted in a doctrine of the church. A communal good of wholeness rather than the sinfulness of communal members is its basic frame of reference. The meaning of the church is understood primarily as the promise and task of recreating an interdependent humanity rather than the maintenance of a religious institution or its programs just to cope with sinfulness. Communal wholeness is realized when differing parties are able to engage one another in respectful, creative problem solving. A negotiating process is a practical means for Christians' "speaking the truth in love" inside and outside church institutions. Its aim is to approximate the biblical vision of *shalom,* wholeness.

A Christian ethic of negotiation repudiates principals' self-fulfillment at others' expense, or self-negation for others' benefit. What is prescribed is self-fulfillment through incorporation of principals' diverse gifts and perspectives into a more holistic community. Principals are led in a process of pursuing their interests in terms of others' interests. Rather than competing with one another to satisfy their partisan interests, they participate with one another in discovering ways to incorporate their interests. Because, as Pogo put it, the enemy is us, principals are led to join in recognizing the enemy within each of them rather than projecting that enemy onto one another. Principals who have faced one another as enemies find one another in a shared enmity of win/lose outcomes.

Another faith meaning informing a negotiating process is the belief that God's creative Spirit may dwell in and transform good faith transactions between human beings. A win/win negotiating process presumes to trust in God's mysterious way of indwelling social processes. Like the feeding of the five thousand, when principals pool their meager personal resources for a common good, all parties may be miraculously fed. Parties engaged in a win/win negotiating process are acting on the belief that their circumstances are not zero-sum. What had been a struggle between them to get a bigger piece of pie now becomes a struggle among them to create a bigger pie for all.

A negotiating process is also informed by a Christian anthropology that holds that being human involves being morally ambiguous. While all people are perceived to be of inherent worth in a Christian perspective, no one is expected to fight fair out of the goodness of his or her heart alone. Human beings are seen to be faulted with dirty fight as well as fair fight proclivities.

One faith meaning informing resolving strategies is that no party to a conflict has enough "purity of heart" to fight fair. All parties to a conflict act out of mixed motives. A Christian understanding of our humanity augments the affirmation of people's goodness in secular models of conflict management of people with a realistic recognition of people's capacities to do evil as well.

As stated earlier, the fair fighting sought in both negotiating and mediating strategies is based more on the moral and psychological impact of principals' covenanting than on their individual virtues. Contracting ground rules expresses the Christian understanding that we are redeemed and re-created through God's covenanting with and for us. Covenanted ground rules serve to reinforce the fair fight proclivities of individual principals with communal sanction and accountability. In contrast to the murderous exchanges between Cain and Abel, the fair fight ground rules covenanted by principals empower them to be one another's moral "keepers." The biblical concept of a covenanting life-style is a fundamental axiom of this model's process for resolving conflicts constructively. The insistence on formulating and contracting fair fight ground rules at the outset of a negotiating strategy reflects such a Christian understanding of the necessity and power of covenants for all human behavior.

Implementing a
Negotiating Issues Strategy

When the combined effects of contextual factors, power ratios, and ethical proclivities informing all parties promise at least a 50 percent probability of good faith negotiation, one intervenes by proposing the formulation and contracting of up to five key fair fight ground rules. Rather than beginning to deal immediately with substantive differences, positive conditions for fair fighting are both tested and reinforced by negotiating standards and procedures for the principals' interactions (see fig. 11.2).

Covenant Ground Rules

While a Preventing Exchanges Strategy seeks to block virtually all exchanges between principals, a Negotiating Issues Strategy seeks to block *only* destructive exchanges between principals (refer back to chapter 8 for Jane and Rensis Likert's list of the most common kinds of destructive behavior in conflicts). This is done by formulating and covenanting ground rules banning such behaviors. When considering what ground rules to formulate, one will focus on choosing rules that set up barriers against the particular forms of dirty fighting found in one's Step Two appraisal of the principals' proclivities. For example, should one of the principals show a track record of interrupting/overriding others verbally, a key ground rule one might propose would be "no interrupting." Or should another principal show a tendency to personalize disagreements, a key ground rule one might propose would be "no personalizing issues." Although it is helpful for a manager to be prepared to propose one or two ground rules to principals, it is also essential that the principals be involved in proposing ground rules as well. When a manager does all the work of formulating ground rules for principals, principals are prone to slip unconsciously into playing cops-and-robbers when it comes to enforcing them.

It is not uncommon for principals to conflicts to seek to bypass or even discount the need for negotiating and covenanting behavioral ground rules. They may protest that such attention to ground rules seems awkward, unnecessary, redundant, impolite, or even insulting. "Why go to such trouble when everyone here is a Christian?" Or "This is insulting. Don't we all already know how to be responsible? Let's get on with what we're here to deal with." From a Christian perspective parties' resistance to setting explicit ground rules seems to reflect their shadow sides of pride and fear—dirty fight tendencies to distrust any shared control or specific ways of being accountable. A manager's answer to such protests is in effect to reframe them by affirming that since parties are responsible selves, there should be no problem in formulating some explicit ground rules expressive of their good intentions.

Again, a manager will want to remember that the collective power to formulate and enforce fair fight ground rules resides only within and between the principals. Bystanders have the collective power to constrain a conflict's destructive resolution. But neither bystanders nor a manager can make principals fight fair. Only principals have the power to choose to behave constructively and deal with one another in good faith.

The ground rules of a negotiating process are meant to facilitate coherent, assertive, self-controlled behaviors by all. In contrast to a Mediating Relationships Strategy, where there is need for ground rules that focus more on principals' emotional self-expression and self-understanding, the ground rules for a Negotiating Issues Strategy focus more on principals' emotional self-control for clear thinking and communication.

Behavioral ground rules are short, simple, and to the point. They are often stated as "do's" or "don't's." Common examples of possible ground rules for principals' self-control and constructive communication are as follows:[5]

- Speak for yourself, not for others.
- Listen to understand, not to refute.
- No labeling.
- Be specific by citing bases or examples of your views.
- Challenge others' behaviors and ideas, not their motives or their worth.
- No blaming of self or others.
- No "people are saying." Give facts or cite names.
- Paraphrase what you heard another say before responding to it.
- When you oppose, go on to say what you propose.
- Address differences, not personal motives, intentions, or character.
- No personalizing of issues.

As agreements on ground rules are reached, the manager puts them in writing on a chalkboard or newsprint. Fair fight ground rules are to be posted and kept highly visible for the rest of a negotiating process. Such visibility strengthens their enforcement collectively by all parties.

Once ground rules have been covenanted, a manager will probably find it necessary to reinforce them in short order. Early on, principals frequently test to see if all parties are serious about the ground rules. One will be alert to intervene when a ground rule begins to be ignored. One's intervention calls attention to the ground rule rather than to its violator. Should one or more principals continue to violate ground rules, the manager calls for all participants to renegotiate ground rules or quit the negotiating process entirely. In a constructive negotiating process ground rules may be changed, but they may not be ignored or discounted.

Identify Interests

Once principals have established behavioral ground rules, a problem-solving process ensues. There are various renditions of the problem-solving process.[6] What follows is an analysis of the problem-solving process centered on concepts of principals' interests and frames of meaning.

Tasks	Processes	Climate	Problems
1. Assessments of principals' interests	Interviewing, research, questionnaires, fact finding	Nonjudgmental, curious, patient	Generalizing, rationalizing
2. Reframing principals' differences	Exploring assumptions, recognizing larger frames of reference, expanding frames	Accepting, imaginative, intuitive	Limited data, polarizing
3. Generating options	"What if" brainstorming, building scenarios, "best of all worlds" dreaming	Fast paced, playful, provocative, collaborative	Premature criticism, ridicule, vagueness
4. Formulating resolutions that maximize all parties' interests	Pro/con assessments, role playing, building scenarios, testing against ethical criteria	Both/and mentality, practicality, clarity, imaginative	Either/or mentality, perfectionism, pessimism

We have already emphasized the key importance of identifying principals' underlying interests when seeking a win/win outcome. Most principals will define a conflict's issues in ways that justify or support their own positions or solutions to these issues. Rather than beginning with principals' definitions of issues, positions, or solutions, a win/win negotiating process begins with principals' perceptions of the interests underlying their definitions of issues, positions, or solutions. A manager leads principals in this process by asking them what interests, needs, values, or convictions they are seeking to serve by the positions they take. Or a manager may ask principals what interests, needs, values, or convictions they expect to realize by a solution they favor. A manager may ask, "What hopes and concerns lie behind your position or your opinion?" or "What interests are you seeking to meet by your solution?" The operating axiom here is that to *understand* one another, principals must communicate about what interests *underlie* their differences. As these interests come to be recognized and validated, principals are equipped with the information they need to solve the puzzle of meeting their interests. Rather than fighting for their differing solutions to their interests, they begin to fight for solutions that meet their differing interests.

Defining Differences

In implementing the second task of a Negotiating Issues Strategy, principals' positions were reframed *de facto* by their identifying the interests underlying such positions. In this third step principals are led in defining their differences in light of all of their competing interests. They define differences rather than standing up over the issues. As they do so, they move from competing to collaborative behaviors. Rather than focusing on issues or positions over which they are in conflict, they focus on recognizing the differing ways they are seeking to realize their interests. What has been a power struggle over opposing interests becomes a pooling of power to formulate ways of dealing with the problems involved in meeting their interests. Their differences begin to look different in light of the underlying interests that have now been made visible to all. Principals now begin a process of problem solving rather than a contest of power.

For example, it was common during the 1980s, when the membership of mainline American Protestant denominations was declining, for parties to assume that the cause was ideological. Conflicts arose when educational program materials were perceived by some parties to be too "liberal" and by others to be too "fundamentalist." Both parties to such conflicts shared at least one underlying interest: the prosperity and numerical growth of their denomination. But both parties' previous positions for meeting their interests pitted them against one another in win/lose, either/or ways. Once their shared interest in the denomination's well-being became clear, parties could define their differences as matters of means rather than ends. Furthermore, parties could see how contextual factors were influencing their perceptions. While one position had reflected a general cultural distrust of centralized authority, another position had reflected a general decline in the dominance of white male culture. Both positions could be seen as appropriate in light of which contextual factors were made to be influential. The principals could agree to define their differences not only in terms of means rather than ends but also in terms of their differing contextual factors. They defined their differences in ways that acknowledged that all were right in the sense of being legitimate ways of interpreting things.

In this third task, a manager expands the awareness of principals by exploring with them larger perspectives or frames of reference bearing on their differing interests. Such additional frames of reference may include such contextual factors as the dynamics of institutional roles, the environmental circumstances bearing on institutions, or cultural, economic, and sociological changes occurring in an even larger social context. These additional ways of viewing differing interests augment rather than replace previous frames of reference. The greater the number of sensible perspectives on their differences that principals acquire, the greater the number of possible responses to their differences will principals be able to consider.

Generate Options

Whether one employs or skips the third task of reframing principals' interests, the task of generating options for meeting principals' interests is mandatory. The creativity that is often brought to bear on this task arises from associating perspectives that have previously been dissociated.

The essential process for this task is brainstorming. Brainstorming is a form of collective pipe dreaming. It is synergistic, as one idea triggers another. A brainstorming process must prohibit any evaluation of ideas while they are being generated, since negative responses tend to shut down the creative energy of the process.

Brainstorming also involves the assumption that the best solutions arise from working with many good ideas rather than finding a single "best" idea or "perfect" solution. Therefore, the more ideas the better, regardless of how outlandish or unfeasible they may seem. The greater the number of ideas principals can generate, the larger the reservoir of ideas they will have from which to draw in formulating realistic solutions.

Finally, brainstorming involves recognition that as principals cross-fertilize their awareness, they acquire new perspectives and new ideas about their situation. The problem has not been that principals have no capacity to imagine new ideas. The problem has been that principals have had no new perspectives with which to imagine new ideas. A manager asks the principals to imagine and list any ideas that might meet many or all of the interests that have been identified.

During a brainstorming process, all ideas are written on a blackboard or newsprint in full view of the principals. Ideas trigger additional ideas. They usually come in waves or bursts of sharing by the principals.

Sometimes, principals resist the task of brainstorming. They may think that they have already found an acceptable resolution of their differences and that there is no need to take the time and energy to imagine any others. Or they may think that they are being asked to suspend all common sense and engage in a useless exercise of "blue skying." A manager may answer these concerns by assuring principals that no valuable solution will be lost in this process and that their critical thinking is only being suspended temporarily.

Formulate Win/Win Resolutions

The art of formulating win/win resolutions consists in maximizing the benefits and minimizing the costs of various options before the principals. Rather than choosing one option in place of another, principals are often able to creatively mix and combine aspects of various options to the maximum advantage of all of the principals and a larger common good. A manager informs the principals that there are four ways, listed in order of declining preference, in which they can *build* from the options they have generated their win/win resolutions of differences:

1. Combine or synthesize options or portions of options; failing that,
2. Bargain for tradeoffs between options or portions of options; failing that,
3. Develop resolutions that are lesser evils than continuing to leave their differences unresolved; and failing that,
4. Formulate temporary agreements with limited time frames for how principals will live constructively with their continuing unresolved differences.

In most church conflicts, the resolution of issues requires a consensus, a support level of at least 70 percent of the principals. Such consensus usually reflects participants' discovery of new solutions by combining options. Consensus is not unanimity, however. Once 70 percent of the principals support a proposed resolution, a manager will briefly explore with the remaining principals what modest changes, if any, would make the resolution more acceptable to them. Acceptance is distinguished from advocacy. Acceptance is required if a conflict is to be resolved. A minority's loyal dissent is to be distinguished from any principal's subversive dissent.

A manager will encourage principals to spend time seeking to combine and build maximal resolutions before accepting less desirable alternatives. Less desirable alternatives are sought as compromises or bargains only after the possibility of maximal resolutions has been seriously explored.

This book's model recognizes that there are situations that seem to admit of no creative solutions. The size of the pie cannot be increased. The conflicting interests cannot all be satisfied. In such situations consensus remains the standard for resolving church conflicts. In such cases consensus involves not only compromise but also agreements about how the principals will deal constructively with their continuing differences.

Should efforts to resolve differences in any of these ways break down, a manager breaks off the negotiating process and intervenes with one or more of the constraining strategies previously described. Further coaching of principals may open the way to resume the negotiating process. A community of bystanders, however, should not be held hostage indefinitely by the effects of principals' unresolved issues. The good of the larger community may require an end to efforts to manage a conflict and the initiation of an arbitration process to resolve principals' differences on their behalf. As previously indicated, such arbitration can settle principals' differences for the benefit of bystanders. Rarely, however, do arbitrated settlements gain the support of the original principals themselves. When efforts to utilize both constraining and resolving strategies of conflict management fail, arbitration is a manager's necessary option of last resort.

Account to Bystanders

The final task of a Negotiating Issues Strategy is to report the provisional resolutions between principals to assess any intended or unintended negative effects of their resolutions on the larger community's wholeness. This can be done in a public meeting or (more commonly) by written communication with a sampling of or representatives of bystanders.

The constructive resolution of principals' differences will benefit the larger community housing the conflict. Principals' energies and resources are freed from their conflictive antagonism for communal activities. Frequently, the constructive resolution of principals' differences also contributes new visions, understandings, and solutions for other communal concerns as well.

When such benefits do not accrue to bystanders from the resolutions of conflicts, the minimal ethical requirement for principals' resolutions is that they not involve the reduction of the larger community's benefits. As a safeguard against resolutions that meet principals' interests at the cost of bystanders' interests, this final task of reporting is necessary. Should a community of bystanders raise objections, a manager will work with them to designate spokespersons for further negotiating processes with the original principals. Bargaining will be needed to accommodate rather than completely reformulate the principals' resolutions.

Two Illustrations of Using a
Negotiating Issues Strategy

Any Keys to the Kingdom?

In chapter 1 we spoke of the rapid formation of thunderclouds of ill will between the traditionalist and modernist factions of the congregation of Good Shepherd Church.

Good Shepherd Church was a hundred-year-old parish of about four hundred members. It was located in the middle city region of a growing metropolitan area of 1 million called Argon. Good Shepherd was a warm, caring, familial congregation that had been deeply influenced by its association with many of the children and staff of a nearby orphanage. In recent years, however, Good Shepherd had been rent apart by bitter conflict over its worship forms and style in Sunday worship services.

Bert Brown was representative of the traditionalist faction who favored formal, familiar liturgy led in a warm and solemn style. Brown's family had been leaders in Good Shepherd for three generations. Alice Dawn was representative of the modernist faction who allied themselves with the pastor, who favored an informal, creative liturgy led in a warm and spontaneous style.

The bitter controversy had finally culminated in the pastor's resignation, leaving only the church secretary and the governing body to work with its interim pastor, Rita Carnes.

When Pastor Carnes arrived, she initiated a Preventing Exchanges Strategy between the traditionalists and the modernists. Her first Sunday in the pulpit she stated that during the interim period the conflict over liturgy would be put on hold while she used the forms and style of Sunday morning worship with which she was herself comfortable. No one would be asked to support or oppose it. After three years of acrimonious exchanges, Good Shepherd collectively breathed a sigh of relief.

Seven months later, however, the congregational calm was abruptly broken when a written petition was circulated demanding that all doors of the church plant be locked immediately. The reason given was a veiled reference to the secretary's fright over a surprising encounter with a stranger in the church's kitchen the preceding week. By the end of Sunday morning worship Good Shepherd Church was a beehive of tension, with little clots of people speaking in lowered voices of alarm. Rita's phone began to ring off the hook.

A brief assessment of the situation led Rita to believe that a Negotiating Issues Strategy might work. Although the neighborhood around the church plant had been changing from suburban to an affluent commercial area, Good Shepherd's emotional rules were responsible and lines of communication and trust between governing body, interim pastor, and members had been strengthening these past seven months. Both representative principals (Brown and Dawn) seemed reasonably balanced in power, with Brown's orientation being barely dirty fight and Dawn's barely fair fight.

At the next evening's monthly meeting of Good Shepherd's governing body, Rita waited until the petition with sixty signatures had been read. Before she could get the floor, Brown made the motion that all church plant doors be locked. Before the motion was seconded, Rita interrupted. "I very much oppose our hastening to judgment on this matter without a much more open sharing of thoughts and feelings among us. I make a motion in two parts: that we vote to become a committee of a whole to discuss this matter, and with that action that we first establish some ground rules for expressing ourselves in that discussion." Her motion was seconded, as was Brown's. The motion about procedure took precedence. A tense, short-spoken debate with muffled anger occurred. Rita's motion passed by a bare majority. She then proposed two ground rules for discussion: no personal attacks over differences and expressing feelings with "I" rather than "You are" statements. A third ground rule proposed was no interrupting. A fourth was no long sermons, which proposal generated a trickle of laughter. All four ground rules were adopted.

Rita then proposed that each board member be given up to three minutes' time to share without interruption or criticism his or her present feelings and thoughts. This process was agreed on and begun. Once when someone began to challenge another's input, the challenger was respectfully prevented from continuing. Once when someone began to run over the three-minute limit, the offender was respectfully prevented from going further. Otherwise, all parties cooperated. By the end of this first round of sharing, the feeling tone of the board meeting had begun to change from fear and hostility to serenity and an almost gentle tenderness.

For an hour and a half board members began to unpack their differing perspectives, concerns, and hopes: their underlying interests. Their sharing quickly moved beyond the question of locked doors to questions of congregational identity, mission, and their changing neighborhood. Toward the end of the time period a board member proposed that board members be paired according to pro and con sentiments about the doors and visit and interview each member who had signed the petition. This idea achieved unanimous support. Arrangements were made for each pair of visitors to use a uniform, open-ended set of interview questions. A brief pastoral letter informing the congregation of the board's action was authorized.

At next month's board meeting the emotional climate was dramatically different—relaxed, hopeful, and even joyful. Visitors reported the appreciation of those they had interviewed. Before the substantive findings from their visits were given, a board member thought aloud about the possibility of challenging the congregation to pledge some $12,000 for remodeling the church office in a way that would make it secure without having to lock the remaining church plant doors. The board became excited about this alternative way of meeting the interests of those who demanded security for staff and the interests of those who strongly believed in continuing to afford the community an open sanctuary for weekday meditation and meetings. The idea became a motion that quickly secured 90 percent support. Three weeks later, members of the congregation had pledged over $13,000. The conflict over locking the church plant had been resolved.

Can We Talk About It?

Old First Church had long since passed its prime. An aged granite building in an aged section of the city, Old First's community had weathered the tides of affluence, out-migration to the suburbs, inner-city blight, and now regentrification.

Each fall the governing body of Old First went on a twenty-four-hour retreat to deepen members' relationships, review the board's role and responsibilities, and address a "tough or sensitive" issue facing Old First. There was no doubt in anyone's mind what that issue needed to be this year: the matter of blessing gay and lesbian unions.

Pastor Charles was clearly a principal. He was strongly in favor and politically active for changing his denomination's policy of denying ordination to self-affirming homosexuals. He had performed elsewhere religious services recognizing homosexual unions. He had neither organized nor blocked a petition from a group of members of Old First to permit gay and lesbian dances and the blessing of homosexual unions at Old First itself. For all these reasons Charles thought it wise to secure an outsider to design and manage the board's retreat. His General Presbyter, Alan, agreed to serve.

In preparing for the retreat, Alan had researched how other churches in the metropolitan area had or were dealing with conflicts over homosexual life-styles. One of Alan's contacts got him in touch with Steve, a gay lay officer who had met three months earlier with the group of Old First petitioners. At Alan's request and with Charles' concurrence, Steve was asked to come to the board's retreat to make a presentation in the final three hours of the event.

As the retreat began, Alan shared the design for the whole event, including the provision for Steve's presentation and participation. At the first break, two board members became upset when they recognized Steve as being the homosexual who had previously met with the Old First petitioners. They requested that Pastor Charles either ask Steve to leave or ask the board to approve Steve's presence and participation.

When the board reconvened, Pastor Charles asked them whether (1) they were willing to permit Steve to be present and participate when scheduled, (2) they wished to excuse Steve until his scheduled presentation, or (3) they wished to excuse Steve altogether. Immediately one member proposed that Steve leave while the board made its choice. For thirty minutes board members discussed with an awkward inhibition whether Steve should even be present while they discussed their choice. Finally the outsider, Alan, asked each board member whether Steve's presence was inhibiting him or her from being open and frank. All responded that Steve's presence would not affect their participation. At that point Steve was invited to introduce himself. Two ground rules were surfaced and affirmed: that members be candid about their thoughts and feelings during the retreat, and that members relate respectfully to everyone regardless of her or his position or orientation.

The board then began to identify and write down on newsprint members' concerns about the petition. A large catalogue of hopes and fears poured out until more than two pages of newsprint were filled. Personal testimonies began to be offered of some members' positive and negative experiences with lesbians/gays. Deep feelings were expressed. "What will my son be subjected to when his friends find out he belongs to a gay church?" "How much longer will we treat homosexuals like modern lepers?"

Next, members identified biblical passages, specific articles and studies, and denominational papers and decisions providing larger perspectives, perceptions, and arguments about the whole matter of homosexuals' participation and place in the life and work of the church. Once these larger frames of reference had been identified and considered, Steve was asked to comment on what he had been seeing and hearing. He was both affirming and challenging, adding both his own perspective and some additional resources. Steve was asked by Charles, "What motivates you to advocate for this cause so passionately?" Steve's response included an account of how, a couple of years earlier, he had learned that a gifted young clergywoman who died prematurely had lived in daily fear that her own secret lesbianism would be discovered and she would be ejected from her profession.

The retreat was drawing to a close. Board members began to affirm that they had all been changed by being able to differ honestly without boiling over emotionally. They agreed that no board member had abandoned ship. They agreed that their response to the petition for blessing gay/lesbian unions had not yet become clear but that their next steps would be to involve all church members in a process of honest, respectful dialogue for the emergence of some kind of communal consensus. This was decided as their next step. They ended their retreat in a circle, affirming their diversity and acknowledging their oneness as children of God. They had begun a Negotiating Issues Strategy, which they were now both prepared and committed to complete.

In Conclusion

A Negotiating Issues Strategy secures a win/win resolution of substantive differences through covenanting constructive behavior and exploring principals' interests. Sometimes this intervention will be aborted when principals do not covenant in word or in fact constructive behavioral ground rules. In such circumstances, the confrontative process is itself stopped, and a manager resorts to one or more of the constraining strategies to prevent destructive exchanges, change contextual factors, and/or coach one or more of the principals. Otherwise, a negotiating process continues until differences are resolved by consensus, bargaining, acceptance of necessary compromise, or temporary agreements for dealing constructively with unresolved differences. When repeated efforts to resolve differences fail, a manager will seek a binding arbitration of principals' differences, which benefits primarily relevant communities of bystanders.

CHAPTER 12

Step Three/Resolving Strategies: Mediating Relationships

The young minister sat in his office alone. His stomach was tied in knots. It had been seventeen months since his spiritual high at his ordination and installation as pastor. He had felt truly called to minister to these people. They had welcomed him with affirmation and affection. Soon, however, he discovered that one fourth of the people listed on the church roll did not even live in the community anymore. Even some people who obviously liked him did not come to worship very often. When he had proposed a new order of worship based on denominational prescriptions, the discussion had been gently and indefinitely postponed. In the spring when he had enthusiastically invited the youth to sign up for the summer's national denominational youth conference, none of them had chosen to go. A number of their parents had explained that plans for summer jobs and family vacations left no room for the conference. And now when he was asking the governing board to participate in a countywide interchurch plan for assisting exconvicts to get jobs, there was hostility toward him personally. His dreams sagged. He felt lied to. He felt discounted. He felt like he was being pulled down by a kind of spiritual undertow in the parish. His trust in these people kept going down too.

Defining Primary Relationships

Obviously, it was time for this young pastor and his congregation to level with each other and clear the air about his dreams and their commitments in order to build a mutually rewarding pastoral relationship. If two parties to a relationship were exactly alike, one of them would be unnecessary. In this fact lies both the glory and the agony of conflicted primary relationships. The Chinese proverb goes, "If you haven't fought each other, you do not know each other."[1]

David Viscott defines a primary relationship as being a commitment to another party.[2] It consists in mutual attachment. Sharon Wegscheider-Cruse speaks of an affectional primary relationship as "a passionate . . . commitment between two people that nurtures both people and maintains a high regard for the value of each person."[3] A primary human relationship for Christians involves a commitment that is second only to one's commitment to God and to self. An affectional relationship is primary when it incorporates the center of one's being. A work relationship is primary when it involves the center of one's doing. Primary affectional relationships are built in families of origin and families of creation: marriages or other committed relationships involving sex, special friendships, bonds between parents and child, or bonds between siblings or other extended family members. Primary work relationships are built in communities of vocation and/or commitment: between long-term employers and employees, athletic team mates, professional colleagues, occupational partners, commercial project groups, or members of civic, political, philanthropic, or religious associations.

Primary affectional and work relationships are not realities one simply discovers. They are realities one builds.

> We all know that falling in love and/or becoming part of a creative work team is ecstasy, but we're also just as convinced that most love and work relationships will wither or even die with time. . . .
>
> All of us hunger for a love or bonding that will stay intimate and secure, yet also encourage our individual fulfillment. Freedom and intimacy are to a person what sun and water are to a plant: both must be present at the same time for a person to flourish. . . . The question is how to overcome separateness, achieve union, and so forth, without losing oneself in the process.[4]

A primary relationship adds a third dimension to one's social being. This third dimension offers interdependence rather than counterdependence or codependence between oneself and the primary other(s). This third dimension can be visualized. In one of their presentations on building constructive coupleships, Sharon and Joe Wegscheider-Cruse invite two people to stand within arm's length, facing each other on separate chairs. These two people are asked to dramatize their coupleship without getting off the two chairs. Typically, they try to embrace each other straddling between the chairs. One or both people put a foot on the other's chair. In so doing, their balance becomes unstable, their pose awkward, and they find it increasingly uncomfortable to stay in such a straddled stance. Their solution, it turns out, is found when a third chair is pulled up so that each party can stand with one foot on his or her chair and the other foot on the third chair. With such an arrangement the couple can embrace with ease, stability, and mutual balance. The third chair, their primary relationship, complements rather than compromises their separate identities. Their commitment is not to invade or take over the separate character/chairs each brings to the relationship. Their commitment is to create and invest a part of themselves in a third reality represented by the third chair: their primary work or emotional relationship, their coupleship or partnership.

A Mediating Relationships Strategy deals with how two parties to a primary affectional or work relationship can create and invest themselves productively in a third-chair relational enterprise: a marriage or a pastoral relationship, a special friendship or a church staff team, a parent/child relationship or an employer/employee relationship, an athletic or work team. Church conflicts over the terms of pastoral relationships, between members of a church staff, between rival congregational factions for control of a parish, or between church authorities and volunteers over basic roles usually require a Mediating Relationships Strategy for their resolution (see fig. 12.1).

In casual relationships the onset of conflicting differences between parties usually results in reducing the investment in or terminating the relationship. Parties simply do not have enough personal investment or

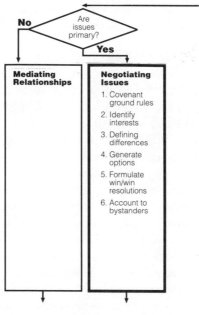

Fig. 12.1

commitment to build a relationship by working through their relational difficulties. In primary relationships where parties care enough to fight, their conflict will either build or diminish the quality of their relationship.

Fisher and Brown define a good primary relationship as "having what we need to get what we want."[5] These authors maintain that whatever the parties may want in the relationship, what they need is the ability to deal with their differences without rupturing their relationship. It is this ability to deal with differences rather than an absence of differences that constitutes a good primary relationship. It is this ability that a Mediating Relationships Strategy seeks to enhance and utilize among parties to conflicted primary affectional and work relationships.

Understanding a Mediating Process

At its core, the Mediating Relationships Strategy of this model addresses the previously unconscious ways in which principals impose or overlay on each other the emotional baggage they acquired in past familial or work relationships. The primary emotional difficulty of the young pastor introduced above was not with the behaviors of parish members but with himself. His primary emotional need was to distinguish between those with whom he was growing in a current pastoral relationship and those he had experienced in the primary relationships of his seminary education. Insofar as the pastor is expecting his congregation to relate to him the way his seminary community did, he and they will not be able to build a realistic and mutually rewarding pastoral relationship.

Unlike the reflective technique of some kinds of pastoral counseling, a Mediating Relationships Strategy is a highly directive process. The director of this process does not exercise control over the thoughts, values, feelings, or commitments of any principal in a conflicted relationship. But the process director does assertively lead the process by which principals' emotional issues are expressed, named, understood, and worked through.

Often principals may collectively undertake a Mediating Relationships Strategy early in building their relationship. However, in situations when such efforts break down or when a malevolent cycle becomes chronic, a principal/manager will no longer be able to manage his or her emotions and the process simultaneously. Just as a physician will not operate on her own child except in emergencies, a principal/manager's own emotional blindspots or compulsions will be too intense for him or her to serve as a mediating process director. Nor may bystanders who are close to one or more of the principals be sufficiently detached to serve well as directors of a mediating process. In common with general concepts of managing conflict, this model holds that an objective third party is usually needed to direct a mediating relationships strategy. The emotional intensity of conflicted primary relationships simply makes it necessary to secure the services of a person who is not a party to the relationship. Once a primary relationship becomes destructively conflicted, a principal/manager will want to secure a third party to oversee and direct the process of a Mediating Relationships Strategy. Such a third party might be a neighboring clergy person, therapist, counselor, or consultant. The term "director" will be used in distinction from a principal/manager while describing how a bystander/manager or third party/manager undertakes and implements a mediating process.

The director of a Mediating Relationships Strategy does not rescue the principals, who must take responsibility for their relationship. Just as in a Coaching Strategy, a director of a mediating process works with principals rather than for them. Margaret and Jordan Paul make clear principals' responsibilities in conflicted primary relationships to do the work of resolving them:

> The first step to meaningful change is to become aware of [one's] intent. . . . The intent to protect is a basic motivation to defend oneself against any threats, real or imagined, of emotional pain. . . . Problems arise when [one's] primary intent is self-protective—to make the other change. . . . Only one response to a conflict breaks the protective circle and opens the door to intimacy: an intent to learn.[6]

Principals alone can make the choice in a conflicted work or affectional relationship to care more about learning than self-protection. Unless or until principals make the choice to learn, a director cannot make the tasks of a Mediating Relationships Strategy yield reconciliation.

For this reason, a Mediating Relationships Strategy is often preceded by a Coaching Strategy with one or more of the principals in order for them to feel sufficiently trusting of the third party to choose to learn rather than to protect themselves in the mediating process. Parties who have low self-esteem, who shame themselves, or who fear a loss of self-esteem will not be emotionally ready to choose to learn rather than to protect themselves in primary relationships. Nor may such parties know how to behave and express themselves respectfully in primary relationships. A third party's coaching can help such parties gain sufficient self-worth and self-assertiveness to participate fruitfully in a Mediating Relationships Strategy.

It is imperative that a Mediating Relationships Strategy be undertaken in privacy and with strict confidentiality. No bystanders may be present. The emotional vulnerability required of principals is difficult enough without subjecting them to observation or an accounting by others. An ethic of conflict management requires accountability to bystanders about the terms of relating that are reached at the conclusion of a mediating process. For the same reason, an ethic of conflict management requires emotional and physical protection from bystanders during the process of revealing, exploring, understanding, and formulating the terms of their primary relationship. Primary relationships are not public matters. The public's stake in primary relationships is their effect on the common good to be constructive rather than destructive.

A Mediating Relationships Strategy addresses the behavioral terms of a relationship but not its emotional substance. Principals to primary work or affectional relationships grow into or out of relationships through emotional interaction over time. A two- to four-hour directed process of engagement does not itself create the healing or trusting needed for a continuing good relationship. The outcome of a Mediating Relationships Strategy is simply the realization of mutual understandings and formulation of mutual terms, which open the way for principals to become reconciled within or without their continuing primary relationship.

Although a Mediating Relationships Strategy does not complete the emotional healing of parties to primary relationships, it begins the journey of healing. A mediating process is as emotional as it is cognitive. Whether the strategy is concerned with work or affectional relationships, it requires the expression and exploration of principals' feelings. Unless principals' feelings are owned, they cannot learn what is going on within and between themselves and others. Until principals express their feelings in constructive, assertive ways, they cannot come to understand each other. Whereas ground rules for principals in a Negotiating Issues process provide for ownership and self-control of their feelings, the ground rules for principals in a Mediating Relationships process provide for ownership and the constructive expression of principals' feelings.

A mediating process is confrontative, but it is not a "no holds barred" kind of confrontation. Principals are not given the freedom to say everything about anything they think or feel. Principals are directed to level with each other about their feelings and perceptions of each other in *specific* incidences. Principals are directed to speak in "I" messages rather than "you are" messages. Principals are directed to communicate about specific experiences rather than in sweeping generalizations. Principals' identifications of critical events in their relationship generate the information about feelings and perceptions that is then used to explore past emotional baggage that is destructively influencing current exchanges between them.

A Mediating Relationships Strategy is therapeutic, but it is not therapy. Principals' identified perceptual distortions are not worked through in the process itself. Instead, principals' distorted perceptions are used to identify previously learned habits of feeling and perceiving so that parties can work out behavioral terms or agreements that will prevent continuing distortions or dysfunctions in the ways they will now relate.

Finally, a Mediating Relationships Strategy is built on a principal of unconditional constructiveness, to borrow a term from Brown and Fisher. Rather than identifying what is wrong and defective about the principals, a Mediating Relationships Strategy focuses on identifying what is right and worthy about the principals. The assumption is that there are always good reasons for destructive behavior. The destructiveness of principals' behavior is not discounted or ignored. However, principals are led to understand rather than shame themselves in light of such behaviors. In a Mediating Relationships Strategy all principals are presumed to be imperfect and sinful, yet worthy and responsible, selves who can learn from their mistakes and brokenness and grow in grace. The terms that resolve their relationship are formulated in light of whom they now seek to become rather than who they have been. The goal is to formulate terms that are good for the futures of both participants and their relationship. Such terms of reconciliation may involve participants' healing by letting go as well as by renewing their primary relationship.

Faith Meanings for a
Mediating Relationships Strategy

The distinction between wrong-being and wrong-doing in a Mediating Relationships Strategy reflects a Christian understanding of the distinction between humanity's creation in the image of God as inherently good and humanity's sinfulness as universally falling short of the will of God. One addresses the destructive behaviors and evil results of principals' experiences in primary relationships. But one addresses these behaviors with an unconditional constructiveness about the humanity of principals to primary relationships. Otherwise human sin is taken as evidence of human defect and the often devastatingly evil results of human sin as the evidence of some satanic character of being human.

A second faith meaning that undergirds a Mediating Relationships Strategy reflects Christian understandings of the atonement. Human responsibility and choice to repent are undertaken as exercises of God's grace that delivers parties from enslavement/compulsion to sin and restores the option of repentance. Parties to conflicted primary relationships are considered able to accept forgiveness for their past sinning rather than to numb or forget their sinning. In accepting their responsibility for missing the mark of God's will, principals are gifted with the choice of seeking God's will. Moral accountability turns out to be accessibility to God's grace. Old wounds between parties are transformed into new opportunities for parties.

Third, a Mediating Relationships Strategy is built on a biblical understanding of the communal origins of individual character defects. Principals are led to understand the interpersonal, systemic sources of their feelings, behavior, and thoughts rather than making a moralistic judgment of personal virtues and vices. The desired outcome of speaking the truth in love is not participants' condemnation but their conversion. It is assumed that troubled relationships are resolved by changing terms rather than by punishing persons.

Finally, a Mediating Relationships Strategy incorporates an ethical recognition of a larger community's care for its members' spiritual well-being. While a mediating process is undertaken apart from communal observation of participation, its results are subjected to communal feedback. The private domain is connected with the public good by accounting for the outcomes of principals' reconciliation. No primary relationship is communal business; but every primary relationship affects communal business.

Implementing a
Mediating Relationships Strategy

Establish Ground Rules and Procedures
for Assertiveness

Because a Mediating Relationships Strategy involves self-disclosure and emotional vulnerability, a physical setting that safeguards with ground rules privacy and privileged communication is required (see fig. 12.1). The director of the process will secure in advance such a physical arrangement. No reporters, observers, or other bystanders are permitted to be present. Precautions should be taken to provide a comfortable setting where principals will not be interrupted, observed, or betrayed by any outsiders.

A director of a Mediating Relationships process prepares principals in advance of their confrontation by giving them instructions and directions. A director instructs principals to bring to the confrontation up to three brief, written descriptions of specific incidents or episodes they have found destructive to the relationship. A director may also advise principals to provide some independent validation of these episodes. A director may also rehearse principals in how to recognize and express their feelings constructively.

A process director will also provide principals in advance of their confrontation directions about the logistics of the confrontation—time, place, physical arrangements. Principals are advised that they need not exchange pleasantries or other normal rituals of introduction when they arrive on site. They are also advised to wear informal clothes and to plan to meet for up to four hours without interruptions from the outside.

A mediating process begins with a director's leading participants in formulating or validating rules for expressing feelings and behaving assertively and accountably. While behavioral ground rules for a negotiating process focus on principals' awareness and self-control of their feelings, behavioral ground rules for a mediating process focus on principals' expression and exploration of their feelings.

Often principals have difficulty recognizing their feelings. Unfortunately, many Americans, especially male Americans, have learned to ignore their feelings. They may not even have learned the words to think about or express their feelings. The cultural injunction to be rational is often taken by Americans as a prescription to reject or ignore emotions rather than balance them. A director may want to give some guidance on this point.

The first language all human beings speak is the sounds of their feelings. With their first breath as infants, they cry. Because feelings are the universal first language of all human infants, feelings are simple. Therapists generally agree that there are six basic feelings human beings may have: three positive ones of peace, power, or joy; three negative ones of mad, sad, or scared. All other feeling words denote combinations or shadings of these basic six. It helps principals to know that there are only six basic feelings from which to choose when identifying their emotions. Principals may also be helped to recognize their feelings by being led in paying attention to their physical states.

> Does my stomach feel tight or upset? Are my palms moist? Are my jaw muscles clenched? Am I making fists or gripping something tightly? Am I raising my voice? These are all possible signals of anger, frustration, or fear. A soft voice, a tendency to move closer, and moist eyes can indicate affection, empathy, or perhaps sadness. Depending on the context, my physical sensations may indicate different emotions. But once I have noted the sensations, identifying the underlying emotion is usually not difficult.[7]

Much of the work a director does in helping principals identify their feelings and express them assertively reflects the director's own work with himself or herself in Step One of this book's model. As one learns how to recognize, explore, understand, and express one's own feelings, one learns how to help others do the same.

A second major focus for behavioral ground rules in a Mediating Relationships Strategy is assertiveness. When all is said and done, the key to being assertive is knowing that one is worthwhile. One cannot assert what one does not want, value, or respect. Often it helps to read to and post in sight of the principals some version of Manuel Smith's Bill of Rights for self-worth.

- You have the right to judge your own behavior, thoughts, emotions, and to take responsibility for their initiation and consequences upon yourself.
- You have the right to judge if you are responsible for judging other people's problems.
- You have the right to change your mind.
- You have the right to make mistakes and be responsible for them.
- You have the right to say, "I don't know."
- You have the right to say, "I don't understand."[8]

Such axioms for accepting, respecting, and asserting oneself provide an emotional bedrock for communicating assertively in the tasks of a Mediating Relationships process. Here are some standards from which principals may be led to formulate two or three of their own ground rules of "do's" and "don'ts":

- Say how you feel, not how you feel about someone else. Use "I" statements, not "You are . . ." statements.
- State feelings; don't load them into your expression of perceptions or opinions.
- Speak for yourself, not for others.
- No interrupting. Care enough to listen before you respond.
- Stay in your own skin and don't claim all of reality when you say what *you* are feeling or perceiving.
- Describe specific behaviors or actual events, not your generalized interpretations or judgments about everything.
- Accept consequences but refuse blaming by yourself or others.

Once principals have agreed on some ground rules for expressing feelings and communicating assertively, it is often helpful to lead them in a "test run." A director can ask each principal in turn to express in no more than three minutes his or her current feelings. This "round" of feelings ventilation is tightly structured. Principals may not interrupt, comment, or argue with what is said. Only the director may intervene to coach a principal having difficulty recognizing feelings or expressing them respectfully. As one or two such three-minute rounds of feelings expression proceed, principals begin to make their ground rules operative. Their trust and respect of both their leader and their ground rules increase. They may wish to add to or change their ground rules before they go on to the next tasks of the mediating process.

Identify Critical Incidents

The next task of principals in a Mediating Relationships Strategy is to identify specific incidents in their relationship that were disruptive or destructive of the relationship for them. Just as principals are guided in a negotiating process to identify their interests rather than declare their positions, so principals are guided in a mediating process to identify their specific experiences rather than declare their judgments.

A director leads principals in describing specific incidents with the other principal(s) that were experienced as being destructive of their relationship. These critical episodes are described and subjected to validation jointly by the principals or by a source independent of the principals. The first task is to get on the table factual accounts of what was said and done in the episode.

After an episode has been described, participants' feelings and thoughts *during* the incident are remembered and shared. Then participants' feelings and thoughts *since* the incident may be shared. Each participant's thoughts and feelings are accepted and respected. No agreement between principals is sought or needed—only the constructive expression of their feelings and coherent accounting of their thoughts. No disputes are permitted.

A director may help principals in this task by inviting them to write down and/or post on newsprint some of their primary feelings or thoughts during or since each incident they identify.

Understand Destructive Patterns

Principals' difficulties and pain in primary relationships usually stem from their past experiences in primary affectional and work relationships. For example, a principal may have learned as a child that big boys don't cry. When he observes another minister on his staff cry, he feels scorn, even derision. When his own son cries, he becomes either angry or scared. When he is grieved himself, he numbs himself or he feels threatened. In each case his past baggage about crying distorts his current ways of responding to others.

Or, for another example, a principal may have learned in her first experience as a church officer that her pastor talked in judgmental ways about members who differed with him theologically. When this principal's current pastor, a clergywoman, protests her sexist language about God, she stands up for her views in the parking lot but withholds her views in meetings of the governing board. Her distrust of any minister who disagrees with her distorts her otherwise constructive perceptions of her current pastor.

The third task of a mediating process is to discern feeling patterns to principals' feelings and thoughts by reflecting on critical incidents in their experiences of their primary relationships. Like a detective seeking to solve a crime, a director leads participants in seeing how previous formative experiences seem to be coloring or distorting current experiences in their relationship. The intent is to understand rather than to judge. The goal is insight rather than critique. A director may ask a principal such questions as these:

- When do you remember first feeling (sad, mad, joyful, etc.) with your parents, your siblings, your teachers, your ministers, your employers, etcetera?
- What important person at work or at home does this principal's behavior remind you of?
- When did you learn to think of this (person, behavior, situation) this way?
- What happened to you in school similar to this episode?
- What in your past experience does this incident remind you of?

Most parties to conflicted primary relationships bring emotional scars and wounds from their pasts that distort their characters. Most parties to conflicted primary relationships are unconsciously seeking to rework these parts of their pasts. David Viscott offers parties to troubled primary relationships a typology of character traits that undermine or enhance the building of primary affectional or work relationships. He classifies parties to primary relationships in four categories of character—dependent, controlling, competitive, and mature. A portion of his typology is as follows.[9]

Trait	Dependent	Controlling	Competitive	Mature
Major defense	Denial	Excuses self, blames others	Pretends not to care	Accepts reality honestly
Defensive position	Helpless, panic	All powerful, all knowing	So what? It doesn't matter	Tries to understand

Self-doubt	I'm unlovable	I'm no good	I'm a failure	I made a mistake
Threatens with	Injuring self	Withdrawing support	Another person	Tries not to threaten
Lies about	What might decrease love	Strength, wealth, influence	Caring, age, confidence, talent	Tells the truth
What starts fight	Threat of abandonment	Disputing their judgment	Embarrassing them	Hurting their feelings
They fear	Losing love	Losing influence	Losing impact	Losing self
Strength	Loyalty	Organization	Ambition	Flexibility
Weakness	Clings	Manipulates	Brags	No fatal flaw
Style of arguing	Abused child	Grand inquisitor	Wounded celebrity	Let the hurt speak
Responsibility	Blames self	Blames partner	Blames circumstances	Accepts role in problem

Viscott's typology provides parties to conflicted primary relationship some fundamental connections between some of their feelings, thoughts, and behaviors. The danger of any typology is its oversimplification. Typologies offer overviews, not diagnoses. The appropriate way to use Viscott's typology with principals is to trigger their understandings of themselves. A destructive way to use Viscott's typology with principals is to label or analyze others. The third task of a mediating process requires principals' acknowledgment of themselves for others' understandings, rather than principals' indictments of others in their own secret understanding.

One recalls the humorous sign posted in a manager's office: "The success of your treatment depends on which one of us is the doctor." In a Mediating Relationships Strategy no one is the doctor. The success of a mediating process depends on how principals come to understand and take responsibility for themselves in their past and current primary relationships.

Often principals are not conscious of many of the thoughts and feelings that motivate their behaviors. In the stress and alienation of ruptured primary relationships, principals are often at their most reactive level emotionally. When principals begin to understand themselves, they are able to change from reacting to others to making choices with others. As principals experience this inner change, they become ready to collaborate in formulating new terms for their relating.

The following adaptation of guidelines for principals from Fisher and

Brown may help principals to be unconditionally constructive with each other during this task of coming to understand themselves and the emotional baggage they have imposed upon themselves and others in their current relationship:

1. Balancing: Even if another principal (or principals) acts irrationally, balance your own feelings with reason.
2. Understanding: Even if another principal (or principals) misunderstands you, focus on understanding the other rather than getting the other to understand you.
3. Communicating. Even if another principal (or principals) is not listening, listen to him or her.
4. Acting reliably: Even if another principal (or principals) is trying to deceive or mislead you, neither trust nor deceive him or her; be reliably truthful.
5. Accepting: Even if another principal (or principals) is rejecting your feelings and thoughts, accept his or her feelings and thoughts, not to agree but to learn from them.[10]

At times principals may experience emotional relapses during this task. They may have a shame attack. They may slide back into blaming accusations rather than angry confrontations. They may fall back into playing victim rather than taking responsibility for themselves and their relationship. They may start acting out rather than stating their feelings. A director intervenes when such relapses occur, coaching them in assertive, responsible ways to stay with the task of coming to understand themselves in the presence of other principals.

Formulate Constructive Terms

Once principals have reached shared understandings of what have been the destructive patterns or terms underlying their difficulties, they can reconcile their relationship. A director leads them in brainstorming (see chapter 11) patterns of behavior and arrangements that would enhance both themselves and their relationship. They will select from these possibilities those terms which will resolve their emotional issues. As these new terms emerge they will learn whether their reconciliation involves dissociating or reassociating with each other. They should dissociate if they cannot find ways to be themselves in their relationship. To use the example of the three chairs, they cannot keep one foot each on a third chair if that foot won't reach from their "self-chair." They may reassociate if they can find ways to be themselves in their relationship—to keep one foot on the self-chair and the other on the third chair.

These new terms are agreements that contribute to each other in light of both their strengths and weaknesses. Whatever the substance of their new terms, the constructiveness of the process stems from the collaboration and mutual accountability the principals achieve with each other. Whatever ways they use to resolve their conflicted relationship, they agree to hold each other accountable. A director may encourage such accountability by ensuring that the principals' new terms are put in writing for the record.

A mediating process involves principals in letting go of previously destructive terms of their relationship. The loss of any relationship is usually painful and frightening. Even though the relationship has been destructive, it has been familiar and has met destructive needs of the parties. The old terms must be surrendered, however, if new terms are to supplant the old. Sometimes old terms are not supplanted. The relationship is concluded by mutual consent because the principals have changed or have become free to be who they really are. Either way, a mediating process involves principals in confronting their current identities so as to be reconciled to God and themselves, if not to each other.

Sometimes what principals learn in a mediating process is that their most constructive alternative lies beyond their relationship rather than within it. They find it impossible to reconcile what is good for each of them with what is good for the relationship. Principals may decide that the most healing solution is for them to let go of each other and move on. Or they may decide that the most healing solution is for them to learn new ways of relating in a continuing primary relationship. In either case, a mediating process seeks reconciliation by providing all principals with healing ways of letting go of the past and choosing a future.

Report Outcomes Only

It has been emphasized that unlike the public character of a Negotiating Issues Strategy, a Mediating Relationships Strategy is a privileged process. What is reported to those who are related to the principals is only the perceived consequences for them of the outcomes of the process. Often the immediate result of the resolution of primary relationships is the necessity and capability of undertaking negotiations of larger communal issues long held hostage by what have been ruptured relationships. A manager will be alert to the mistake of letting principals to conflicted relationships negotiate substantive issues that involve others. Larger communal issues are neither private nor appropriately negotiated in privileged contexts. Only the terms of relationships are to be resolved in a Mediating Relationships Strategy. Substantive issues are resolved in the public and accountable processes of a Negotiating Issues Strategy. A director or manager is responsible for ensuring that this distinction is made and kept in conflictive situations.

Three Illustrations of Using a
Mediating Relationships Strategy

The Stuck Search Committee

Jennifer was at the end of her rope. As chair of the committee to find and call a new pastor, she felt completely blocked. Every time she spoke positively about a candidate, her nemesis, Sheila, spoke negatively. The whole committee could feel the deep anger just beneath the surface between the two women. After seven months of this feuding, Jennifer was ready to resign the chair. She simply could not figure out how to work with Sheila. As she said to the interim pastor, "Something's got to give here if we are ever going to get a candidate we can all support."

"Are you willing to confront her?" the interim pastor asked.

"Yes, I am," Jennifer replied.

"Okay," he said, "I'll call Sheila and see what might be possible."

When the interim pastor called Sheila and indicated that Jennifer was upset with her, Sheila began to cry on the phone. Hers were tears of rage, not grief. "I just don't know if there's any point in even trying to talk to Jennifer," Sheila said. The manager listened. By the end of the conversation Sheila had agreed to attempt a constructive confrontation. The arrangements were made for the two women to meet with the director of the process for a three-hour confrontation at Jennifer's home on a weekday morning when no one would be around. The phone was to be taken off the hook. Pleasantries were to be suspended.

Two ground rules were established: no interrupting and no personal attacks. Each woman took five-minute turns in expressing her frustrations over and perceptions about a string of destructive incidents over the more than twelve months of the committee's existence. Feelings were acknowledged and shared constructively. Both women shared their hurts and frustrations with each other over the conflicting positions they had taken in the congregation-wide split over the preceding pastor. Both women acknowledged that the emotions and substantive issues of this preceding lose/lose communal conflict had not been resolved for them. Both women began to make connections between those unresolved issues from the congregation's conflict and their perceptions and feelings toward each other on the search committee.

As the women began to see the connections between what had happened between them in the congregation's conflict and what had happened between them in committee meetings, the emotional climate between them changed. Anger gave way to insight. Defenses gave way to open-minded interviewing. They began to agree to disagree about the previous pastor. They also began to distinguish between what each of them had actually said and done in the congregation's warfare and what each of them had attributed to the other in the fray.

The two women then began to propose some agreements for dealing with each other on the current search committee. They agreed to let bygones be bygones, to let go of previous grudges and hurts. They also agreed to level with each other when either of them began to harbor the old kinds of perceptions and interpretations of each other. Once they agreed to let go of their past experiences of each other and to check out current experiences with each other, their conflicted work relationship was resolved. Four months later, the search committee made a unanimous recommendation of a candidate to become pastor of the congregation.

Telling Time

In a staff meeting, the head of staff exploded. "Walter, I've been asking you for ten months why we cannot get a comfortable temperature in the sanctuary for worship service. This is the 1990s, man. Surely we can solve this problem. So when are you going to get off your butt and solve it?"

Walter stared at John in silent rage. Then Walter walked out. The rest of the staff sat in embarrassment and discomfort. The weekly staff meeting was soon adjourned.

John felt shame tugging his sleeve of consciousness. He went into his study and began to engage in self-recrimination for his outburst. He knew that he had good reasons to be frustrated over the situation. He also knew that his outburst had been inappropriate. It made him squirm inside.

He got up and walked to Walter's office. "Come on, let's deal with what just happened," John said.

The two men walked back to John's office, closed the door, and sat down opposite each other. "Look, Walter, I apologize for jumping you in there, but I get so frustrated with you. Every time I bring this temperature business up, you go into this twenty-minute explanation of how the heating/cooling system works and what all the difficulties are about getting the temperature right."

"Damn it, John," Walt replied. "You ask a question and then flatly refuse to listen to its answer. All I've been doing is trying to help you understand the complexity of solving this temperature problem. Rather than listening so you can understand and look at the options with me, you just jump on my case as if I'm incompetent. You want a staff, then you better learn how to utilize a staff."

There was silence.

"Okay, I'm listening now. What would help me is if you could summarize the problem and give me the bottom line. I know I'm impatient with technical things. That's your aptitude, not mine. In fact, it occurs to me that you're probably a sensate on Myers Briggs while I'm an intuitive. It's just that when I ask you as an associate what time it is, I want the time, not an explanation of how your watch works."

"Well, John, to use your metaphor, I would tell you the time if my watch worked. My problem is that I don't have a properly operating time machine. I will be willing to work on condensing my explanation if you will work on trying to understand what's not working."

Both ministers laughed. They were understanding each other.

"Actually, Walt," said John, "one of my faults is not only not understanding mechanical things but getting anxious and impatient over not understanding. Somehow I learned that *real* men know how to fix anything that's broken. Chalk one up to my childhood."

"Yeah," said Walt. "I learned the same thing, which is probably why I get so uptight over not being able to fix the situation yet."

"Okay," said John, "it's a deal. Give me the bottom line, and I'll learn to hear you out."

Later both men realized that, in itself, the issue over the sanctuary's temperature was not a major problem. What was at risk was their collegial relationship. Each man had begun to question the trust and good faith of the other. Out of the resolution of their relationship had come both deeper understanding and goodwill.

I Heard the Preacher Is an Alcoholic

Maxey Church has been anything but tranquil during its fifteen-year history. It was the result of a merger of two former congregations in the same community. After experiencing difficulties with their first two ministers, Maxey called Ruth as pastor three years ago.

About eighteen months into this pastoral relationship, the chair of Personnel approached Ruth to inform her that rumors were traveling through church and community that she was an alcoholic. The chair's efforts to track down these rumors had revealed that at least three persons were gossip mongers: the church treasurer (male), the church day care director (female), and a community alcohol rehabilitation counselor (female). The treasurer and day care director had both been opposed to calling a clergywoman in the first place. Ruth called her regional denominational office. She asked for the regional executive to serve as third-party director for intervention to deal with her rapidly deteriorating pastoral relationship. Harriet agreed.

Harriet called the Maxey's Personnel chairperson. Together they asked Ruth to undertake an assessment for chemical dependency from a respected center for the treatment of alcoholics. In three weeks Ruth received a written medical statement that completely cleared her of any signs of alcoholism or alcohol abuse.

Harriet then arranged for a meeting of the governing board and Harriet to confront the rumor mongers. Harriet opened the meeting by describing the serious legal jeopardy of character assassination. The written report clearing Ruth of alcoholism was shared. The director then introduced the concept of behavioral ground rules by reading to board members portions of the vows to which they had subscribed when they were ordained and installed as church officers:

> Will you be governed by our church's polity . . . and abide by its discipline? Will you be a friend among your colleagues in ministry, working with them, subject to the ordering of God's Word and Spirit? . . . Do you promise to further the peace, unity, and purity of the Church?[11]

Harriet then proposed four ground rules:

1. Be accountable.
2. Be factual.
3. Be respectful.
4. No "people are saying" comments allowed.

The church treasurer was unable to contain himself. He broke in by informing all present that truth was not being served by such moral browbeating nor by some outsider paid to write a fancy assessment. Harriet immediately interrupted him, asking the board to vote on the proposed ground rules. An affirming vote of all was taken.

After silence, Harriet asked the treasurer to share the facts he had. He responded, "I would never share any information with *you!*"

More silence. Harriet said, "Please share the facts of which you have knowledge." Silence. Harriet then said, "I am going to ask this governing body to read your silence not as unwillingness to share information but as an inability to do so." Silence once more. Harriet then asked the governing board to dismiss the rumors about Ruth as having been motivated by something other than Ruth's behavior. By voice vote, all but one member agreed to do so. The day care center director never spoke. Harriet then worked with the board and its personnel committee to plan how they would deal with further encounters of the rumors about Ruth. They decided to inform the congregation by word of mouth rather than by a formal meeting that might seem to give more credence to the rumors than was fitting.

Following the departure of the treasurer and the day care director, Ruth cried and prayed with the governing board members. The following day she called her accusers and asked for their support. The secretary has been reasonably cooperative. The day care center director has kept her distance, and the community alcohol rehabilitation counselor has quit attending Maxey. Trust and openness in the pastoral relationship between the congregation and Ruth have been increased.

In Conclusion

Not all mediating strategies succeed in reconciling relationships. Senior pastor John, who resolved issues with Walt, failed to resolve a conflicted relationship with another member of his staff. When John acknowledged his tendency to be overly aggressive in this second incident, he was met with hostility rather than reciprocity. In Ruth's case, she was never really reconciled with either the day care director or the church treasurer. While Ruth's governing body supported a constructive process of tracking down and refuting false rumors, another congregation in a similar situation simply asked their pastor to resign without explanation. As with a negotiating process, when principals in a mediating process choose not to participate in good faith, the process will be aborted so that neither constraining strategies nor arbitration can be initiated to manage the conflictive situation constructively.

As we shall see in a concluding chapter, the primary missional purpose of a resolving strategy is the realization of justice and compassion in human life. We have more to live for as Christians than just our private affairs or happiness. A public life of human solidarity is our best hope for private lives of fulfillment. While a Mediating Relationships Strategy enriches our lives personally, it is even more valuable as a means of building healthy faith communities in which members can become one without discounting or power struggling over their differences. As we build healthy primary relationships, both individually and corporately, we are empowered to partner with God in seeking God's rule in all human affairs: the ultimate goal of all Christian conflict management.

CHAPTER 13

Fighting for
God's *Shalom*
as Mainline Christians

The prophetic tradition of the Christian faith calls us to pursue God's justice and compassion in all human affairs:

> *Shalom* is a comprehensive word, covering the manifold relationships of daily life, and expressing the ideal of life. . . . The kernel of *[shalom]* is community with others, the foundation of life. . . . Peace is central to the preaching of the prophets, who from Micaiah to Ezekiel engage in conflict with false prophets on the question of Peace or No Peace. . . . They interpreted political and social turmoil as the necessary judgment of God, in the face of which to prophesy security is to pass over sin. . . . The mission of Jesus brings no easy harmony but division (Matt. 10:34, Lk. 12:51), which will be reproduced in the mission of the Twelve as his representatives to announce the Kingdom as a gift to be accepted and taken back (Matt. 10:12–15, Lk. 10:5–9).[1]

Because God's peace seeks social wholeness rather than harmony, the pursuit of it plunges us into conflicts with fracturing forces within ourselves, our faith communities, and the public sector. We tangle with evil forces and structures that isolate, oppress, exploit, and deceive part or all of this world and its inhabitants. The evil of these forces consists in how they maim our own and others' physical and spiritual solidarity in Christ, plundering God's image within us. "Glory to God in highest heaven, and on earth peace, goodwill among [people]" is a call to arms, not to tranquillity.[2]

At first, the idea of fighting for God's *shalom* seems a contradiction in terms. We think of the medieval crusades, when Christians killed babies in the name of a God of love. We also think of crusading mentalities since, throughout history, from witch hunts in New England, to patriotic claims of manifest destiny or holy war, to virulent hostility between many who call themselves pro-choice or pro-life.

Dirty fighting for God's peace is a contradiction in terms. When power is used in the service of righteous dogmatism, whatever its ideology, it becomes destructive of the wholeness of God's creation. Ideology and ego become the gods primarily served, however God's name is claimed. When people, whether Christian or not, believe that the moral goodness of their purpose permits the use of *any* means in its pursuit, they have begun to play god themselves. When people, whether Christian or not, mistake the evil people do as the evil-ness of the people themselves, they have begun to judge others in un-godly fashion. Aggressive and manipulative uses of power in whatever spiritual or religious cause fracture the Peace of God within and between people.

On the other hand, the pursuit of God's peace in a meantime world involves the use of power. We do not have the moral safety of forsaking the exercise of power as a necessary means of restraining divisiveness and pursuing goodness. While social crusades often evidence reactive uses of power in dirty fighting, healing social change movements require proactive uses of power in fair fighting. In a meantime world, violent uses of power will usually need to be constrained before they may be transformed. Moreover, no human exercises of social power, however well intended, will be morally perfect. Power may not be inherently corrupting, but sinful human beings are inherently fallible in its exercise. Fighting fairly for God's peace is therefore both a requirement of and judgment on all responsible selves. As responsible selves, we are called both to exercise power and to repent of its misuse by us and others, subject to the grace of God. The paradox is that until we risk fighting fairly for God's peace, we do not seem to experience the redeeming gift of God's peace for our efforts.

The Pain of Conflict
in Mainline American Churches

Since the 1950s, mainline American churches have often been caught up in the contradiction of fighting dirty for God's *shalom,* within both the church and the larger society. Hostility has exuded from both liberals and conservatives alike. Denominations and congregations have split because of win/lose power plays between militant social activists on one hand and militant pietists on the other. Virulent forms of sexism, racism, and class-ism have splintered Christian solidarity and often plunged mainline church members into win/lose power struggles to control their church policies and practices. As Richard Osmer observes,

> Throughout the past decade, the mainline Protestant churches in this country
> have gone through a period of significant self-doubt and reassessment. . . .
> Congregations and denominations have continued to struggle with the ves-
> tiges of the civil rights and antiwar movements, which challenged and di-
> vided mainline churches.[3]

Tossed by relentless gales on a sea of massive social change, the spirit and
the resources of mainline churches have been severely curtailed by various
behavioral expressions of righteous partisanship.

Staggering from such divisiveness, mainline churches today stand in
critical need of fair fight ways of responding to forces of destruction within
and without their boundaries. Committed to be inclusive faith communities, mainline Christians stand in special need of learning ways to deal
constructively with deeply rooted differences among them. Committed
from an inheritance of civil religion to shape the public sector with Christian values, mainline Christians also stand in special need of devising new
ways of doing social good collaboratively with nonchurch partners of
shared moral and social interests. In other words, at least one important
component of a recovery of the integrity, mission, and credibility of American mainline churches will be members' learning how to constrain dirty
fighting and secure fair fighting within and without their bounds. This final
chapter explores how this book's model might contribute to such a recovery through (1) fighting for God's *shalom* within ourselves to serve rather
than consume the gospel, (2) fighting for God's *shalom* in congregations to
incorporate rather than just tolerate our diversity, and (3) fighting for
God's *shalom* in the public sector to sustain rather than destroy the earth
and all its creatures.

Fighting for God's *Shalom* Within,
as Maturing Christians

This book's model reminds us that we harbor within ourselves both fair
and dirty fight proclivities. Fair fighting requires our choosing to act out of
our fair fight proclivities. When we fight fair, we repent of the sinfulness of
our human-doing while claiming the goodness of our human-being. This
distinction between behavior and character saves us from enemy making
of ourselves while making us ethically responsible for ourselves. This distinction also confronts us daily with the decision to trust God and live
responsibly or to trust false gods and live compulsively. As Gerald May
reminds us,

> Saint Augustine once said that God is always trying to give good things to us,

but our hands are too full to receive them. If our hands are full, they are full of the things to which we are addicted. . . . We may not be able to make our hands completely empty in order to receive the gifts of grace, but we can choose whether to relax our hands a little or to keep clenching them ever more tightly.[4]

In conflictive situations we struggle between trusting God for shared control of living with others or trusting ourselves and seeking to unilaterally control everyone and everything that gets in our way. When we trust God, our hands relax a little, and we work through differences with others. When we trust ourselves, our hands tighten into fists to overcome others' differences.

The book's model also reminds us that life is difficult because it is conflictive. While mainline Christians may often evidence a regrettable lack of religious enthusiasm or visible intensity about their faith, they have shown a commendable appreciation for the moral and spiritual complexities of the Christian tradition. Basically, mainline Christians will not settle for fast spiritual fixes or easy answers. As a faith community, mainline American Christians know that spiritual as well as physical life requires that people grow up: "We must no longer be children, tossed to and fro and blown about by every wind of doctrine, by people's trickery, by their craftiness in deceitful scheming. But speaking the truth in love, we must grow up" (Eph. 4:14–15a).

Mainline Christians have recognized, however imperfectly, that God's agenda with us is not only to sustain us when we are in pain but also to redeem us through it. In conflicts, speaking the truth in love is almost always painful. God's agenda with us is not only to nurture us as spiritual infants on the milk of God's mercy but also to wean us for discipleship that entails our chewing on the tough meat of complex, risky, ethical decision making. By and large, it is to the credit of mainline Christians that we have not been satisfied simply with being born again. We aim to grow up spiritually as well.

This book's model offers us a process in conflictive situations for updating our theologies enough to help us serve a God we love more than use a God we need. As mainline Christians we seek, however imperfectly, to live the Christian life in light of twenty centuries of Christian tradition rather than just in light of our own feelings and personal histories. A fair fight process of self-talk provides a means to do so. As mainline Christians we seek, however imperfectly, to grapple with the paradoxical character of biblical faith rather than using scripture in simplistic or authoritarian ways to proof text our limited perspectives. A fair fight process that leads us to contract and share behavioral controls as peers and that opens us to seeing and thinking in new ways provides a means to do so. As mainline Christians we seek, however imperfectly, to resist destructive acts of religious enemy making, labeling, and dogmatic intolerance apparent among some televangelists and demagogic leaders of secret religious sects. A fair fight process that outlaws such behaviors provides a means to do so.

Fighting for God's *Shalom*
in Faith Communities of Diversity

This book's model prescribes the processes of constructive conflict resolution as a primary means for creating corporate solidarity out of diverse Christian individuals. It is by means of fair fighting that mainline Christians can incorporate rather than just tolerate members' increasingly visible differences of race, sexuality, ethnicity, and socioeconomic class. It is by means of fair fighting that mainline Christians can formulate communal positions and commitments with enough specificity and solidarity to be of serious political and economic consequence in the public sector. Fair fighting for God's *shalom* provides promising ways for mainline Christians to recover both their integrity as inclusive communities and their influence as responsible corporate players in national and global affairs.

Because of its previous cultural establishment in North America, many mainline Christians of white-individualistic-Anglo-Saxon-male cultural heritage are neither sensitive to nor skilled in working out differences with others as equal partners. Many mainline Christians are in the habit of telling like parents other members what they should think and do, rather than exploring, as adults, with other members what they believe and feel called to do. Such habitually hierarchical ways of declaring church beliefs and policy have not only violated minorities but left the currently disenfranchised majority in disarray and confusion. Often one senses that the malaise of mainline church leaders now stems more from the bankruptcy of former controlling leadership styles than from any malevolent intentions. By and large, mainline church leaders are not practiced in respectfully communicating their underlying interests in open, accountable processes of communal decision making. By and large, mainline church leaders are not experienced in active listening and dialogue with colleagues as ways of discerning the mind of the Lord of the church. For both these reasons mainline faith communities have handled their diversity with mutual forbearance while their potential power of corporate witness and action against evils deplored by most mainline Christians has not been realized. This book's process provides ways mainline church leaders can exercise participative leadership without simply resorting to polling popular sentiment and can formulate creative solutions without simply hammering out reluctant compromises.

As we have emphasized repeatedly, this book's model prescribes ways to establish personal respectfulness rather than emotional closeness as the measure of Christian solidarity. The ground rules and procedures of resolving strategies lead parties in asserting and working through their differences rather than hiding and manipulating because of their differences. The procedures of both resolving strategies direct parties in discovering a commonality by getting to the bottom of their concerns rather than by harmonizing superficial perceptions of their concerns. Parties are given ways to incorporate their differences rather than to minimize them. Christians come to see their differences as valuable ingredients for corporate ministry, rather than as a costly dismantling of corporate-activity ministry.

This book's model makes clear that real relationships between uniquely differing people are built through constructive conflict rather than through harmonious dishonesty. Perhaps much of the malaise of mainline churches stems from the illusion that human beings can have conflictless community. Christian community building involves more than social companionship. Christian community building requires incorporation in Christ, which comes through surfacing and working through individual and group differences.

The book's model reminds us that true Christian community is labor intensive: It requires working differences into corporate wholeness rather than passively tolerating them. This book's model instructs us that what we seek in Christian community is useable communal solidarity in ministry, rather than simple general assent for each member to go his or her separate way. The book's model challenges us to fight out differences fairly until a majority of members in our community can honestly commit to standing and working together in specific corporate ministries. Such commitments to corporate ministry arise not because members agree but because they have been respectfully heard and participated creatively in that policy's emerging formulation. It appears that until the members of mainline congregations and denominations become so incorporated in Christ through fair fighting processes, they will not become an embodiment of Christ to one another or the world.

Stories of congregations in this book that achieved constructive management of their conflicts provide some supporting evidence for what is said above. In each case where communal conflicts were resolved, mainline congregations experienced resurgent vitality. The energy and resources members had previously invested in win/lose power struggles became available for positive mission activity. As these congregations became more safe emotionally, members could honestly question and creatively brainstorm about putting their convictions to work. Members began to experience one another as stimulating rather than critical. As members' differing perspectives and commitments mingled in the flow of conversations, new visions and ministries sprang up without tedious planning or programming processes. The *shalom* happening within their community began to spill over the boundaries of the community.

In one case, a congregation whose members had been at loggerheads over social action found themselves working side by side to remodel the home of a family in crisis over a life-threatening illness. Hardly had they finished this labor of love for one of their own than they began to participate in a community program to restore homes for the homeless. In another case, a congregation that had been afraid of racial differences found themselves increasingly drawn into a tutoring ministry for slow learners. Children of every color and class began to come into members' lives and the church plant. To be sure, there remained members who resisted and criticized each and every "change of color" that was happening. But these members no longer represented or sapped the community's spirit.

We recall that the first step in this book's model for managing a conflictive situation leads us to work with ourselves before working with other parties. In parallel fashion, Christians seem not to be able to work God's *shalom* outside their faith communities until they have worked God's *shalom* within. Until faith communities resolve their own emotional issues constructively, they will tend to project these communal issues and feelings onto others outside. Parishes that suppress diversity within tend to act in judgmental, hostile, or critical ways with outsiders who disagree with them. Fear rather than hope seems to motivate whatever changes such parishes make in grudging adaptation to irresistible social changes in their environments.

By the same token, as we learn to make constructive peace within our congregations, we become more competent for prophetic ministries of reconciliation beyond our congregations. We also become sufficiently incorporated that we can act in the public sector as corporate agents of the gospel rather than only as associations of Christian individuals.

Fighting for God's *Shalom* in an Endangered Public Sector

There is no need to describe the evil forces that threaten to extinguish our spaceship earth and all its species. The wages of social sin are social deaths. The results of dirty fighting in the public domain are evil corporate structures and megatrends that mock the goodness of God and of all God's creatures. We have already proposed that a church's prophetic ministry in such a public context will require corporate, disciplined, focused communal action if it is to have an impact.

When fighting for God's *shalom* within generates sufficient corporate solidarity for Christian influences on public affairs, this book's model then offers a way of understanding church ministries of reconciliation in the public sector. In our time, no single social agent can overcome the combined social forces of entrenched social privilege, unaccountable processes of social policy-making, the adversarial procedures of civil process, and the complexity of global interdependence. Prophetic power to change contemporary societies requires action more than rhetoric. Due to the cultural disestablishment of mainline Christianity in twentieth-century America, previous elitist ways of effecting social change through persuasion of political and business leaders seem increasingly out of date and impotent. Prophetic power to change contemporary societies will best be found through coalition building. If principals fighting for God's *shalom* are to achieve even an approximate power parity with social agents of injustice, greed, deceit, and violence in public life, we must build coalitions with non-Christians.[5] When one is on a sinking ship, one has little time to quiz others about their belief systems. One coalesces with them around shared values for saving the ship.

Coalitions are temporary alliances around shared values or shared agendas. They are not permanent, all-embracing communities of agreement. The basis for building coalitions for Christian ministries of reconciliation is selecting partners with shared values, not shared beliefs. Forming such coalitions to fight for God's *shalom* in public life seems to mean that mainline Christians should know how to advocate their interests rather than defend their beliefs. A negotiating process offers mainline Christians guidance for such coalitions forming.

Fighting for Public Shalom
by Constraining Malevolent Cycles

Many concepts of this book's model for managing conflicts seem to apply to reconciling ministries that involve the constraint of destructive forces and structures in the public sector. We are reminded that destructive conflicts are power struggles and that they follow a predictable cycle of latency, triggering, and escalating power struggles that result in win/lose or lose/lose outcomes. Ministries that block destructive public policy exercise the economic and political power of bystanders rather than the use of persuasive power with the principals. Unfortunately, Christian efforts in our time to fight for peace in the public sector have not always understood this. Many Christians have tried to make peace through interpersonal communication rather than supra-personal constraint. We have tried to change the minds of the powerful rather than mobilize the power of bystanders to set limits on the behavior of the powerful. We have proposed win/win solutions to global problems when the power and positive ethical orientations to implement such solutions were lacking.

In our adversarial time of staggering imbalances of economic and political power, this book's model suggests that the first task in fighting for public *shalom* lies in mobilizing a global community of bystanders to constrain malevolent cycles of evil. Rather than following habits of a bygone era of first seeking to change the mind of the elites, mainline Christians may gain more success through working with bystanders to prevent destructive exchanges or change destructive contextual factors. A Christian initiative might identify human survival as a value on which to unite as bystanders in fighting for social structures that prevent partisan gain at public expense.

In this regard mainline Christians disagree over the moral legitimacy of using violence to constrain evil forces. Such Christian disagreement involves, of course, the whole question of a just war. While this is not the place to pursue that question, this is the place to assert that almost all Christians agree that nonviolent forms of power are forms of ethical choice and should be utilized first. Almost all Christians also agree that violent forms of power are but stopgap measures until nonviolent forms of power can be utilized to resolve social conflicts.

Fighting for Public Shalom *by Initiating Benevolent Cycles*

Once destructive forces have been constrained by communities of bystanders, fighting for God's *shalom* in public life will go the second mile of seeking the resolution and reconciliation of all parties' interests. While those who fight for God's *shalom* in public life may be cynical enough to seek first to prevent destructiveness, they remain hopeful enough to work toward a community of incorporated human solidarity rather than simply sterile coexistence. Miraculously, a Berlin Wall can come down, and amidst its debris Beethoven's Ninth Symphony can be performed. Peace keeping is not an end in itself. Peace keeping is to provide opportunity for peace making. It is by peace making that Christians realize the goal of fighting for God's *shalom* in national and international affairs.

We do not seek a punitive vengeance against global principals who have fought dirty. We seek reparation for and reconciliation with global victims of dirty fighting.

Christians believe that God loves and claims the world. God's church is just God's provisional arrangement. Christians recognize that human solidarity is already a given in God's creation of this world. In this reality lies the hope for resolving rather than simply constraining conflicts in the public sector. It is a created solidarity that no differences of religion, ethnicity, language, or culture can completely erase. As the twentieth century comes to a close, humanity's inherent connectedness becomes increasingly apparent as global structures of business, communication, science, and political cooperation develop. It is this basic human solidarity, rather than our particular Christian perceptions of it, that provides a ground of commonality around which Christians can mobilize bystanders and build coalitions with other principals of good will. It is also this fundamental human interdependence that intensifies both the threat to and will for human survival, which can energize a global movement to preserve this planet's fragile ecology. While Christian perspectives on human creation validate human solidarity, Christian ministries of reconciliation seek the resolution of conflicting differences rather than the subjection of conflicting differences to Christian ideas. Fighting for God's *shalom* witnesses to God in Christ by reflecting God's love rather than by controlling God's love for all people.

This book's model for intervening in the public sector prescribes fighting for realizing Christian values in the processes of management rather than in the substance of Christian beliefs. In this model, a prophetic Christian ministry consists primarily of reconciling processes rather than evangelizing contests. If we are able to be agents of God's reconciliation, non-Christian parties will want to know of the God whose *shalom* we have sought. When Christian values are experienced in public processes, Christian beliefs may be believable.

Experiencing the Gift
of God's *Shalom*

In a book that prescribes a model of intentional efforts to manage conflictive situations, it is easy to forget that God's *shalom* is God's gift. Our difficulty is often one of half-truths due to either/or thinking. We miss the whole truth when we think that our efforts as managers are all that can happen in conflictive situations. We also miss the whole truth when we think of God's gift as something we passively receive rather than as Someone we actively risk following. The whole truth is that God's *shalom* is both God's gift and our response-ability.

We discover both dimensions of *shalom* as we experience managing conflicts. When we experience a constructive conflict, we are surprised by a creativity or by an inner healing we never thought to hope for. Miraculously, we experience God's indwelling in the process. When we experience the power of bystanders to prevent destructive exchanges, we change. Obviously there is more power here than simply the sum of the parties. New courage and hope are born in us and in our faith communities. When we risk fighting for *shalom* in the public sector, we learn about trusting God in a deeper way. We experience being proactive change agents for God's rule, rather than reactive victims of overwhelming forces and structures. Even though we often fail to achieve the changes we seek, we are changed by the process itself.

When we do our part to manage conflicts, God does far more than we can ask or think. As we work the steps of a Christian ethic of conflict management, we are graced by a Christ we had not thought to be present and by a hope we had not expected to realize. The gap between our Christian beliefs and our Christian experiences narrows. Having undertaken a conflict's management in fear and trembling, we find ourselves receiving what Paul Tillich called the courage to be. We receive a fresh sense of the liveliness of God. We receive a humility that stems from being grateful to God rather than hateful toward ourselves.

In all such ways we find ourselves gifted by God's *shalom* in increasing ways. For most Christians, the fear and the risks of managing church conflicts are never completely eliminated. But the courage and the trust that come from managing church conflict increase in us. We know that when we act responsibly, we receive a peace that transcends the limits of any behavioral model. In the final analysis, what makes conflict management Christian turns out to be our realizations that God is making of our efforts more reconciliation than we can ever know or imagine. Thanks be to God.

Flowchart for Managing Church Conflicts

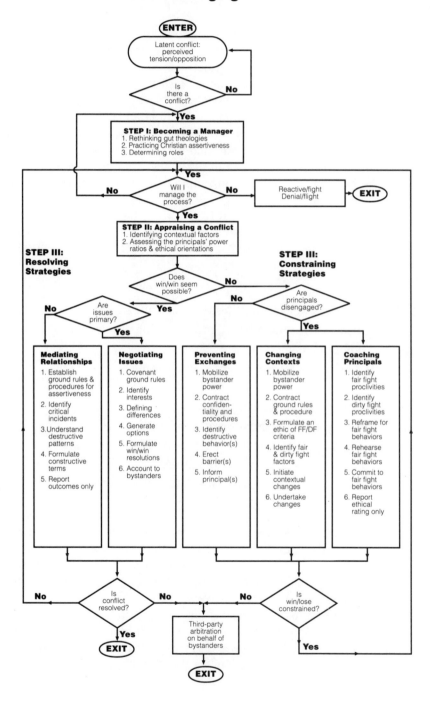

An Inventory of One's Gut Theology of Conflict

All of us have operating "gut" theologies about conflict. Our gut theologies are feeling-based ideas about conflict. We acquired these feeling-based ideas from our *experiences* of conflict between birth and ten years of age. How our parents dealt with each other, with us, and with our siblings generated how we came to *feel* about conflict. As we grew older and learned Christian teachings, we tended to adapt our Christian beliefs to fit with our feeling-based assumptions about conflict. Even today, our gut theologies continue to be our immediate, emotional *assumptions* about conflict, regardless of what we have learned to think. Assess your gut theology about conflict by indicating from 1 to 6 your immediate, unthinking reactions to each statement below.

Strongly Disagree	Disagree	Tend to Disagree	Tend to Agree	Agree	Strongly Agree
1	2	3	4	5	6

_____ 1. Fighting is unchristian. Jesus never got into fights.

_____ 2. "Turning the other cheek" means letting others win.

_____ 3. Conflict is mean: One wins, others lose.

_____ 4. If I love like Jesus did, I can make peace with anyone.

_____ 5. In conflicts, God is in control.

_____ 6. Conflicts are good. They push us to learn and grow up.

_____ 7. Jesus died on the cross because he was victimized.

_____ 8. God wants everyone to stand up for his or her rights.

_____ 9. Heaven is where there is no fighting.

_____ 10. If I fight fair with others, they will fight fair with me.

Romans reminds us, "Think of God's mercy, and worship God in a way that is worthy of thinking beings. . . . Do not model yourselves on the behavior of the world around you, but let your behavior change, modeled by your new mind. This is the only way to discover the will of God and know what is good" (12:1–2, selected versions).

Christian maturity involves reassessing as an adult our feeling-based thoughts from childhood. We do not ignore our childhood beliefs, but we do go on beyond them. We balance what we learned in our families of origin with what we now learn in our family of faith.

A Primer for Updating Gut Theologies

We often use a Bible verse as a proof text or anchor for our childhood feelings. Rather than being informed by the verse, we inform the verse. The following inventory may help one become aware of and intentional about one's inner Christian messages.

Bible Verse	Childhood Script	More Mature View
Be quick to listen but slow to speak and slow to arouse your temper; God's righteousness is never served by a person's anger."—James 1:19–20	It's bad to get angry. Jesus doesn't want me to be angry. Being angry is sinful.	You must speak the truth to one another. . . . Even if you are angry, you must not sin.—Ephesians 4:25a–26

Reflection: Anger is not sinful. Expressing one's anger assertively is loving others enough to present oneself honestly to them, even at the risk of their rejection. Expressing one's anger is caring enough to speak honestly about and for yourself. It is sinful to express anger aggressively or manipulatively, but not to do so assertively.

Bible Verse	Childhood Script	More Mature View
If anyone hits you on the right cheek, offer him the other as well.—Matthew 5:39b	Good Christians don't fight. Fighting is evil.	You shall love your neighbor as yourself.—Mark 12:31

Reflection: In conflicts, we are to act in ways that love ourselves *and* others; we are not commanded to act in ways that love others at the expense of ourselves or love ourselves at the expense of others.

Bible Verse	Childhood Script	More Mature View
Love your enemies and pray for those who persecute you.—Matt. 5:44	Give your enemies whatever they want. Be a doormat.	Jesus rebuked Peter and said, "Get behind me, Satan!"—Mark 8:33

Reflection: In conflicts, we are to love persons but not love or accept all of their behaviors. Because we love persons, we assertively challenge and constrain any aggressive or manipulative behaviors by them. The Christian ethic in conflicts is to love ourselves and our enemies, while despising anyone's destructive behaviors.

Bible Verse	*Childhood Script*	*More Mature View*
Anyone who wants to save his life will lose it; but anyone who loses his life for the sake of the gospel will save it. —Mark 8:35	Don't ever defend, protect or fight for your life. Submit to violence.	Can any of you, for all his worrying, add one single cubit to his span of life? —Matthew 6:27

Reflection: We are created as limited beings. We can control ourselves, but we cannot unilaterally control others. When we lose the illusion that we can safeguard ourselves by controlling others, we can discover the idea of gaining our lives by losing unilateral control over others. Seeking to save ourselves by controlling others is hopeless. Seeking to preserve ourselves by collaborating with others is hopeful. Sooner or later we all die, but not of our deciding. In a conflict, we can act realistically by seeking to share behavioral control for constructiveness, while trusting God to preserve our living on this side of the grave or the other. We are not called to give up our lives for God, but to entrust our lives to a God we cannot control.

Work Sheet for Step One Self-Talk for Assertiveness

1. List your current feelings over this conflictive situation.
   POSITIVE FEELINGS: (various ways of feeling glad, peaceful, or powerful)

   NEGATIVE FEELINGS: (various ways of feeling mad, sad, or scared)

2. What are your thinking, believing, or expecting in this conflict that gives you these feelings?

3. Recall the sounds, images, and family rules of conflicts at home or at school when you were a child (1 to 10 yrs.).

   SOUNDS:

   IMAGES:

   FAMILY RULES:

4. What negative messages about yourself and others in conflicts do you think you learned from such childhood experiences?

5. Which of these childhood messages about yourself and others in conflicts seem to connect with thoughts behind your current feelings?

6. What positive Christian messages for assertiveness do you now choose to give yourself about self and others in this conflictive situation? (See examples in chapters 2 and 6.)

7. Have your negative feelings changed? If so, how? If not, work further with items 2 through 6, above.

Work Sheet for Appraising Conflictive Situations

Contextual Factors	Principals	Power Assets Personal (✓)	Role (✓)	Ratio H/M/L	Ethical Proclivities Dirty Fight	Fair Fight	Rating DF/FF/BF
A. Key Communal Rules							
B. Key Communal Structures							
C. Key Environmental Circumstances							

Overall +/- = ___
(+1/0/-1)

A Glossary of
Working Terms

AGGRESSION: A destructive use of power that violates others by controlling their resources for one's purposes.

ARBITRATOR: An individual or group authorized to resolve substantive differences on behalf of the original parties to a conflict.

ASSERTIVENESS: A constructive use of power by which one stands up for one's rights by expressing one's thoughts, feelings, desires, or beliefs in direct, honest, and appropriate ways that do not violate another person's rights (see Lange & Jakubowski, *Responsible Assertive Behavior*), p. 7.

BYSTANDER: In distinction from a principal, a party who is primarily invested in the effects of a conflict on its hosting social system.

CANDOR: Honestly accounting for oneself with others without fully disclosing oneself (e.g., "I choose not to tell you about X").

CONFLICT: A power struggle over actual or perceived interdependent differences.

CONSTRUCTIVE BEHAVIOR (FAIR FIGHT): Win/win ways of resolving differences toward greater wholeness of parties and the larger social systems hosting them.

DESTRUCTIVE BEHAVIOR (DIRTY FIGHT): Win/lose ways of resolving differences for one party's interests at the expense of others.

ETHICS: "The moral life of the Christian community *in response to God,* the Creator, the Governor, and the Redeemer" (H. Richard Niebuhr, *The Responsible Self,* p. 40).

GUILT: In contrast to shame, taking responsibility for one's wrongdoing that violates one's values, principles, beliefs, or agreements.

MANAGING CONFLICTS: Coping by assertively proposing and negotiating processes that constrain win/lose or obtain win/win resolutions of conflicts.

MANIPULATION: A destructive use of power that violates others by deceptively using their resources for one's purposes.

PARTY: An individual, group, faction, or role incumbent related to a conflict as principal, bystander, or third party.

PRINCIPAL: In distinction from a bystander, a party to a conflict who is primarily invested in the differences at issue.

PROCESS: A pattern of social interaction (e.g., how parties are fighting as opposed to what they are fighting about).

RESPONSIBLE SELF: Acting in the image of God in response to others as made in the image of God (H. Richard Niebuhr, *The Responsible Self,* p. 65).

SHAME: In contrast to guilt, perceiving oneself as wrong-being and defective as a person, which must be kept secret at all costs.

SIN: Any violation of oneself or others as beings of intrinsic worth who are created for community.

THEOLOGY: Reflection on the action and nature of God (H. Richard Niebuhr, *The Responsible Self,* p. 40).

THIRD PARTY: A conflict manager from outside the social system hosting a conflict.

Notes

PREFACE

1. David Viscott, *I Love You, Let's Work It Out* (New York: Pocket Books, 1987), p. ix.

CHAPTER 1

1. Morton Deutsch, "Conflicts: Productive and Destructive," reprinted in Fred Jandt, ed., *Conflict Resolution Through Communication*, (New York: Harper & Row, 1973), p. 156.

2. Jay Hall, *Conflict Management Survey* (The Woodlands, Tex: Teleometrics, 1969), p. a.

3. Jack L. Stotts, *Shalom: The Content of the Peaceable City* (Nashville: Abingdon Press, 1973), p. 98.

4. See here H. Richard Niebuhr, *The Responsible Self* (New York: Harper & Row, 1963), and Dietrich Bonhoeffer, *Ethics* (New York: Macmillan Co., 1949).

5. See Stotts's discussion of the ethical principle of incorporating penultimate values in the context of ultimate values, in *Shalom: The Content of the Peaceable City*, p. 41.

6. See Konrad Lorenz, *On Aggression* (New York: Bantam Books, 1966), and Anthony Storr, *Human Aggression* (New York: Bantam Books, 1968).

7. See Kenneth C. Haugk's definition: "Antagonists are individuals who, on the basis of *non-substantive evidence, go out of their way* to make *insatiable demands,* usually attacking the person or performance of others. These attacks are *selfish in nature, tearing down rather than building up,* and are frequently directed against those in a leadership capacity" (*Antagonists in the Church* [Minneapolis: Augsburg Publishing House, 1988,] pp. 25–26).

8. See, for example, Richard E. Walton, *Interpersonal Peacemaking* (Reading, Mass.: Addison-Wesley Publishing Co., 1965); Amitai Eztioni, *The Active Society*

(New York: Free Press, 1968); R. R. Blake and J. S. Mouton, *Managing Intergroup Conflict in Industry* (Houston, Tex.: Gulf Publishing Co., 1964); Virginia Satir, *Peoplemaking* (Palo Alto, Calif.: Science and Behavior Books, 1972); and M. Scott Peck, *The Different Drum* (New York: Simon & Schuster, 1987).

9. "Religious conflict requires different modes of resolution than either bargaining or game theory. Value integration is required" (Clagett G. Smith, ed., *Conflict Resolution: Contributions of the Behavioral Sciences* [Notre Dame, Ind.: University of Notre Dame Press, 1971], p. 28).

10. See Morton Deutsch, *The Resolution of Conflict* (New Haven, Conn.: Yale University Press, 1973): Alan Filley, *Interpersonal Conflict Resolution* (Glenview, Ill: Scott, Foresman & Co., 1975); and D. Stanley Eitzen, *In Conflict and Order: Understanding Society*, 2nd ed. (Newton, Mass.: Allyn & Bacon, 1982), as examples.

11. See especially H. Richard Niebuhr's formulation of man the responder in *The Responsible Self*, p. 60f.

12. Charles Perrow, *Complex Organization: A Critial Essay* (Glenview, Ill.: Scott, Foresman & Co. 1972); Edgar H. Schein, *Organizational Psychology* (San Francisco: Jossey-Bass, 1985); Terrence E. Deal and Allen A. Kennedy, *Corporate Cultures: The Rites & Rituals of Corporate Life* (Reading, Mass.: Addison-Wesley Publishing Co., 1982); and John D. Adams, ed., *Transforming Leadership* (Alexandria, Va.: Miles River Press, 1986). It is axiomatic in the literature of organizational development and transformation that social systems have both formal and informal patterns/rules for participants' behavior. These structural and cultural understandings of organization are wedded with concepts of familial emotional process in social systems, among which Edwin H. Friedman's *Generation to Generation* (New York: Guilford Press, 1985) is currently receiving wide acclaim.

13. Amitai Etzioni, *A Comparative Analysis of Complex Organizations: On Power, Involvement, and Their Correlates* (Chicago: Free Press of Glencoe, 1961).

14. See unpublished Xenos lectures by Edward Campbell, available from McCormick Seminary, April 1983; Robert C. Worley, *Change in the Church: A Source of Hope* (Philadelphia: Westminster Press, 1971); and above all Joseph Haroutunian, *God with Us: A Theology of Transpersonal Life* (Philadelphia: Westminster Press, 1965).

15. Virtually all theorists of conflict management agree that parties to a conflict must share larger or ultimate values in common as a basis on which to resolve their differences. Deutsch's *The Resolution of Conflict* is exemplary of such a fundamental theoretical concept.

16. See Gerard I. Nierenberg, *The Art of Negotiating: Psychological Strategies for Gaining Advantageous Bargains* (New York: Cornerstone Library, 1978), and Rensis Likert and Jane Likert, *New Ways of Managing Conflict* (New York: McGraw-Hill Book Co., 1976), as models that typically involve outside consultants as conflict managers in profit-based organizations.

CHAPTER 2

1. David Viscott, *The Language of Feelings* (New York: Pocket Books, 1976), p. 49.

2. See Albert Ellis and Robert Harper, *A New Guide to Rational Living* (Hollywood, Calif.: Wilshire Book Co., 1975).

3. David Burns, *Feeling Good: The New Mood Therapy* (New York: Signet Books, 1980), p. 49.

4. Ibid., pp. 40–41.

5. This way of thinking is challenged by J. B. Phillips's classic little book on Christian dogmatism, *Your God Is Too Small* (New York: Macmillan Co., 1953). See also Milton Rokeach, *The Open and Closed Mind* (New York: Basic Books, 1960).

6. There is a wealth of literature on early childhood development that supports this book's axiom that we basically formed emotionally in our first six years of life. See particularly Erik H. Erikson's *Childhood and Society* (New York: W. W. Norton & Co., 1963) and W. Hugh Missildine's *Your Inner Child of the Past* (New York: Pocket Books, 1963).

7. "Because a child is dependent on adults for survival, he or she cannot choose to leave—thus precluding mutuality. . . . In other words, for intimacy to unfold, there must be a balance of power" (Stephanie Covington and Liana Beckett, *Leaving the Enchanted Forest: The Path from Relationship Addiction to Intimacy* [San Francisco: Harper & Row, 1988], p. 26).

8. Doctrinal themes are symbols of meaning claimed by Christian communities as normative for all their members. In this section of the book such claims are simply admitted and used to explore a Christian understanding of conflict. No attempt is made to speak here as a systematic theologian.

9. H. Richard Niebuhr, *The Responsible Self*, p. 133.

10. Ibid., p. 133.

11. See L. L. Welborn, "On the Discord in Corinth: I Corinthians 1–4 and Ancient Politics," *Journal of Biblical Literature* 106, no. 1 (1987): 85–111.

12. Haroutunian, *God with Us*, p. 212; gender-inclusive language added by author.

13. This faith concept is consistent with the ideas of theorists like Lewis Coser, who, in disputing the harmonious goal of Parsonian sociology, values conflict as the energizer for social vitality and creativity. See Lewis Coser, *The Functions of Social Conflict* (New York: Macmillan Co., 1956).

14. See Walter Bruggemann, Sharon Parks, & Thomas Groome, *To Act Justly, Love Tenderly, Walk Humbly: An Agenda for Ministers* (New York: Paulist Press, 1986).

15. Randolph Sanders and H. Newton Malony, *Speak Up! Christian Assertiveness* (Philadelphia: Westminster Press, 1985), pp. 33–34.

16. Ibid., p. 39. These messages have been adapted in light of Burns's list of distorted ways of thinking in *Feeling Good*, pp. 40–41.

CHAPTER 3

1. Arthur J. Lange & Patricia Jakubowski, *Responsible Assertive Behavior* (Champaign, Ill.: Research Press, 1976), p. 7.

2. Sanders and Malony, *Speak Up! Christian Assertiveness*, p. 25.

3. Michael Emmons and David Richardson, *The Assertive Christian* (Minneapolis: Winston Press, 1981), pp. 47–48.

4. James Gustafson, "Introduction," in H. Richard Niebuhr, *The Responsible Self*, pp. 35–36.

5. Lange and Jakubowski, *Responsible Assertive Behavior*, p. 7.

6. Emmons and Richardson, *The Assertive Christian*, pp. 2–30.

7. Douglas Sturm, *Community and Alienation* (Notre Dame, Ind.: University of Notre Dame Press, 1988), p. 89.

8. Ibid., p. 50.

9. Merle A. Fossum and Marilyn J. Mason, *Facing Shame: Families in Recovery* (New York: W. W. Norton & Co., 1986), pp. 5–6.

10. Haugk, *Antagonists in the Church*, pp. 25–26.

11. Reinhold Niebuhr, *The Nature and Destiny of Man*, Vol. 1, (New York: Charles Scribner's Sons, 1932), p. 255.

CHAPTER 4

1. Again the reader is put on alert that this may be a debatable proposition. In a manuscript to be published by Westminster/John Knox Press under the working title of *Conflict Mediation Across Cultures: Conflict and Dispute Pathways and Patterns*, David W. Augsburger observes, "The second basic proposition that becomes obvious in cross-cultural studies is that the parties most directly invested in a dispute are usually less able . . . to settle the dispute constructively. . . . A third party becomes essential . . . to resolve conflict" (chapter 1, p. 7).

2. See such theorists as Morton Deutsch, Allan Filley, Richard E. Walton, William Ury, Jack Nussan Porter, and Jacob Bercovitch.

3. See an unpublished paper by Robert C. Worley, "A Polity Which Promotes Faithfulness to God," presented at Reunion Day Lecture, McCormick Seminary, April 1984.

4. See Anne Wilson-Schaef's discussion of white male culture in *Women's Reality: An Emerging Female System in a White Male Society* (Minneapolis: Winston Press, 1981).

CHAPTER 5

1. H. Richard Niebuhr, *The Responsible Self*, pp. 56–57, 60.

2. The following table of comparisons is based on unpublished material provided by Dr. Judy McDonald, a family therapist who has served on her presbytery's Committee on Ministry, the work group that represents a presbytery as the third party in all Presbyterian pastoral relationships.

3. A church system's culture is here understood to be the interaction of at least four variables: its primary symbols of meaning, emotional climate, status figures, and ritual activities. See Deal and Kennedy, *Corporate Cultures*, and Schein, *Organizational Culture and Leadership*.

4. This numbered question and others below have been adapted from material in Friedman, *Generation to Generation*, pp. 272–73.

CHAPTER 6

1. Paul Tillich, *Love, Power, and Justice* (London: Oxford University Press, 1954), p. 87.

2. Herbert Goldhamer and Edward Shils, "Types of Power and Status," American Journal of Sociology 45, no. 2 (September 1939): 171–82.

3. In Etzioni, *A Comparative Analysis of Complex Organizations*, p. 4ff.

4. See Dennis H. Wrong, *Power: Its Forms, Bases, and Uses* (New York: Harper & Row, 1979), for a more extended discussion of the kinds of power opponents may exercise in conflictive situations.

5. For a general discussion of the flow and relativity of power in social relationships see especially Peter M. Blau, *Exchange and Power in Social Life* (New York: John Wiley & Sons, 1967), pp. 19–31.

6. See such representative thinkers as Kurt Lewin, *Resolving Social Conflicts* (New York: Harper & Row, 1948); Deutsch, *The Resolution of Conflict*; and William Ury, Jeanne Brett, and Stephen Goldberg, *Getting Disputes Resolved* (San Francisco: Jossey-Bass, 1988).

7. Sissela Bok, *Lying: Moral Choice in Public and Private Life* (New York: Vintage Books [Div. of Random House], 1978), pp. 6, 14.

8. Ibid., p. 96.

9. Lange and Jakubowski, *Responsible Assertive Behavior*, pp. 58–59.

10. Sturm, *Community and Alienation*, pp. 50, 89.

11. Tillich, *Love, Power and Justice*, pp. 57, 60.

CHAPTER 7

1. Likert and Likert, *New Ways of Managing Conflict*, p. 59.

2. See James E. Dittes, *When the People Say No* (New York: Harper & Row, 1979).

3. See Wilson-Schaef, *Women's Reality*, pp. 124–25.

4. Friedman, *Generation to Generation*, pp. 35–36.

5. These axioms have been selected from those on pp. 36–39 of Friedman's book and reformulated in the language of this book's model of conflict management.

6. For an extensive discussion of this concept, see Richard Bandler and John Grinder, *Reframing: Neuro-Linguistic Programming and the Transformation of Meaning*, (Moab, Utah: Real People Press, 1982).

7. Examples borrowed from a presentation by Judy McDonald of Lubbock, Texas.

CHAPTER 8

1. Likert and Likert, *New Ways of Managing Conflict*, pp. 65–66.

2. For this critical distinction between behavior and personhood see works by Haim Ginott, particularly *Between Parent and Child* (New York: Avon Books, 1976).

3. This principal of truthfulness through accountable dialogue with others is the central thesis of Sissela Bok's ethic in *Lying: Moral Choice in Public and Private Life*. It is also found in the thinking of James Gustafson's *The Church as Moral Decision Maker* (Boston: Pilgrim Press, 1970), M. Scott Peck's *People of the Lie* (New York: Simon & Schuster, 1985), and Hans Kung's *Truthfulness: The Future of the Church* (New York: Sheed & Ward, 1968).

4. See section on "Preventing Ignition of a Conflict Interchange" in Richard Walton, *Interpersonal Peacemaking: Confrontations and Third Party Consultation* (Reading, Mass.: Addison-Wesley Publishing Co., 1969).

CHAPTER 9

1. Among many sociological descriptions of American individualism, see especially Robert N. Bellah, *Habits of the Heart: Individualism and Commitment in American Life* (New York: Harper & Row, 1985).

2. Haroutunian, *God with Us*, p. 72; gender-inclusive language inserted by author.

3. Material adapted from a D. Min. course offered by Rev. John Swyers in 1990.

4. See especially the discussion of fear of authority by Richard Sennett in *Authority* (New York: Alfred A. Knopf, 1980), pp. 15–27.

CHAPTER 10

1. See Friedman on the laws of emotional triangles in *Generation to Generation*, pp. 35–39.

2. From Milton Mayeroff, *On Caring* (New York: Harper & Row, 1971), pp. 41–42; gender-inclusive language inserted by author.

3. See Burns, *Feeling Good*, pp. 40–41.

4. Many books for assertiveness training exist. Especially recommended here is Lange and Jakubowski, *Responsible Assertive Behavior*.

5. See Bandler and Grinder, *Reframing: Neuro-Linguistic Programming and the Transformation of Meaning*, p. 143.

CHAPTER 11

1. Roger Fisher and William Ury, *Getting to Yes: Negotiating Agreement Without Giving In* (Boston: Houghton Mifflin Co., 1981), pp. 20, 21.

2. Ibid., pp. 3–14.

3. Ibid., p. 40.

4. Adapted from Edward M. Stack, *Reading in the Arts and Sciences*, 4th ed. (Boston: Houghton Mifflin Co., 1987), p. 41.

5. Sources of these suggested ground rules include Robert A. Bacher, Judith L. McWilliams, and Allan Jahsmann, eds., *Congregational Conflict: A Guide to Reconciliation* (Philadelphia: Parish Life Press, 1983).

6. There are various renditions of the problem-solving process. For example, Aubrey Fisher speaks of four phases: phase I, orientation to the problem; phase II, dispute/differentiation of positions about the problem; phase III, emergence of alternatives to win/lose resolutions of the problem; and phase IV, political adoption of preferred emergent alternatives. See B. Aubrey Fisher, "Decision Emergence: Phases in Group Decision-Making," in Fred E. Jandt, comp., *Conflict Resolution Through Communication* (New York: Harper & Row, 1973), pp. 198–220.

CHAPTER 12

1. David W. Augsburger, "Conflict Mediation Across Cultures: Conflict and Dispute Pathways and Patterns," manuscript to be published by Westminster Press in 1991, chapter 2, p. 1.

2. Viscott, *I Love You, Let's Work It Out*, p. 3.

3. Sharon Wegscheider-Cruse, *Coupleship: How to Have a Relationship* (Deerfield Beach, Fla.: Health Communications, 1988), p. 23.

4. Jordan Paul and Margaret Paul, *Do I Have to Give up Me to Be Loved by You?* (Minneapolis: CompCare Publications, 1983), pp. 1–2.

5. Roger Fisher and Scott Brown, *Getting Together: Building a Relationship that Gets to Yes* (New York: Penguin Books, 1988), p. 7.

6. Paul and Paul, *Do I Have to Give up Me to Be Loved by You?* pp. 7–9.

7. Fisher and Brown, *Getting Together: Building a Relationship that Gets to Yes*, p. 49.

8. Selected from a list in John Bradshaw, *Healing the Shame That Binds You* (Deerfield Beach, Fla.: Health Communications, 1988), pp. 162–63.

9. Viscott, *I Love You, Let's Work It Out*, pp. 206–31, selected and adapted.

10. Selected and adapted from a list of principles by Fisher and Brown, *Getting Together: Building a Relationship that Gets to Yes*, pp. 38–39.

11. *Book of Order* 1987–88 (Louisville, Ky.: The Office of the General Assembly, Presbyterian Church [U.S.A.], 1987), G-14.0207, selected portions.

CHAPTER 13

1. Alan Richardson, ed., *A Theological Word Book of the Bible* (New York: Macmillan Co., 1960), pp. 165, 166.

2. This is the alternative ancient reading of the text, Luke 2:14. It is here used because it better communicates the fact that God-in-Christ "favors" all humanity.

3. Richard Robert Osmer, *A Teachable Spirit: Recovering the Teaching Office in the Church* (Louisville, Ky.: Westminster/John Knox Press, 1990), p. 3.

4. Gerald G. May, *Addiction & Grace* (San Francisco: Harper & Row, 1988), pp. 17, 19.

5. See Hugh F. Halverstadt's dissertation, *"The Church as Organization: A Theological Argument"* (Ph.D. diss., Northwestern University, 1973).

Bibliography

Adams, John D., ed. *Transforming Leadership: From Vision to Results.* Alexandria, Va.: Miles River Press, 1986.

Augsburger, David W. *When Caring Is Not Enough.* Ventura, Calif.: Regal Books, 1983.

Bach, George R., and Wyden, Peter. *The Intimate Enemy: How to Fight Fair in Love and Marriage.* New York: Avon Books, 1981.

Bacher, Robert A., McWilliams, Judith L., and Jahsmann, Allan, eds. *Congregational Conflict: A Guide to Reconciliation.* Philadelphia: Parish Life Press, 1983.

Bandler, Richard, and Grinder, John. *Reframing: Neuro-Linguistic Programming and the Transformation of Meaning.* Moab, Utah: Real People Press, 1982.

Beattie, Melody. *Codependent No More.* Minneapolis: Hazelden, 1987.

Becvar, Dorothy Stroh, and Becvar, Raphael J. *Family Therapy: A Systemic Integration.* Newton, Mass.: Allyn & Bacon, 1988.

Bercovitch, Jacob. *Social Conflicts and Third Parties: Strategies of Conflict Resolution.* Boulder, Colo.: Westview Press, 1984.

Berkowitz, M.N., and Owen, J. *How to Be Your Own Best Friend.* New York: Ballantine Books, 1981.

Blake, Robert, and Mouton, Jane. *Solving Costly Organizational Conflicts.* San Francisco: Jossey-Bass, 1984.

Blake, R.R., and Mouton, J. S. *Managing Intergroup Conflict in Industry.* Houston, Tex.: Gulf Publishing Co., 1964.

Blau, Peter M. *Exchange and Power in Social Life.* New York: John Wiley & Sons, 1967.

Bok, Sissela. *Lying: Moral Choice in Public and Private Life.* New York: Vintage Books (Div. of Random House), 1978.

————. *Secrets: On the Ethics of Concealment and Revelation.* New York: Vintage Books (Div. of Random House), 1983.

Bolton, Robert. *People Skills.* New York: Prentice Hall Press, 1979.

Bonhoeffer, Dietrich. *Ethics.* New York: Macmillan Co., 1949.

Bradshaw, John. *Bradshaw on: The Family.* Deerfield Beach, Fla.: Health Communications, 1988.

————. *Healing the Shame That Binds You.* Deerfield Beach, Fla.: Health Communications, 1988.

————. *Homecoming: Reclaiming and Championing Your Inner Child.* New York: Bantam Books, 1990.

Bramson, Robert. *Coping with Difficult People.* New York: Ballantine Books, 1981.

Bridston, Keith. *Church Politics.* Cleveland: World Publishing Co., 1969.

Burns, David. *Feeling Good: The New Mood Therapy.* New York: Signet Books, 1980.

Burns, James MacGregor. *Leadership.* New York: Harper & Row, 1978.

Cameron-Bandler, Leslie, and Lebeau, Michael. *The Emotional Hostage: Rescuing Your Emotional Life.* San Rafael, Calif.: FuturePace, 1986.

Coser, Lewis. *The Functions of Social Conflict.* New York: Macmillan Co., 1956.

Covington, Stephanie, and Beckett, Liana. *Leaving the Enchanted Forest: The Path from Relationship Addiction to Intimacy.* San Francisco: Harper & Row, 1988.

Deal, Terrence E., and Kennedy, Allen A. *Corporate Cultures: The Rites & Rituals of Corporate Life.* Reading, Mass.: Addison-Wesley Publishing Co., 1982.

Deutsch, Morton. *The Resolution of Conflict: Constructive and Destructive Processes.* New Haven, Conn.: Yale University Press, 1973.

Dittes, James E. *When the People Say No.* New York: Harper & Row, 1979.

Dudley, Carl. *Making the Small Church Effective.* Nashville: Abingdon Press, 1978.

————, and Hilgert, Earle. *New Testament Tensions and the Contemporary Church.* Philadelphia: Fortress Press, 1987.

Eitzen, D. Stanley. *In Conflict and Order: Understanding Society.* 2nd ed. Newton, Mass.: Allyn & Bacon, 1982.

Ellis, Albert and Harper, Robert. *A New Guide to Rational Living.* Hollywood, Calif.: Wilshire Book Co., 1975.

Emmons, Michael, and Richardson, David. *The Assertive Christian.* Minneapolis: Winston Press, 1981.

Erikson, Erik H. *Childhood and Society.* New York: W. W. Norton & Co., 1963.

Etzioni, Amitai. *The Active Society: A Theory of Societal and Political Processes.* New York: Free Press (Div. of Macmillan Publishing Co.), 1968.

————. *A Comparative Analysis of Complex Organizations: On Power, Involvement, and Their Correlates.* Chicago: Free Press of Glencoe, 1961.

Filley, Alan. *Interpersonal Conflict Resolution.* Glenview, Ill.: Scott, Foresman & Co., 1975.

Fisher, Roger, and Brown, Scott. *Getting Together: Building a Relationship that Gets to Yes.* New York: Penguin Books, 1988.

Fisher, Roger, and Ury, William. *Getting to Yes: Negotiating Agreement Without Giving In.* Boston: Houghton Mifflin Co., 1981.

Fossum, Merle A., and Mason, Marilyn J. *Facing Shame: Families in Recovery.* New York: W.W. Norton & Co., 1986.

Friedman, Edwin H. *Generation to Generation: Family Process in Church and Synagogue.* New York: Guilford Press, 1985.

Fromm, Erich. *The Anatomy of Human Destructiveness.* New York: Fawcett Crest, 1973.

Gamson, William A. *Power and Discontent.* Homewood, Ill.: Dorsey Press, 1961.

Gilligan, Carol. *In a Different Voice.* Cambridge: Harvard University Press, 1982.

Ginott, Haim. *Between Parent and Child.* New York: Avon Books, 1976.

Goulding, Mary McClure, and Goulding, Robert L. *Changing Lives Through Redecision Therapy.* New York: Grove Press, 1979.

Gustafson, James. *The Church as Moral Decision Maker.* Boston: Pilgrim Press, 1970.

Halverstadt, Hugh F. "The Church as Organization: A Theological Argument." Ph.D. diss., Northwestern University, 1973.

Haroutunian, Joseph. *God with Us: A Theology of Transpersonal Life.* Philadelphia: Westminster Press, 1965.

Harris, John C. *Stress, Power and Ministry.* Washington, D.C.: Alban Institute Press, 1977.

Haugk, Kenneth C. *Antagonists in the Church: How to Identify and Deal with Destructive Conflict.* Minneapolis: Augsburg Publishing House, 1988.

Hendrix, Harville. *Getting the Love You Want: A Guide for Couples.* New York: Harper & Row, 1988.

Hopewell, James F. *Congregation: Stories and Structures.* Philadelphia: Fortress Press, 1987.

Kaufman, Gershen. *Shame: The Power of Caring.* Rev. ed. Rochester, N.Y.: Schenkman Books, 1985.

Kelly, Colleen. *Assertion Training, A Facilitator's Guide.* La Jolla, Calif.: University Associates, 1979.

Krantzler, Mel. *Creative Divorce: A New Opportunity for Personal Growth.* New York: Signet Books, 1973.

Kung, Hans. *Truthfulness: The Future of the Church.* New York: Sheed & Ward, 1968.

Lange, Arthur J., and Jakubowski, Patricia. *Responsible Assertive Behavior: Cognitive/Behavioral Procedures for Trainers.* Champaign, Ill.: Research Press, 1976.

Leas, Speed B. *Leadership and Conflict.* Nashville: Abingdon Press, 1982.

———. "Should the Pastor Be Fired?" Washington, D.C.: Alban Institute, 1981.

Leas, Speed B., and Kittlaus, Paul. *Church Fights.* Philadelphia: Westminster Press, 1973.

Lerner, Harriet. *The Dance of Anger: A Woman's Guide to Changing the Patterns of Intimate Relationships.* New York: Harper & Row, 1985.

Lewin, Kurt. *Resolving Social Conflicts.* New York: Harper & Brothers, 1948.

Likert, Rensis, and Likert, Jane. *New Ways of Managing Conflict.* New York: McGraw-Hill Book Co., 1976.

Lorenz, Konrad. *On Aggression.* New York: Bantam Books, 1966.

McCormick, Richard, and Ramsey, Paul. *Doing Evil to Achieve Good: Moral Choice in Conflict Situations.* Chicago: Loyola University Press, 1978.

McSwain, Larry L., and Treadwell, William C., Jr. *Conflict Ministry in the Church.* Nashville: Broadman Press, 1981.

May, Gerald G. *Addiction & Grace.* San Francisco: Harper & Row, 1988.

May, Rollo. *Love and Will.* New York: Dell Publishing Co., 1969.

———. *Power and Innocence.* New York: Dell Publishing Co., 1972.

Menninger, Karl. *Whatever Became of Sin?* New York: Hawthorn Books, 1975.

Mickey, Paul A., and Wilson, Robert L. *Conflict and Resolution.* Nashville: Abingdon Press, 1973.

Miller, John M. *The Contentious Community: Constructive Conflict in the Church.* Philadelphia: Westminster Press, 1978.

Missildine, W. Hugh. *Your Inner Child of the Past.* New York: Pocket Books, 1963.

Moore, Christopher W. *The Mediation Process: Practical Strategies for Resolving Conflict.* San Francisco: Jossey-Bass, 1986.

Niebuhr, Reinhold. *Moral Man and Immoral Society.* New York: Charles Scribner's Sons, 1932.

———. *The Nature and Destiny of Man.* New York: Charles Scribner's Sons, 1941.

Niebuhr, H. Richard. *The Responsible Self: An Essay in Christian Moral Philosophy.* New York: Harper & Row, 1963.

Nierenberg, Gerard I. *The Art of Negotiating: Psychological Strategies for Gaining Advantageous Bargains.* New York: Cornerstone Library, 1978. Reprint.

Nouwen, Henri. *The Wounded Healer: Ministry in Contemporary Society.* Garden City, N.Y.: Doubleday & Co., 1972.

Palmer, Parker J. *The Company of Strangers: Christians and the Renewal of America's Public Life.* New York: Crossroad Publishing Co., 1981.

Paul, Jordan, and Paul, Margaret. *Do I Have to Give up Me to Be Loved by You?* Minneapolis: CompCare Publications, 1983.

Peck, M. Scott. *The Different Drum: Community Making and Peace.* New York: Simon & Schuster, 1987.

———. *People of the Lie.* New York: Simon & Schuster, 1985.

———. *The Road Less Traveled.* New York: Simon & Schuster, 1987.

Perrow, Charles. *Complex Organization. A Critical Essay.* Glenview, Ill.: Scott, Foresman & Co., 1972.

Phillips, J. B. *Your God Is Too Small.* New York: Macmillan Co., 1953.

Porter, Jack Nussan, and Taplin, Ruth. *Conflict and Conflict Resolution: A Sociological Introduction.* Lanham, Md.: University Press of America, 1987.

"Presbyterians and Peacemaking: Are We Now Called to Resistance?" Paper adopted by the 121st General Assembly of the Presbyterian Church (USA). 1985.

Rokeach, Milton. *The Open and Closed Mind.* New York: Basic Books, 1960.

Rubin, Theodore Isaac. *Compassion and Self-Hate.* New York: Ballantine Books, 1975.

Russell, Letty M. *The Future of Partnership.* Philadelphia: Westminster Press, 1979.

Sandole, Dennis, and Sandole-Staroste, Ingrid, eds. *Conflict Management and Problem Solving: Interpersonal to International Applications.* New York: University Press, 1987.

Sanford, John A. *Evil: The Shadow Side of Reality.* New York: Crossroad Publishing Co., 1981.

Satir, Virginia. *Peoplemaking.* Palo Alto, Calif.: Science and Behavior Books, 1972.

Schein, Edgar H. *Organizational Culture and Leadership.* San Francisco: Jossey-Bass, 1985.

———. *Organizational Psychology.* 2nd ed. Englewood Cliffs, N.J.: Prentice-Hall, 1970.

Sennett, Richard. *Authority.* New York: Alfred A. Knopf, 1980.

Shaw, Graham. *The Cost of Authority: Manipulation and Freedom in the New Testament.* Philadelphia: Fortress Press, 1982.

Smith, Donald P. *Clergy in the Cross Fire: Coping with Role Conflicts in the Ministry.* Philadelphia: Westminster Press, 1973.

Smith, Hedrick. *The Power Game: How Washington Works.* New York: Ballantine Books, 1988.

Sparks, James Allen. *Potshots at the Preacher.* Nashville: Abingdon Press, 1977.

Stone, Ronald, and Wilbanks, David. *The Peacemaking Struggle: Militarism & Resistance.* Lanham, Md.: University Press of America, 1985.

Storr, Anthony. *Human Aggression.* New York: Bantam Books, 1968.

Stulberg, Joseph B. *Taking Charge/Managing Conflict.* Lexington, Mass.: Lexington Books, 1987.

Sturm, Douglas. *Community and Alienation: Essays on Process Thought and Public Life.* Notre Dame, Ind.: University of Notre Dame Press, 1988.

Tillich, Paul. *Love, Power, and Justice.* New York: Oxford University Press, 1954.

Trueblood, Elton. *The Humor of Christ.* New York: Harper & Row, 1975.

Ury, William, Brett, Jeanne, and Goldberg, Stephen. *Getting Disputes Resolved.* San Francisco: Jossey-Bass, 1988.

Viorst, Judith. *Necessary Losses.* New York: Fawcett Books, 1986.

Viscott, David. *I Love You, Let's Work It Out.* New York: Pocket Books, 1987.

———. *The Language of Feelings.* New York: Pocket Books, 1976.

Walton, Richard E. *Managing Conflict: Interpersonal Dialogue and Third Party Roles.* 2nd ed. Reading, Mass.: Addison-Wesley Publishing Co., 1987.

Wegscheider-Cruse, Sharon. *Coupleship: How to Build a Relationship.* Deerfield Beach, Fla.: Health Communications, 1988.

Welborn, L. L. "On the Discord in Corinth: I Corinthians 1–4 and Ancient Politics." *Journal of Biblical Literature* 106/1 (1987): 85–111.

Wilson-Schaef, Anne. *Co-Dependence: Misunderstood—Mistreated.* San Francisco: Harper & Row, 1986.

———. *Women's Reality: An Emerging Female System in a White Male Society.* Minneapolis: Winston Press, 1981.

Worley, Robert C. *Change in the Church: A Source of Hope.* Philadelphia: Westminster Press, 1971.

———. *Dry Bones Breathe!* Chicago: Center for the Study of Church Organizational Behavior, 1978.

———. *A Gathering of Strangers.* Philadelphia: Westminster Press, 1976.

———. "A Polity Which Promotes Faithfulness to God." McCormick Theological Seminary, 1984.

Wrong, Dennis H. *Power: Its Forms, Bases, and Uses.* New York: Harper & Row, 1979.